Gyeongju
The Capital of Golden Silla

Gyeongju, the capital of the ancient Korean kingdom of Silla, is known for its majestic gold crowns and earrings excavated from mounded tombs. Recent archaeological findings from Silla sites demonstrate a culture that extends far beyond these gold adornments. Nelson's book highlights the implications of archaeological contexts and gendered perspectives to shed light on the intersection of archaeology and written texts. This book is an excellent addition to the field, challenging genderless perspectives of material culture in the study of early historic Asia.

Professor Junko Habu, University of California at Berkeley, USA

Gyeongju, the capital of the Kingdom of Silla, grew from a loose confederation of villages called Saro, to become the capital of most of the Korean peninsula. Its relationships with Japan, the Eurasian Steppes, and countries along the Silk Road leading to Europe helped to make the city one of the most prosperous and significant in ancient East Asia. In this seminal new volume, Sarah Milledge Nelson draws on over 30 years' experience to offer the first complete history of this fascinating city. *Gyeongju* explores culture, class and rank, industry, international relations, rulers, and socio-cultural issues such as gender, and examines in detail the complex systems of class and rank, Gyeongju's position as the royal seat of Silla, and the influence and legacy of the ancient city.

Excavations in Gyeongju have provided evidence not only of the wealth and power of the monarchy, but also of production and agriculture, and the reach of Gyeongju's trade routes, making this city a fascinating case study for the region. Augmented with an extensive range of maps and images which illustrate the city's rich history, this volume is crucial reading for anyone interested in the city, the kingdom of Silla, the history and archaeology of Korea, and early urbanism and state formation in East Asia.

Sarah Milledge Nelson is Distinguished Professor of Anthropology at the University of Denver, USA. Some of her authored books are: *The Archaeology of Korea*; *Shamans, Queens and Figurines*; and *Spirit Bird Journey*, a novel about Korean archaeology, as well as several other books and journal articles. She has been working in Korean archaeology since 1970.

Cities of the Ancient World

Cities of the Ancient World examines the history, archaeology and cultural significance of key cities from across the ancient world, spanning northern Europe, the Mediterranean, Africa, Asia and the Near East. Each volume explores the life of a significant place, charting its developments from its earliest history, through the transformations it experienced under different cultures and rulers, to its later periods. These texts offer academics, students and the interested reader comprehensive and scholarly accounts of the life of each city.

Damascus – Ross Burns

Miletos – Alan Greaves

Aleppo – Ross Burns

Forthcoming:

Cádiz – Benedict Lowe

Ebla – Paolo Matthiae

Carlisle – Mike McCarthy

Palmyra – Michael Sommer

Elis – Graham Bourke

Carthage – Dexter Hoyos

Memphis, Babylon, Cairo – David Jeffreys and Ana Tavares

Paphos – Scott Moore

Antioch – Andrea De Giorgi and Asa Eger

Salamis – Giorgos Papantoniou

Gyeongju
The Capital of Golden Silla

Sarah Milledge Nelson

LONDON AND NEW YORK

First published 2017
by Routledge
2 Park Square, Milton Park, Abingdon, Oxon OX14 4RN

and by Routledge
711 Third Avenue, New York, NY 10017

Routledge is an imprint of the Taylor & Francis Group, an informa business

© 2017 Sarah Milledge Nelson

The right of Sarah Milledge Nelson to be identified as author of
this work has been asserted by him/her in accordance with sections 77 and
78 of the Copyright, Designs and Patents Act 1988.

All rights reserved. No part of this book may be reprinted or
reproduced or utilised in any form or by any electronic, mechanical,
or other means, now known or hereafter invented, including
photocopying and recording, or in any information storage or
retrieval system, without permission in writing from the publishers.

Trademark notice: Product or corporate names may be trademarks
or registered trademarks, and are used only for identification and
explanation without intent to infringe.

British Library Cataloguing-in-Publication Data
A catalogue record for this book is available from the British Library

Library of Congress Cataloging-in-Publication Data
Names: Nelson, Sarah M., 1931–
Title: Gyeongju: the capital of Golden Silla / Sarah Milledge Nelson.
Description: Milton Park, Abingdon, Oxon: Routledge, 2016. | Series:
    Cities of the ancient world | Includes bibliographical references and index.
Identifiers: LCCN 2015041387| ISBN 9781138778702
    (hardback: alkaline paper) | ISBN 9781315627403 (ebook)
Subjects: LCSH: Kyæongju-si (Korea) – History. | Kyæongju-si
    (Korea) – Antiquities. | Kyæongju-si (Korea) – Social life and customs. |
    City and town life – Korea (South) – Kyæongju-si – History – To 1500. |
    Kyæongju-si (Korea) – Politics and government. | Silla (Kingdom) –
    History. | Korea – History – To 935.
Classification: LCC DS925.K9 N45 2016 | DDC 951.9/01—dc23
LC record available at http://lccn.loc.gov/2015041387

ISBN: 978-1-138-77870-2 (hbk)
ISBN: 978-1-315-62740-3 (ebk)

Typeset in Times New Roman
by Swales & Willis Ltd, Exeter, Devon, UK

Contents

List of figures	vi
List of maps	vii
Preface and acknowledgments	viii

1	The ancient city of Gyeongju	1
2	Saro/Silla and the historical record	18
3	Gyeongju archaeology	35
4	Production: ceramics, bronze, iron, and gold	53
5	Silk roads and trade routes	64
6	Ranking and sumptuary rules	78
7	Rulership in Silla	86
8	Religions in Gyeongju	99
9	Gyeongju and Japan	110
10	Gyeongju in an East Asian perspective: a summary	119

References	134
Index	145

Figures

1.1	Gold crown from Tomb 98 north mound (Hwangnam Daechong)	3
1.2	US satellite image of tomb mounds in Gyeongju	4
1.3	Cheomseongdae, possible astronomical observatory in Gyeongju	5
1.4	Large bronze bell, Gyeongju	6
3.1	Horse trappings from Silla tombs	37
3.2	Horse buckle and tiger buckle excavated in North Gyeongsang Province	38
3.3	Gilded saddlebow from royal grave in Chaoyang	41
3.4	Two clay vessels in the shape of horses with riders	48
3.5	Painted white horse from the Heavenly Horse Tomb	49
4.1	Silla pottery	54
4.2	Jewelry from Silla tombs	57
4.3	Gold belt from Tomb 98, north mound	59
5.1	Early Indonesian beads found in Korean sites	67
5.2	Face bead from a tomb in Wolseong-ro, Gyeongju	69
5.3	Glass vessels from Silla tombs	72
5.4	Silver bowl from Hwangnam Daechong, south mound	75
6.1	Large chest ornament of gold and glass from Tomb 155 (Heavenly Horse Tomb)	79
7.1	Kinship chart showing early kings and queens of Silla	96
7.2	Kinship chart showing lineage of male kings of early Silla	97
7.3	Kinship chart showing only queens of early Silla	97
8.1	The Mountain Spirit and his tiger, a common image in Buddhist temples in Korea	101
8.2	Crown from the Lucky Phoenix Tomb, with gold cut-out birds	102

Maps

1.1	The sites of Gyeongju	2
1.2	The Three Kingdoms of Korea	12
2.1	The Korean peninsula in the mid third century CE	20
3.1	Topological map of Bronze and Iron Age sites in and near Gyeongju	36
3.2	Numbered tombs in Gyeongju	46
5.1	"Highways" of the Eurasian Steppes	65
10.1	Korea's place in East Asia	131

Preface and acknowledgments

I have been fascinated with the polity of Silla since I first visited the museum in Gyeongju and learned that gold crowns had been unearthed from burials under giant mounds; even more intriguing to me was the fact that the woman with the finest crown of all was an unknown queen—or at least a personage not found in the recorded histories as a queen. I have written several papers and chapters about that mysterious queen, and in the process I have acquired an ever-expanding knowledge of the Silla polity over the two decades that I have been prodding this particular conundrum.

While learning more about both the archaeology and the history of Gyeongju as the seat of the Silla polity, I discovered that Silla was a polity unlike the other two of Korea's historic Three Kingdoms: Baekje and Goguryeo. State formation trajectories were varied in Korea. One pattern, one explanation, does not suit all of the Three Kingdoms. Thus, this book became both a description of the city of Gyeongju and an investigation of the roots of Silla's differences from Baekje and Goguryeo.

It has been observed (by too many Korean archaeologists to name them all) that not only did the mounded tombs in Silla and their contents apparently spring up on Gyeongju soil without local precedent, but the astounding amount of gold used for adornment of the Silla dead also had no antecedents. While some archaeologists continue to look for a developmental trajectory in Gyeongju (which I acknowledge also can be found), the exogenous nature of the tombs that begin to appear in the third century is not easy to explain under that paradigm alone.

My hope for this book was to explore the various kinds of information that should inform our understandings of early states, as well as to try to picture Gyeongju as it grew and changed through the ten centuries that it served as a capital city. Therefore, it became tempting to search for a migratory group or an invading force, but I needed to explore more thoroughly both the archaeology and the histories of the Silla polity. The fierce discussions over the "horse-riders" that it has been suggested dashed through Korea on their way to Japan advocated a cautious approach. However, as I am an archaeologist rather than a historian, I tend to prefer archaeological evidence. Archaeological tidbits discovered by the unearthed history have led to new perspectives on the ethnicity of the people buried in the mounded tombs.

It will come as no revelation to archaeologists that trying to pin down the archaeology of Gyeongju is like coping with a shifting target, with new surveys

Preface and acknowledgments   ix

and excavations occurring every season. I try to keep up with ongoing archaeology by correspondence with my peers in Korea, and below I thank them for their help, but they have no blame for any deficiencies of mine, or for my occasionally non-standard interpretations of the sites. As a foreigner, I feel free to explore such ideas, and I do not mind if new evidence appears that requires a new perspective on previous explanations. That's just how it works. Learning about the archaeology of Gyeongju, and interpreting its history, are works in progress, and I expect they always will be.

In the process of writing this book I realized that I needed to know more about Dongbei/Manchuria in the centuries contemporaneous with Silla/Saro in Gyeongju, in order to explore the possibility of a new group of people arriving in Gyeongju in the third or fourth century. I had barely touched upon this topic previously, other than noticing the northern implications of many archaeological discoveries.

Although I worked at the site of Niuheliang near Chaoyang, Liaoyang, China for most of a decade, it is an earlier site where I concentrated on the Neolithic period, all but ignoring sporadic evidence of a much later Han presence here. Thus, for this book I needed to delve into both the archaeology and history of the shifting ethnicities in Manchuria. My numerous sources are cited in the references and, since it is a lively archaeological scene, I am sure there is much more to come. This is an exploration of possibilities.

Writing the book took much longer than it should have, not only because I extended my reach, but I also had an unfortunate event with my good eye, which left me unable to read (or even see the figures on the carpet) for a month. Thanks to modern medicine and modern technology, I can now read and write again.

Discussions with Korean friends about which form of transliteration of the Korean language should be used left me undecided. I like the McCune–Reichauer system because it makes it possible for English speakers to understand how Korean is pronounced. On the other hand, the new official system transliterates the Korean letters, rather than their sounds, into Roman letters, thus the English reader can know how a word is spelled in the Korean alphabet. Since at present the official manner of rendering Korean into the Western alphabet is used on street signs and in museums, I decided to use the official form.

While I am always grateful to Korean colleagues for their work, there are many people to thank for their specific aid. Archaeologists Bong Won Kang, Sung Joo Lee, and Martin Bale were extraordinarily gracious, supplying me with both data and ideas. James Lankton commented on the chapter that includes glass. I pestered other friends in Korea to help me with permissions for the figures— Professor Sung Joo Lee (again!), Professor Yangjin Pak, and Hwajon Lee gave help beyond measure. Rachel Lee sent me an aerial view of Gyeongju. My other Korean archaeologist friends, too numerous to mention, have been supportive with their data over the years.

Putting together a book takes many people. Thanks to the team at Routledge for tackling this complex book. Lizzi Thomasson handled finding the figures in the public domain or obtaining permissions. Krysia Johnson executed the copy-editing with a sure eye and an understanding mind. Julie Willis spear-headed the final copy.

1 The ancient city of Gyeongju

William Griffis, who taught at the Imperial University of Japan in the nineteenth century, but never visited Korea, describes Gyeongju as depicted in ancient documents from the vantage point of Japan across the Tsushima Strait. He was impressed with everything he read about Gyeongju at the height of its glory and describes it as,

> a brilliant center of art and science, of architecture and of literary and religious light. Imposing temples, grand monasteries, lofty pagodas, halls of scholars, magnificent gateways and towers adorned the city. Its campaniles, equipped with water-clocks and with ponderous bells and gongs, which, when struck, flooded the valleys and hill-tops with a rich resonance, and the sciences of astronomy and horoscopy were cultivated.
>
> (Griffis 1882:14)

Although this paean to Gyeongju is not an eyewitness description of the city, Griffis was envisioning the past based on what he had read and perhaps heard, rather than his own experience or memories, for he never visited Gyeongju. Nevertheless, his poetic yearning for a Gyeongju of the past can stand as a record of the way Gyeongju was perceived to have been "before a ruthless Japanese torch laid them in ashes in 1596" (continuation of quotation above).

Homer Hulbert, a keen observer of Korea and avid historian, who in contrast to Griffis actually lived in Korea, wrote, "The Kingdom of Silla was by far the most highly civilized of the Three Kingdoms [of Korea]. She was an eminently peaceful power, and paid more attention to the arts of peace than to those of war" (Hulbert 1969 [1906]:72).

As Silla's capital, Gyeongju prospered for a thousand years, and indeed was highly civilized, but as for its peacefulness, Silla first conquered the nearby towns, then all of the Gaya kingdoms one by one and, finally, joined with the Tang dynasty in China to defeat the other Korean kingdoms, Baekje and Goguryeo. So, Hulbert's description, too, must be taken as more ideal than real. Nevertheless, the quotation is useful for understanding how thoroughly the early Western writers were mesmerized by the mystique that Gyeongju and the kingdom of Silla continued to radiate even after the ravages caused by intermittent raids and wars, and Gyeongju's fall from the position of capital city.

2 *The ancient city of Gyeongju*

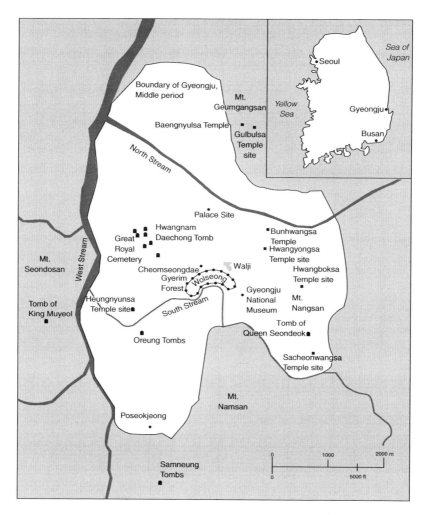

Map 1.1 The sites of Gyeongju. Redrawn from Leidy and Lee 2013, *Silla, Korea's Golden Kingdom*, p. 14.

In 1920, decades after both of the above descriptions of Gyeongju were written, a remarkable excavation enhanced Silla's reputation still further and also the world's understanding of the Silla polity in a new and unanticipated way. Accidental digging into one of the mounded tombs in the center of the city revealed a beautifully crafted gold crown covered with dangles of jade and gold, accompanied by a plethora of gold jewelry, as well as precious objects from distant realms. These objects made world news, even enticing the Crown Prince of Sweden to visit Korea. Purposeful excavations of a few other mounded tombs followed, producing another gold crown, gilded shoes, and other dazzling artifacts with which the royal dead were laid to rest. Even with these striking artifacts, Gyeongju's fame did not spread as widely as was deserved. However, the gold of Silla made an impact with a brilliant exhibit of Silla gold artifacts in 2014, which brought the beauty and sparkle of Gyeongju's tombs to the attention of the American public.

The Metropolitan Museum of Art in New York mounted an exhibit on Silla gold, including its gold crowns, gold jewelry, objects from the Silk Road, and much more. Soyoung Lee and Denise Leidy write of the Mounded Tomb period:

> The royal tombs of this period, magnificent visual markers of political dominance, have preserved the rich artistic and cultural traditions of Silla's elite. Excavations of these impressive burial sites in the capital city of Gyeongju . . . have yielded a dazzling array of gold regalia, pottery, metalwork, and other objects meant to accompany the deceased in afterlife.
>
> (Lee and Leidy 2013:6)

Figure 1.1 Gold crown from Tomb 98 north mound (Hwangnam Daechong)
Source: Alamy

4 The ancient city of Gyeongju

Even to this day there is a mysterious aura of antiquity surrounding the tomb mounds that loom over the center of the city like an unnatural range of hills.

Careful sifting of the earth by archaeologists has increasingly revealed important features and artifacts, which add incrementally to knowledge about the city in all its eras. Other surprises, too, may lie in the numerous unearthed tombs.

In addition to the imposing tomb mounds, Buddhist monuments large and small are scattered seemingly randomly around the city of Gyeongju, some of them remnants of bygone buildings. Many of the large temples were destroyed by a variety of foreign invasions mostly from Japan and Mongolia, but even after Silla's power was ceded to the Goryeo dynasty, some ancient buildings still stand, a few unfathomable until they are explained, such as a bottle-shaped building said to have been an astronomical observatory built by the clever Queen Seondeok (Figure 1.3).

Several brick and stone pagodas, an icehouse, a pond that was part of a pleasure palace, Buddhist shrines, temples, and a grotto with a giant Buddha gazing out toward Japan, as well as many unexcavated royal tombs, still grace the city. One of the world's largest bronze bells also hangs outside the museum, where it can be struck with a log from the outside (rather than a clapper) so it resonates in booming tones (Figure 1.4).

The footprint of Hwangyongsa, an enormous Buddhist temple that was erected in a field on the eastern edge of the city, has been outlined by archaeologists digging around the pillar bases on which the roof rested. It has a square footprint, about 280 meters in each direction. Huge dragon roof ornaments emphasize the

Figure 1.2 US satellite image of tomb mounds in Gyeongju

Source: Alamy

Figure 1.3 Cheomseongdae, possible astronomical observatory in Gyeongju
Source: Alamy

power of the building, and a pair of stone buttresses that braced a tall flagpole is guaranteed to make the visitor feel dwarfed by this phantom building. It had a nine-story wooden pagoda 68 meters high, the skyscraper of the time. It is said that when Hwangyongsa was constructed it was the largest Buddhist temple complex in Asia. This temple also had a renowned bell which measured about 3 meters high, but was destroyed in a fire.

Both the Buddhist grotto of Sokkuram and the monastery of Bulguksa needed restoration in the twentieth century. Invaders had burned the wooden halls and temples of Bulguksa, but graceful stone bridges and elegant pagodas were

Figure 1.4 Large bronze bell, Gyeongju
Source: Alamy

indestructible by fire. Other Buddhist monuments are in the process of excavation. The earlier glories of Geumseong, the "golden fortress," as the Silla capital was known in its prime, are being revealed bit by bit.

Even with its golden crowns, shimmering with golden leaves and jade jewels, its majestic Buddhas, and its Silk Road treasures, Gyeongju is not well known as a tourist destination outside of Asia, in spite of having been the capital of the state of Silla for a thousand years. World history has unjustly passed over much of the rich field of Asian history before European contact, especially East Asia. Therefore, some basic facts are needed for most readers.

The ancient city of Gyeongju 7

Gyeongju is unique among East Asian capitals for the length of its continuity in one location without any hiatus in occupation. The earliest polity in the valley was known as Saro, by tradition founded in 57 BCE, and the city was called Seorabeol. It grew to become Geumseong, a city of nearly one million people in its heyday as the capital of the peninsula. The kingdom of Silla deferred peacefully to the Goryeo dynasty in 935 CE, when the capital of the Korean peninsula moved to Gaesong. The city of Geumseong, now a secondary capital, was renamed Gyeongju at that time, and so it has been called in the more than one thousand years that have elapsed since the days of its glory, as described in the opening quotation. The length of Gyeongju's reign as a capital city may be partly explained by its topography, which provided a defensible area for farmers, miners, and artisans, and the rulers who taxed them, to lead mostly uninterrupted lives in this sheltered valley.

Environment of Gyeongju

A wide valley with deep, rich soil for crops, plentiful water, as well as both iron and gold resources (Park 1998), must have been attractive to the immigrant families who settled there, fleeing from the draconian policies of the Qin dynasty in the second century BCE. The valley as the first settlers saw it was welcoming, with the confluence of five river valleys providing an abundance of water for growing rice and other crops. Along the edges of the hills there was plenty of water too, and the winters were warmer than elsewhere in southern Korea, thanks to the protecting mountains.

The mountains are not especially high, but they are rugged, with steep escarpments above dusty trails leading into the larger river valleys. Mt. Tohamsan (the eminence where both Sokkuram and Bulguksa are located) is the highest of the eastern mountain range that screens the city from the East Sea, with an elevation of 745 meters. The western mountains rise to more than 400 meters, and an even higher peak of 500 meters helps to guard the narrow valley approaches from the direction of the Naktong River, the major river of south-eastern Korea. A national park has been created in this scenic area. These mountains provided both iron and gold, but archaeological evidence suggests that iron was mined and smelted centuries earlier than gold. All along the east coast of the Korean peninsula, gold, iron, and other metals have been extracted. To give an idea of the extent of its gold, Korea was still exporting gold in the nineteenth century (Griffis 1882: 426–427), and as late as the twentieth century it was the fifth largest gold producer in the world (Bartz 1972).

Incheon stream, which rises from the Taebaek mountain range in the north, splits around the southern mountains, dividing them into two ranges, with Mt. Namsan between the two branches of the stream. Mt. Kumosan, 494 meters high, rears its peaks west of the stream.

Mt. Namsan rises steeply between streams south of the city. It remains a sacred mountain, marking the spot where the original villages decided to band together for protection against raiding neighbors. In the Buddhist era, Mt. Namsan became a virtual gallery of Buddhist stone carvings (Adams 1979). Carvings of Bodhisattvas and Buddhas may appear suddenly as one rounds a bend on the mountain path. It seems

8   *The ancient city of Gyeongju*

that a lifetime of hiking around Mt. Namsan would not be enough to encounter all the Buddhas that inhabit it.

Even in the north, where the Hyeongsan River flows, the Gyeongju valley is guarded by peaks of 300 meters and more (Park 1998). The settlers in this site must have selected it as a well-protected valley, off the beaten track, where a band of refugees would be unlikely to be discovered and disturbed. Still, a small tributary gave access to the Naktong River, 526 kilometers long, the largest river of South Korea with 340 kilometers navigable from the south in the rainy season.

In spite of the seclusion of the valley, raiders appeared over the years, from nearby villages as well as from the Japanese islands and, latest of all, Mongols from the far-off Eurasian Steppes. After the villages of Saro discovered that they were not completely protected by their natural topography, mountain fortresses were erected on three of the mountains, two overlooking both sides of the narrow entrance from the Naktong River region into the flat land in the center of Saro's territory, further protecting the valley. Exactly when they were built is unknown, but as Gyeongju grew more prosperous, more fortresses were added to protect the wealth of the city.

A path from Gyeongju followed the Hyeongsan River north to a protected harbor at Pohang, on the East Sea. Another trail led south toward the present city and port of Ulsan. A large bay to the south-east at Busan was also reachable from Gyeongju.

While it is easy to understand the selection of this valley by a beleaguered, weak polity, as even the combined villages of Saro initially must have been, reasons for Gyeongju to flourish are not as clear. Early documents explain that six villages joined together because of "strong enemies nearby" (Ha and Mintz 1972:49). But the same defensible characteristics made the city an unlikely spot for the important trade center that it became, with exotic goods coming from the northern and southern Silk Roads and goods arriving by sea from South-East Asia as well, bringing foreign objects for the royal lifestyle which would ultimately be placed in lavish royal tombs.

Silla is recorded as having done more than its share of raiding and conquering. Silla's early conquests may have been attributable to the fortress-like situation of its capital and heartland, which made it difficult for other polities to retaliate to Silla's raids. However, Gyeongju was vulnerable to predation from the sea. Raids on Gyeongju originating from the Japanese islands were recorded several times in the Silla annals. One attack successfully raided the royal castle of Wolseong-ro in the center of Gyeongju. Even the Goguryeo kingdom was a threat, raiding Gyeongju at least once. Mostly, however, the valley was left in peace to farm, produce iron tools, and by the time of the mounded tombs, to pan for gold and create exquisite gold artifacts.

The continuation of Gyeongju as an important capital when the peninsula was becoming more connected with the outside world is not obvious. Elegant artifacts from distant lands were buried in elite tombs, but no major transportation route ran through the Gyeongju valley, or even to the city. Lacking easy access to either the East Sea or the Naktong River, the location cannot originally have been chosen for trading, although artifacts of stunning beauty reached Gyeongju from at least as far away as Java and Bactria.

The ancient city of Gyeongju 9

On the other hand, the population could flourish within the wide plain and into its narrower valleys, where land and water for rice agriculture were plentiful. Rich sources of iron and gold also contributed to Saro's prosperity, although the ores as well as the elaborate artifacts became draws for marauders. Exactly where iron and gold were mined is not precisely known, but it is often said that the gold was panned from the rivers. Even in the twentieth century gold was being mined in Korea's eastern mountains and shipped to Japan (Grajdanzev 1944).

A brief history

Through time the city was known variously as Seorabeol (when six villages of Saro joined together), Geumseong as the capital of Silla, and Gyeongju after the capital was moved to Gaesong at the beginning of the Goryeo dynasty. It is believed that early on the name Seorabeol came to mean "capital" in a generic sense, becoming the root of the name of the capital of South Korea, Seoul (Kim W. Y. 1982b). The longevity of this term suggests the importance of the name Saro even in the early stages of the polity, although using the name as a term for capital city may only have been applied later, as a memory of vanished glory.

Each stage in the city's thousand-year history has left its imprint on the landscape, but the city did not simply grow larger or merely add accretions of one stage upon the previous one. As Seorabeol, in the first century BCE and later, the city was well defended, which is evident from the daggers and spears bristling in the burials. As Geumseong, imposing royal tombs with rich burial gifts dominating the center of the valley proclaimed the ascendancy of the Kim family. But the center of the city moved north and east as Geumseong enlarged and took on the characteristics of the Chinese capital city at Chang'an, including a pattern of gridded streets and possibly a city wall with gates.

The experience of living in this city must have changed dramatically through time, as the landscape itself was altered by huge constructions. After the time of the mounded tombs, a Buddhist temple was endowed to rise where marshes had probably been used to grow rice, an ambitious monastery was founded on the lower slopes of Mt. Tohamsan, and a giant Buddhist shrine looked out to the East Sea from the top of the same mountain. The new grid pattern of the city, replacing ancient, wandering paths, must have changed the way citizens walked around and rode their horses through the streets, and added structure to the lives of the inhabitants. More and more Buddhist schools were founded, while shrines created by the pious proliferated on Mt. Namsan. By the end of Geumseong's reign as capital, the contours of the city were so altered that its new center would have been unrecognizable to Saro's earlier inhabitants.

The ultimate decline of Great Silla (as it became known) turned Gyeongju into a backwater town, a relatively unimportant destination. Under the Japanese occupation (1910–1945), infrastructure was added in Korea, including railroads, one of which transected Gyeongju. The glory of Ancient Silla was mostly unknown until the addition to a house in 1920 required one of the tomb mounds of the Kim family cemetery in Hwangnam-dong to be removed. To everyone's

10 *The ancient city of Gyeongju*

astonishment, perhaps including the excavators', the officials', and the inhabitants', the tomb turned out to be rich in gold artifacts, containing a glittering gold crown covered with curved beads (*gogok*) made of jade and glass. This tomb is known as the Gold Crown Tomb, as it was the first to come to light, although other gold crowns have since been excavated.

At present, Gyeongju is a composite of all its previous configurations, even though much evidence of earlier times must still be buried beneath later buildings. Like other ancient cities, stones have been reutilized from previous buildings, and walls that had been erected were later torn down. Only the general outlines of the earlier cities can be known. Gyeongju continues to be a living city, now visited for its monuments and museum with grandly displayed artifacts.

The changes in Gyeongju can be divided into stages. The details will be discussed in the chapters that follow; a brief historical overview may be helpful to begin to sort out the complexities of the time.

The Samhan period

Historical documents designate the beginnings of the Three Kingdoms period as precisely 57 BCE, but most archaeologists consider the first three centuries of the Common Era to be merely formative for Silla, and have named it the Samhan (Three Hans) period, sometimes also referred to as the Iron Age. During the Chinese Han dynasty (206 BCE to 220 CE), the northern part of the Korean peninsula was occupied by Chinese commanderies. Presumably, the expansionist Han dynasty was hoping to pacify the population and exploit the land for sources of iron and other materials (Kim J. H. 1978). Only Lelang, the commandery located near the present North Korean city of Pyongyang, remained into the fourth century. The other commanderies were withdrawn because harassment by the local populations made them untenable.

A subsequent decline in the strength of China and its break-up into smaller states in the period called Six Dynasties, gave the Three Kingdoms of Korea breathing room to form themselves. They began to struggle with each other for control of the Korean peninsula, while Xiongnu and Xianbei groups were jostling with each other and with China for land in the north and north-east of China. The larger world of East Asia was being carved out of battles, diplomacy, and trade, in which Silla was only a local participant at this stage. International turmoil allowed groups forming states in Manchuria to send traders and migrants into the Korean peninsula. Even the Xiongnu, the nomadic forerunners of Kubla Khan, made an impact on Korea (Hong 2012).

In 57 BCE, during the time of the Lelang commandery, the city of Seorabeol was formed by consent from six villages located around the edges of the steep hills that protected the valley. The settlements probably consisted of agricultural fields, workshops, and houses, eventually to be surrounded by fortified palaces. The forts followed the Korean pattern of meandering walls, rather than approximately square-walled enclosures, the shape preferred in China. Some recent excavations have unearthed iron workshops and domestic houses, but archaeological methods have not yet systematically been used to pursue the detritus of daily lives in this region, so there is still much to learn.

The population must have been sparse, with no more than 10,000 inhabitants (Kang 2000a). Intrusive elements seen archaeologically can be attributed to Han China (e.g. pieces of chariots, mirrors decorated with patterns in Han style, bells, and horse trappings), but most of the bronze artifacts are epi-nomadic, that is, they come from the nomadic world but were not used by nomadic people (Seyock 2014). Little evidence of direct interaction with China is apparent in archaeological sites.

Nevertheless, Gyeongju was connected to the Asian world and beyond. Burials from the earliest times show that, far from being isolated on its edge of the peninsula, the elite of Seorabeol were connected to a vast trade network. Beads from South-East Asia and exotic items from Central Asia were found in graves from the Samhan period. Participation in a "Yellow Sea Interaction Sphere" (Barnes 1997) is a relevant but not sufficient way to describe the selection and omission of elements that made up the artifacts of the Silla kingdom. Gyeongju had connections with Japan and South-East Asia, as well as Manchuria, Mongolia, and beyond, that were unaffected by China.

The Three Kingdoms period in the Korean peninsula

The appearance of great mounded tombs in the center of Gyeongju, beginning in the early fourth century, is taken as the beginning of the kingdom of Silla as a regional power. The other two kingdoms were Goguryeo and Baekje. Goguryeo arose entirely within Manchuria (now Jilin and Liaoning provinces of China) and later spread to include the northern part of the Korean peninsula. Baekje was founded on the Han River, but later was pushed farther south by Goguryeo, and absorbed the former polity of Mahan. A loose grouping of autonomous cities with a material culture similar to that of Silla was collectively known as Gaya. The Gaya polities arose west of the Naktong River valley and its delta in the earlier part of the Three Kingdoms period (see Map 1.2).

A new burial ground with small mounds appeared in Gyeongju next to the palace of Wolsong-ro in the Gyerim Forest, on land belonging to the Kim clan. During this time the city became known as Geumseong, the "golden fortress."

Whereas, in the beginning, barely visible in archaeological terms, buildings were clustered near South Stream and South Mountain, by the fourth century enormous new tombs were constructed in the middle of the plain, creating a "mountain range" of tombs north of the center. Artifacts in the tombs bespeak connections with north-eastern shamanism (Nelson 2012).

Chinese artifacts are rare in Gyeongju burials, but imports from elsewhere were lavish. Glass and silver vessels are particularly notable. A population of perhaps one hundred thousand people was necessary to support the elites' conspicuous consumption that is evident in the grave goods. Silla had conquered some of its neighboring towns, and used the produce and corvée labor thus acquired to increase its strength.

12 *The ancient city of Gyeongju*

Map 1.2 The Three Kingdoms of Korea

An important difference between Silla and the other kingdoms was that Goguryeo and Paekche both adopted some facets of continental culture much earlier than Silla, while Silla preferred to cling to its epi-nomadic heritage, such as shamanism and gender equality, for much longer. These traits are particularly evident in the artifacts from the royal tombs.

Among the Three Kingdoms of Korea, the Silla state was the farthest from China and, therefore, the most distant from central Chinese influence. This remoteness has been used to explain its unique culture, but Silla was well connected to the other contemporaneous Korean kingdoms, alternately as enemies and allies, and had relationships with polities in the Eurasian Steppes and Manchuria, as well as the Japanese islands.

Polities that formed in the southern areas of the Japanese islands, Tsushima and Kyushu in particular, were in close contact with Silla, and they, too, made sporadic contact with China. Isolation from foreign ideas was not a characteristic of either the state of Silla or its capital city. Creation and preservation of the unique Silla culture must be attributed to other factors.

Buddhist Silla

Buddhism appeared in Goguryeo in 374 and Baekje in 384, but not until the sixth century did Silla become enthusiastically Buddhist. The effect on reorganizing the landscape once again was striking, especially the founding of massive Buddhist temples and schools of Buddhist thought in and near the city, and monasteries too, as well as countless smaller shrines throughout the hills and valleys on all sides, especially on Mt. Namsan. Several Buddhist schools of thought created academies for study, and traveling monks brought scriptures back from India. A grid system was also imposed on the city, north of the huge burial mounds that could not be included in the grid. There are some remnants of a wall in old maps, and some say the city was walled at this time, with four gates like Chinese cities, but this has not been demonstrated on the ground.

Silla unites Korea

The Three Kingdoms were constantly battling each other, but it was Silla that unified the peninsula in the end. Goguryeo pushed Baekje south of the Han River, and harassed Silla. For a time, Silla and Goguryeo were allies, leaving Silla free to gobble up the Gaya states, becoming stronger. Baekje and Silla had border skirmishes, especially as Baekje tried to protect Gaya. During the reign of Queen Seondeok, closer ties were sought with Tang China, where the Empress Wu would hold sway. The alliance of Silla and Tang was successful, conquering both Baekje and Goguryeo officially in 668, bringing the Three Kingdoms period to a close. Silla became known as Great Silla, or sometimes Unified Silla, having unified much of the Korean peninsula under its capital of Geumseong. A few more battles were required for Silla to convince Tang to withdraw from the Korean peninsula, and then peace descended, allowing Silla to flourish in arts and civilization for a few centuries.

A new city was laid out in the style of Tang China, with a grid pattern of streets that is still visible in the Gyeongju of today. It is estimated that the city had nearly one million inhabitants (Kang 2000a). This estimate is derived from census data reported in the *Samguk Yusa* (Iryeon 1972), presumably gleaned from lost Silla annals. The custom of the time was to report population by households rather than individuals, suggesting that households were the basis of taxation. In one census, 178,936 households were counted in Geumseong (Gyeongju) (Kang 2000a).

The city was said to be so rich that tile-roofed houses (contrasted with the straw roofs of farmhouses) reached from the plain to the sea. The *Samguk Yusa* proudly enumerates 35 houses of the elite, which we might call palaces or mansions, so fine that they had gold decoration on the exterior. It must have been a splendid city, as imagined by Griffis in the opening quotation.

14   *The ancient city of Gyeongju*

These changes in the city of Gyeongju reflect growth in the population, but the city had become something different, not merely a larger version of the previous cluster of villages guarded by palaces and forts. The expanding wealth and influence of Silla in the East Asian world is another important product of Gyeongju's growth. Population expansion coincided with changes in the external relationships of Silla, when it joined with Tang China to unite the peninsula.

The very different regimes visible within the present city are a result of the interplay between internal and external change. Internally, Silla experienced an expanding population, increasingly powerful elites, and more complex political organization. External influences included the constantly shifting powers of the "nomadic" Xianbei and Xiongnu, both with Chinese polities, between themselves, the intermittent expansion and power of China, as well as clashes within the Korean peninsula and on the nearby Japanese islands. However, in spite of influences from elsewhere, the character of the city kept a distinctly local flavor. Even when Buddhist monuments provided the dominant theme, the imposing royal tombs continued to make a statement about the past, as they do still. The Buddhist art and architecture developed into a local style, characterized by its monumentality. The Buddhist impetus is clear, but local permutations are also evident.

In the end, the kingdom of Silla destroyed itself with internal divisions caused by the branching of kinship groups of the upper ranks. Instead of creating new forms of government, Silla's elite fought among themselves. The capital city of the new Goryeo dynasty became Gaesong. Now renamed Gyeongju, the city declined into a regional capital.

Gyeongju in world history

Not only the capital of Silla but even Korea itself have seemed "off the beaten track" for East Asia. This is the result of historical events, especially the fact that Korea was the last East Asian country in the region to be "opened" to the West in the nineteenth century (Griffis 1882). However, perhaps the fact that Korea has been understudied in Western scholarship is more relevant to this impression than any intrinsic reasons for Korea to have been perceived as a backwater. Korea has been known through the medium of Japanese and Chinese historical writing rather than being perceived on its own terms. This phase of historical studies on Korea is coming to a close. Archaeological excavations have revealed close and constant connections between the peninsula and the wider world of Asia since well before the beginnings of the Korean Three Kingdoms in the first century BCE.

The closest connections of the Korean peninsula are now known to be with the region that was once called Manchuria and is now north-eastern China, another region also just coming into its own through archaeology. The connections are archaeologically attested by items of material culture such as dolmens, bronze daggers, mirrors, and horse trappings, and materials such as gold and iron.

Before the Chinese Qin and Han dynasties set their sights on the Korean peninsula for exploitation, the areas to the north were populated by distant Korean relatives, Xianbei in Manchuria and Xiongnu in the Eurasian Steppes. While it was

The ancient city of Gyeongju   15

considered to be "barbarian" territory when seen through the eyes of Chinese historians, other perspectives are more useful. The tripolar history of East Asia, and Silla and Gyeongju's negotiation within it for a place in the Asian sun, is the perspective that will be followed in this book. Gyeongju cannot be understood except in its largest context—all of East Asia.

Contents of the book

The next two chapters address the formative period of the city of Seorabeol. Chapter 2, "Saro/Silla and the historical record," focuses on writings pertaining to Gyeongju in this period, while Chapter 3, "Gyeongju archaeology," describes the contributions that archaeology has made to piecing together the history of Gyeongju. Together, these sources of data provide a sense of the early development of the polity, at that time called Saro in some documents and Gyerim in others. An identity was just beginning to form.

Chapter 4 discusses the industries that defined the city. Iron appears to have been the earliest metal industry in Gyeongju. Although bronzes made in Korea are found in local graves, there is no evidence of a bronze industry there. Apparently, the iron ore was only used for agricultural tools and ingots for trade, as no molds for weapons or horse trappings have been found in Gyeongju.

The southern part of the peninsula was well known for its iron ores, but gold made Silla distinctive. It was apparently discovered in the third century, right in the middle of Gyeongju. Exquisite items for trade and royal consumption were produced for local consumption. Very likely, gold nuggets were traded, financing Silla's raids on nearby polities. The pottery industry created jars and bowls for daily use as well as more decorative vessels for use in rituals.

Long-distance trading in beads began as early as the third century BCE, with decorative beads from the Indo-Pacific region. Chapter 5 examines this trade. By the third century, glass and silver vessels also flowed into Gyeongju from across the Eurasian Steppes. Chapter 5 traces the trade routes, and describes the scientific activity that has revealed the specific avenues by which exotic artifacts reached Gyeongju.

Silla was a ranked society from its beginning. Chapter 6, "Ranking and sumptuary rules," takes a closer look at the ranks within the Silla polity, and the way the clan system divided the population into strictly policed ranks, with the royal families at the top. The ranks were visually expressed in the sumptuary rules that regulated the amount and kinds of possessions that each rank could display. The need for such rules must have been partly the result of many exotic items flowing into Gyeongju, as well as the gold jewelry and other precious items that were created within the city.

Chapter 7, "Rulership in Silla," takes a look at the kings and queens of Silla, who they were and how they came to rule. The ruling queens of Silla receive particular attention. The mystery of which king and queen were in the unmarked tombs of Hwangnam Daechong is discussed. It was a time when women could rule, and the reasons for such gender openness are explored.

The changing religions of Silla are reviewed in Chapter 8. The earliest beliefs were animistic, including goddesses of mountains, and shamanism which

16 *The ancient city of Gyeongju*

was artistically portrayed in followers' gold crowns. Buddhism arrived later, as an introduced religion that the elite of Silla at first rejected, and then enthusiastically adopted.

The final two chapters again place Silla in its East Asian context, this time in more detail. Chapter 9 speculates about Silla and the Yamato polity in Japan, particularly the region of Izumo. In spite of some enmity, there were many similarities between Silla and Yamato. Chapter 10 discusses relationships between Silla and the Eurasian Steppes, particularly its Xianbei and perhaps Xiongnu relatives.

Gyeongju's place in East Asia is a glimpse of the wider world. No area developed all on its own. While fairly distinct groups of people inhabited East Asia in the last few centuries BCE—Xiongnu, Xianbei, various polities in China, polities in the developing Korean Three Kingdoms, and various incipient polities in Japan—during the thousand years of Gyeongju considerable mixing occurred, while some clung to a particular ethnicity.

New perspectives on Gyeongju

Although I have been studying and writing about the Silla polity for many years, by focusing precisely on the city of Gyeongju, writing this book has provided me with several new ways to think about the Silla dynasty in the Korean peninsula during the thousand years that Gyeongju had an important role to play in the political and economic systems of entities there. I list the elements of this perspective as a reader's guide:

1 The early records have to be taken seriously, even if not entirely literally. At the very least they are clues to the attitudes of their times.

2 Some people in the Korean peninsula were literate in Chinese even in the last few centuries BCE. We should not allow the Chinese documents to lead us to consider the inhabitants of the Korean peninsula to be "barbarians."

3 The Korean peninsula should be perceived in the Samhan period as a land divided into pockets of fertile, inhabitable valleys by rugged but not high mountains. The ingredients for a good life were available in most of these valley pockets: adequate water, deep soil, and warm summers for growing crops. Travel between the pockets of fertile land was not easy, but it was possible over narrow trails through the rugged hills that divided the valleys.

4 When iron deposits were discovered in various areas of the peninsula, especially in the south-east, many aspects of village life changed. Some people became full-time mining specialists to obtain iron ore, others learned to forge the iron into ingots for trade, or into tools, weapons, and armor. Iron became an industry, requiring managers and workers, and changing the relationship of the leaders to some of the populace. The same occurred with the discovery of gold, with some workers panning in the rivers, and others, who were more skilled, making delicate jewelry and royal paraphernalia.

5 Iron weapons and armor changed warfare, in conjunction with the horse, which made raiding other distant states possible. No one could endure wearing heavy iron armor as a foot soldier, but on horseback the horse took some of the weight.

The speed of horses provided the ability to make quick raids. The intent was to gain new sources of revenue and labor. The Xiongnu to the north of China had pioneered these techniques, and Xianbei peoples possibly invented stirrups, which made fighting from horseback possible. Silla was quick to adopt stirrups.

6   When Han China declared a monopoly on iron, nearby areas not under their jurisdiction, such as in the Korean peninsula, could profit from trade in iron. To whatever extent the Han commanderies in the Korean peninsula were intended to control the iron trade, they were unsuccessful. Southern Korean polities prospered by trading their own iron, which China could not prevent.

7   The loosely populated Korean peninsula in the Jeulmun period became increasingly dense as various groups from northern China, Inner Mongolia, and Manchuria left difficult situations created by Chinese policies, and found their way into the Korean peninsula. Most of these newcomers spoke related Tungusic languages, although some may have spoken Turkic dialects.

8   People were proud of their distant ancestors and remembered groups of their own speech communities for generations. They preserved genealogies, in written form.

9   Seafaring was dangerous, but boats of many sizes, from fishing boats to trading boats, could journey from South-East Asia bringing beads across the sea, and from China carrying silks and other commodities. Japan used the seas for raiding missions. Shrines to goddesses of the sea helped calm the travelers' fears, whether or not they had any effect on the waves.

10 Although gold was not highly valued in China, the northern peoples of the Eurasian Steppes prized it above other metals and precious stones. When the gold of Gyeongju was discovered, it attracted people who already knew how to extract it, and how to fashion it into exquisite jewelry.

11 The Kim family that came to Gyeongju was responding to the gold discoveries. Gold probably funded Silla's conquests.

12 Three branches of Kim clans settled in Gyeongju, Daegu, and near Pusan. They all became prosperous. The name means "gold" and perhaps each region was founded on the exploitation of gold. The branches of the Kim clans became intertwined in Unified Silla.

13 The Gyeongju branch of the Kim clan began to conquer the other branches, one relatively independent village at a time.

14 Crowns were symbols of leadership for the Kim clan, and they allowed (or gave) gilt bronze crowns to the more distant family branches, but saved the best gold crowns for their own royal leaders.

15 Another symbol of leadership was the *gogok*, the curved jewel which was an ancient form of bead used on the Eurasian Steppes to mark leadership, and which was associated with spirits and shamans.

16 The royal mounded tombs began between 420 and 520 according to C14 dates. The earlier dates are more likely. A consensus seems to be forming around the reign of King Naemul and Queen Poban as the beginning of the very large mounded tombs.

17 These topics are pursued in subsequent chapters.

2** Saro/Silla and the historical record

It may seem surprising that there is any written history for the early part of the kingdom of Silla, more than two thousand years ago, but it must be remembered that even at the beginning of the record of Silla, writing in East Asia was already more than a thousand years old. Chinese characters provide the early records on south-eastern Korea, and the tradition of keeping records came from China as well. However, the accuracy of these records has been questioned in a variety of ways (Best 2006; Byington 2016; Davey 2016). One way to check on the validity of ancient records is to compare them with archaeological discoveries, which are outlined in the next chapter. Another is by comparing the documents with each other, revealing discrepancies of various kinds.

The documents that pertain to the earliest eras of the Silla polity have a number of deficiencies that cause some historians to ignore them altogether, and others to treat them with considerable caution. These documents, unfortunately, are the only known descriptions of events in the southern part of the Korean peninsula in the first three centuries BCE and the early centuries CE, so they cannot be simply jettisoned. My stance regarding the documents is that we need to accept that the histories have been manipulated and are incomplete, but there is useful information to be gleaned from even faulty and partial documents, especially when they are supported by archaeological material.

Embedded in the Chinese documents are discussions of three polities we might call chiefdoms, each called Han (Mahan, Byeonhan, and Jinhan), giving them the combined title of the Three Han (Samhan). In contrast, Korean annals begin the story of Gyeongju in 57 BCE, with the organization of a state ruled by kings. These are incompatible versions of the past.

Most historians accept that the territory that became the city of Gyeongju was the seat of a polity called Jinhan, one of the Samhan, and many Korean archaeologists refer to the first to third centuries CE as the Samhan period. This is one perspective in a crowded field of ways to understand the development of the Silla state in Gyeongju, but it is a useful way to begin exploring the documents. The archaeological discoveries in Gyeongju, discussed in the next chapter, are helpful in sorting out material differences through time, but still leave room for

Saro/Silla and the historical record   19

discussion and debate about what polity left these remains. Ju (2009) provides a full discussion of the historical difficulties for readers who would like to delve further into the details. Here, I offer a sketch of those first three centuries from an archaeological viewpoint. I have not read the reports written in ancient Chinese, except in various translations.

Overview of the Samhan period

The polity that is known to history as Silla was called Saro-guk, the state of Saro, in its earlier days, because the first joining of six villages in the Gyeongju plain created a small polity known as Saro, presumably taking its name from the most prominent of the villages. At first, the six villages were scattered around the valleys leading out of the central plain, each village with its own name. Other documents tell of two leaders, one a political leader and the other a spiritual leader. When the leading families of the six villages joined together for defense in 57 BCE, they selected a nominal leader of all the villages, but they continued to meet together to make important decisions. Subsequent leaders were chosen from three families, none of which were the same as the original six clans as recorded in the *Samguk Yusa*, presumably named after the villages. It appears that there was no concept of primogeniture, or a necessary gender of the ruler, although the author of the *Samguk Sagi* did his best to obscure such attitudes.

By the time Silla began to be an important player in peninsular politics, in the third to fifth centuries, the enlarged city was called Geumseong, literally the "golden fortress," but perhaps implying the stronghold of the Kim clan. At that time the city was built around fortified palaces of the ruling families, with mountain fortresses for the first line of defense. At that time Silla was in the process of subduing and incorporating its neighboring polities. When Geumseong was no longer the capital of the Korean state, the city became Gyeongju, as it is still known. The city still had the honor of being a provincial capital.

The Korean Han polities were located in the regions of southern Korea where the states of Silla (Jinhan) and Baekje (Mahan) arose later, with the unaffiliated Gaya (Pyonhan) cities between them. Mahan was said to be the largest and strongest polity at that time, comprised of more than 50 walled towns (Seyock 2004:71). The *Wei Zhi Dongyichuan* lists the *guo* "states" in each polity by name, and enumerates their populations. A city called Saro is included among places in Jinhan, which makes identifying Saro with Silla reasonably secure. The *guo* are interpreted as walled towns, as is implied by the Chinese character that depicts a wall around a spear; the modern meaning of the character is "country." Archaeological surveys have located hundreds of walled towns, and toponyms suggest that at least some were present by the third century. For example, several towns in Korea are named Toseong-ri, meaning "earthen fort village." Archaeologists have also located several previously unknown forts and castles near Gyeongju with possibly early dates.

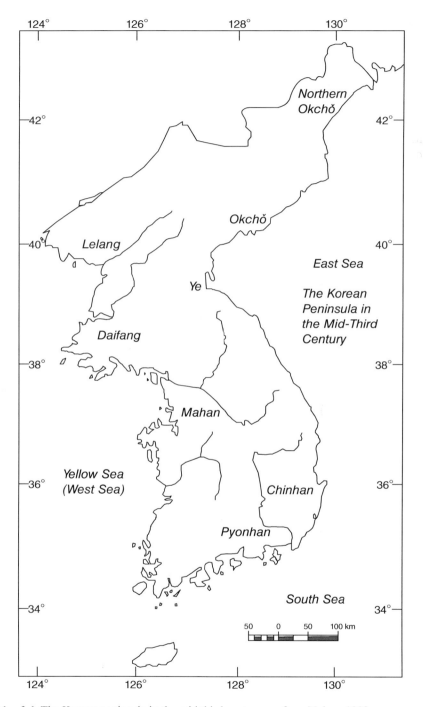

Map 2.1 The Korean peninsula in the mid third century CE, from Nelson 1993

The written record

Several ancient histories describe the early days of Saro, the flowering of Gyeongju, and the emergence of Silla as temporarily the strongest polity in the Korean peninsula. Although the various documents have different emphases and different purposes, and sometimes different "facts," a sense of Gyeongju at the center of the polities of Saro, and later Silla, emerges.

The only written language in the entire East Asian region was Chinese. Although an attempt was made to use Chinese characters as phonetics in the Korean language, it was too clumsy to be widely adopted, as the grammar of Korean is very different from that of Chinese. The Korean language did not have its own script, *hangul*, until the fourteenth century, and even after *hangul* was invented Chinese characters were used in official documents and scholarly writing, even into the 1970s in South Korea. The alphabetic script of King Sejeong was considered women's writing. Real men could read Chinese.

In 108 BCE the former Han dynasty of China conquered some of the Xianbei states in Korea, including the state of Joseon, which is seen as a historic forerunner of current Korean polities by both North and South Korea. To control this territory and exploit the inhabitants, the Han Chinese government established four commanderies within the Korean peninsula and nearby Manchuria, including Liaoning Province. The inhabitants of these conquered regions, however, were unruly. Three of the commanderies were quickly driven out by uprisings of the native peoples. Only Lelang, with its center near the present city of Pyongyang, was able to survive. Lelang, planted in the heart of the peninsula with excellent access from China across the Yellow Sea, lasted about four centuries, long enough to interact with and affect the other inhabitants of the Korean peninsula. Later, a short-lived commandery called Daifang was established south of the former Lelang commandery.

The Lelang commandery was governed by Han Chinese officials who, according to the furnishings in their tombs, lived luxuriously with imports of silk, lacquerware, and objects made of gold and precious stones. The elite rode in horse-drawn vehicles with umbrella-like canopies, and occupied palatial dwellings. Several tombs, forts, walls, and other constructions from the centuries of occupation were left for the archaeologist's spade, although the buildings had been left in ruins. Tombs of local Korean elites as well as Chinese officials have been excavated, with simpler and local artifacts being found in Korean graves, making it possible to discriminate between the natives and the conquerors by the types of their grave goods (Pai 1992, 2000).

The commandery of Lelang was ultimately conquered by the energetic and growing state of Goguryeo in 331. Lelang had had a presence in Korea for roughly the same length of time as the Roman occupation of Britain. The long-lasting presence of Chinese culture in the Korean peninsula may have influenced the development of states in southern Korea, but to whatever extent, the influence was indirect, leaving the local cultures and languages basically the same. The persistence of Korean culture may have been made possible by further immigration into the peninsula of related peoples, a topic to be discussed in Chapter 10.

22 *Saro/Silla and the historical record*

Documents

The documents upon which those who study early Korean history depend stem from several sources. The Chinese dynasties did not attempt to incorporate the Korean peoples, among whom they had planted their commanderies, into their own polities, nor did they ignore them altogether. Chinese officials were recording events in the Korean peninsula. While the accuracy of the reports in those parts of Chinese annals relating to the Korean peninsula is often debatable, the tidbits reported provide an otherwise unavailable perspective on early Korea.

Han and Wei documents on the Samhan

The Chinese governments must have been curious about the possibilities for exploitation of the unconquered people, for they seem to have sent scouts to explore the lands and resources of the southern part of the Korean peninsula, an area which the Lelang commandery did not have under its sway. Records of two of these expeditions give sketchy accounts, but they drop useful hints about village life.

The first of these documents was written during the former Han dynasty and the second in the Wei dynasty, both of them for the purpose of reporting on the peoples and their villages in the rest of the Korean peninsula. The resulting reports have an ethnographic flavor, but they are not systematic in reporting the same data about each region. Population size was frequently noted, which suggests that the strength of possible uprisings was relevant, as well as the existence of resources that might be exploited by China. The Han dynasty had declared state monopolies on iron and salt (Gale 1931) and it was probably of considerable interest to the Chinese government that iron ore was plentiful in southern Korea.

The earliest known documents regarding southern Korea are thus not only written in Chinese, they were created with a Chinese perspective that looked down on "barbarians," meaning any people who did not follow Chinese rituals (Pines 2005). These tantalizing bits about early Korea are embedded in the national histories of the former Han dynasty, the *Hou Han Shu Dongyichuan* (HHS) in the first century CE, and the Tuoba Wei dynasty, the *Wei Zhi Dongyichuan* (WZ) in the late third century. The *San Guo Zhi* (SGZ), translated by Mark Byington (2009), is the earliest of these partial histories. The Wei rulers were a people neither Chinese nor Xiongnu. Known as Xianbei, they may have spoken a language related to that spoken in Gyeongju. A third document referred to as the *Weiliie* was written earlier, but it only exists as quotes in later documents.

The *Dongyichuan* (DYC) was meticulously translated into German by Barbara Seyock (Seyock 2004:25–50) and I have made use of this resource. A translation by Mark Byington (2009) has also been helpful, as well as an arrangement of the three ancient sources displayed beside each other for comparison, including fragments from the *Weiliie*. A translation made by E. H. Parker (1890) is a source I have used in the past, but is less than ideal, because Parker's lectures to his peers simply rendered various texts into English prose without specifying

Saro/Silla and the historical record   23

references, so that it is impossible to be sure of the exact documents he was drawing from. However, there is no reason to doubt that this nineteenth-century English gentleman was paraphrasing Chinese sources to which he had acquired access. A useful comparison of three texts has recently been published (Barnes and Byington 2014), which demonstrates differences among the texts, and shows that parts of later texts are simply copied or paraphrased from earlier annals. Nothing in these reports mentions southern Korea before the second century BCE, when the HHS asserts that Chun, formerly king of Joseon, fled from the Chinese attackers of his citadel, defeated the Mahan, and set himself up as king. However, the same document later says that the "Mahan people again set themselves up as Kings of Chin" (p. 101) suggesting some uncertainty about the events. However, for understanding early Gyeongju these early writings are largely irrelevant.

No further mention of the Han (or Chin) polities of southern Korea is made in any of the Chinese histories until the second century CE, when both the HHS and the SGZ report that "the Han and Ye people grew strong and the commandery districts could not support them" (p. 103). The Ye people seem to have occupied land north of Gyeongju along the east coast. During this time, the *Samguk Sagi* relates that the Daifang commandery was established south of Lelang, and "the Wa and Han eventually became subject to Daifang" (p. 104). The extent and content of such subjugation are not elaborated upon.

The first mention of the "Three Han, Mahan, Chinhan and Pyonhan" occurs in a document of the third century. It is also the first explicit statement about these polities having formerly belonged to the kingdom of Chin (HHS). During the third century, there were different sizes of polity in each of the Samhan. The larger regions of Chinhan and Pyonhan had 4,000–5,000 families, and small regions had 600–700 families. Chinhan was made up of 12 polities, according to the SGZ. The people are said to speak a different language from the Mahan, having come from Qin in order to avoid its harsh laws. They speak a language like that of the Qin (p. 105), which is another suggestion of the possible Xianbei roots of Silla.

Further descriptions in the HHS comment that the Han have walled towns, and that detached villages have chieftains, with titles according to the size of their polity. The people cultivate the five cereals, raise silkworms, and weave fine silk (SGZ), and make silk brocade cloth (HHS). They have carts pulled by horses or oxen. They produce iron and use it as currency. They enjoy singing and dancing and playing a stringed instrument. The SGZ adds an interesting observation: "they use large bird feathers to send off their dead, the intent being to allow the deceased to fly upward. Furthermore, they produce fine-tailed chickens, all of which have tails more than 5 chi long" (p. 106).

Both say that babies' heads are pressed to make them narrow, but the SGZ adds that "Chinhan people all have narrow heads" (p. 107). They live in clay houses with thatched roofs. The SGZ says that horses are sacrificed for the dead. It also says that the people value beads, and wear them on their clothes, ears, and necks. The two documents disagree about whether their sandals are made of leather or straw, but possibly the farmers wore straw sandals and the elite wore leather. Leather production is discussed in Chapter 4.

24   *Saro/Silla and the historical record*

Both versions tell of rites that occur after planting, with singing and dancing and drinking spirits "all day without rest." One person (gender not specified) was in charge of the sacrifice to the spirit of heaven. A sacred area called a *sodo* was set apart with drums and bells suspended from a large log.

These three documents were all written from the perspective of curious outsiders. The WZ is specific about the inhabitants of the south, naming three separate confederations of such polities—Jinhan in the east, Byeonhan on the southern coast, and Mahan in the south-west. (The Han character in Samhan (the Three Han) is not the same character as the one that means the Chinese Han dynasty).

Judging by the WZ portion of the SGZ as well as the HHS, the Chinese scouts found the inhabitants of Korea to be people with strange clothing, unusual houses, and peculiar but interesting habits. For example, one observation was that, "When a son was born they liked to flatten his head by pressing it with stones." This practice has been verified in a Neolithic burial ground at Yeanni, a site that was on the southern coast of Korean prior to a late rise in sea level, in which some skeletons had artificially deformed heads (Kim J. H. 1978), but it has not otherwise been found in north-east Asia, except in a very distant archaeological site of the Boisman culture near Vladivostok in the Russian Far East (Kuzmin 2006a). These observations may reflect settlers from the south. However, human remains of any time period are rarely preserved in Korea, and negative evidence in this case is meaningless. Certainly, the early peoples of the coastal regions of East Asia were fisher folk who were accustomed to using boats and could travel long distances (Ikawa-Smith 1986; Nelson 2008b). It is likely that various groups of people with different languages and ethnicities encountered each other, and some fisher folk from the south could have settled on the south coast of the Korean peninsula. The bead trade makes it evident that trade with southern peoples occurred (see Chapter 5).

Concepts of spirits and the otherworld

The HHS records that the people on the east coast of the Korean peninsula venerated mountains and streams. Furthermore, "they knew how to observe the stars, and could prophesy the abundance or scarcity of the year" (Parker 1890:205). References to astronomical events in the *Samguk Sagi* have recently been published (Stephenson 2013), showing that the leaders of Saro/Silla had an interest in naked-eye astronomy, but the list lacks any indication of the inhabitants perceiving events in the sky as portents.

Some other scraps of information apply specifically to the area of Gyeongju. The Samhan made sacrifices to the spirits of heaven at an annual festival with singing, dancing, and drinking rice wine, and made sacrifices to tigers. Siberian tigers still existed in parts of the Korean peninsula into the twentieth century (Zaichikov 1952), so it is not surprising that tiger spirits were feared and respected. Folk paintings of tigers are still popularly placed on gates, and are often used as protection against destructive spirits (Zozayong 1972). In fact, the Mountain Spirit and his tiger often have a shrine in Buddhist temples (see Figure 8.1, p.101), so pervasive was this concept before the coming of Buddhism. Spotted leopards, which appear with tigers in Korean folk paintings, were said to be plentiful. However, no references to tiger or leopard attacks are found in the Silla annals, and the presence of tigers is not one of the stresses that the Silla people chose to record in their annals (Kang 2000a:878, Table 2). Perhaps the tigers did not live as far south as Gyeongju, preferring the higher mountains of Taebaeksan and Baekdusan.

The WZ describes sacred groves called *sodo*, marked by a tall pole, drums and bells. The HHS further relates that the people of Mahan were shockingly egalitarian, and "drew no distinction of age or sex." The Han villages worshiped the spirits twice a year—after planting and after harvest. These times are still important holidays in Korea. The rituals were described by a Chinese writer, perhaps with disapproval or with envy, as consisting of "a drinking bout night and day, assembling in groups to dance and sing" (Parker 1890). It appears that hard work was rewarded by the spirits with another kind of spirits!

Who were the settlers in Gyeongju?

The question of where various people of Silla migrated from will be raised in a later chapter, but in the context of these documents it is useful to note that the HHS recounts a tale implying that the elite had come from the north-eastern region of China—an area that currently includes Liaoning Province and Inner Mongolia in China, which at that time was settled by a branch of the Xianbei tribe, and later became a part of Goguryeo. The WZ says that the Chinhan and Pyonhan people emigrated from elsewhere, which is why they had been subject to Mahan (p. 104). The WZ further says that,

> the old men of Chinhan used to say that they had been refugees from the Qin dynasty (221–206 BCE) who had fled to the (Korean) Han states in order to escape the misery of forced labor instituted by the draconian governments of the Qin dynasty, who were building part of the Great Wall through Xianbei territories.
>
> Translated in Parker 1890:209

Parker further adds, "Mahan cut off the eastern portion of their state for them" (Parker 1890:209). Thus, Jinhan, which was located in Yeongnam, the south-eastern part of the Korean peninsula, was probably centered on Gyeongju. Most Korean scholars agree that the name Jinhan applies to the area that became the state of Silla in the Three Kingdoms period. After Silla conquered Baekje and Goguryeo, Unified Silla nominally ruled over most of the Korean peninsula.

Korean histories

The early history of Korea is told by Korean authors in two documents: the *Samguk Sagi*, "History of the Three Kingdoms," composed in the twelfth century by a

26 *Saro/Silla and the historical record*

Confucian scholar named Kim Pusik (1145); and the *Samguk Yusa*, "Memorabilia of the Three Kingdoms" (Iryeon 1972), which was written by Iryeon, a Buddhist monk fascinated by miraculous tales and wonders, in the thirteenth century. Both histories were written long after the events occurred, but presumably the *Silla Pon'gi* (annals of Silla), were based on annals extant in the twelfth and thirteenth centuries that have since been lost.

The two histories were written for different purposes, with different emphases, and describe not quite identical historical events. Even the lists of kings in the two histories do not precisely coincide. In addition to the Chinese documents already discussed, these are the most cited writings pertaining to the rise of the Three Kingdoms. However, a few other fragmentary documents exist. There are parts of a village census and an incomplete description of the sumptuary laws (Kim Chong Sun 1965). These sources together provide a variety of kinds of information about earlier times in the Korean peninsula, but each was written for a different purpose and they offer different views on the people and their activities, based on the authors' perspectives and prejudices.

In spite of their differences, the *Samguk Sagi* (1145) and the *Samguk Yusa* (1278) are the most reliable written sources for early Korea. They were written from the hindsight of the successful kingdom of Silla which ultimately became dominant over the other two Korean kingdoms, but that fact in itself does not make the writings biased. Silla had attained and lost hegemony over most of the Korean peninsula by the twelfth and thirteenth centuries, and power had shifted to the Goryeo dynasty when the histories were written. However, Gyeongju was still a regional capital of the Goryeo dynasty, and had retained its splendor as a center of Buddhism until Confucian iconoclasts and foreign invaders destroyed it. The transfer of the capital to Gaesong had been peaceful, and it was not until the Joseon dynasty that Confucianism became ascendant (Deuchler 1992).

Silla's successes may have biased some interpretations in the records of the Three Kingdoms in favor of Silla, especially the *Samguk Sagi,* whose compiler was the great grandson of a "Lord of Gyeongju" (Schulz and Kang 2011:11), but there is no evidence that Kim Pusik did so. Because the similarities between the two accounts of the Three Kingdoms are more compelling than the differences, it is reasonable to assume that ancient annals of the Three Kingdoms underlie the *Samguk Sagi* and *Samguk Yusa*, rather than supposing that the authors relied on folklore or copied Chinese models.

The *Silla Pon'gi* were not written down in their present form in either of the two historical compendia until many centuries after the events they presume to report, allowing some slippage of accuracy due to copying errors and selectivity of what was included. However, it is reasonable to suppose that both books are based on writings that were contemporaneous with the times described. It was customary to keep records, and writing such annals must have been within the capabilities of scribes of Ancient Saro from the beginning of the polity. It is, therefore, surprising that many scholars of early Korea have been skeptical about the timing of the founding of Silla. Increasingly, archaeology tends to uphold the accuracy of the *Samguk Sagi* and the *Samguk Yusa*. Even the inherent biases of the Chinese and Japanese perspectives as written in their own narratives allow their reports to shed some light on early Gyeongju writing.

All writing in East Asia at the time of the founding of Silla was in Chinese characters, Chinese having already been a written language for more than a thousand years. Although the Manchu and Mongol languages did not have scripts until much later, it would be a mistake to consider any of the leaders of East Asian polities in the first century BCE as illiterate, whatever language they may have spoken. The Xiongnu and Xianbei leaders received and sent messages to China as early as 200 BCE (Parker 1890:184), and the Korean states are known to have corresponded with each other (Osgood 1951:176). However, the material on which characters were painted or carved was largely perishable—bamboo and silk before paper was invented. Some stone monuments have survived in Silla, carved with Chinese script. Likewise the Gwanggaeto monument in Goguryeo uses only Chinese to boast about the conquests of the king in 402.

Writing brushes from the first century BCE were preserved in a tomb near the south coast of Korea at Dahori (Yi et al. 1989), opening up the possibility that the lost Silla annals could have been written down close to the time the events occurred, and still been available to the writers of the Korean histories in the eleventh and twelfth centuries. Perhaps perishable materials would have required the annals to be periodically reinscribed, introducing possibilities for error. The Yamato court brought scribes from the Korean peninsula (Paekche) in the early fifth century, and brought their chronicles with them. Granted that this event is later than the founding of Gyeongju, nevertheless a long tradition of keeping records in the Korean peninsula is reflected.

Spoken languages

For the inhabitants of the Korean peninsula, speaking a language unrelated to Chinese in both vocabulary and grammar, the effort of mastering the meanings of Chinese characters must have been enormous. Indeed, for all the Turkic and Altaic speakers on China's borders, learning to read Chinese writing must have been a challenge. The meanings of nouns and verbs could be understood without necessarily absorbing the grammar of Chinese, which in any case is simple compared to the Tungusic, Altaic, and Turkic languages. Besides, all trading peoples would have been familiar with the spoken languages of the peoples with whom they exchanged goods. One branch of the Silk Road ran to the north of China, and many languages must have been spoken en route. Early peoples had to be polyglots.

Gyeongju history

The history of Gyeongju is often divided into time periods, which are visible in the city to this day. The earliest segment is the time of the creation of Saro from the six villages. Gyeongju is replete with cemeteries from this time period. After the rule of King Michu (261–284), the Kim family dominated the rulership.

28 *Saro/Silla and the historical record*

By the time of King Naemul (356–402), enormous funeral monuments, which loom over the middle of the city, were constructed, creating the Mounded Tomb period. With the advent of Buddhism, monuments both large and small sprang up all around the city. While many of the Buddhist buildings have vanished, traces of Buddhism can still be found throughout the city.

The six villages of the confederacy of Saro

Korean documents declare that the state of Silla began in Gyeongju in 57 BCE, with the organization of six villages into a polity that took the name of Saro (Kim W. Y. 1982b) specifies their names and locations. The confederation of six villages was concerned with the need for defense against strong enemies nearby. The leaders of the six villages met along streams or on mountains, which were probably particularly sacred places (Iryeon 1972).

The first discussions among the "leaders and their families" (*Samguk Yusa*), who gathered by the Hyecheon stream to select a central leader, seem to have been motivated by defense. Not only are "strong enemies" mentioned as a specific threat, but also the annals of all the Three Kingdoms cite many incursions, raids, and battles. Bong Won Kang (2000a:878) notes that during the first four centuries of the existence of Saro, 67 incidences of warfare are recorded. The region had no power strong enough to enforce peace, and raiding of other cities must have been mostly for loot or labor power, not for land. Contests for dominance were typical of the cultures of the Eurasian Steppes. Given the amount of raiding recorded in the *Samguk Sagi*, it is no wonder that the villages needed to unite. Quite soon after being founded, Saro began absorbing or conquering nearby small polities, participating in frequent raiding of many of the small states. Clearly, there were no rules.

Warfare was not the only challenge faced by the villages of Saro. The records show flood or heavy rain, typhoons, snow, plagues of locusts, unusually high temperatures, hail, frost, epidemic disease, and crop failure, creating 76 "stresses" in the first four centuries of the existence of Saro (Kang 2000a:878). We read that at one time the king had to open his storehouses to the people because of severe famine.

However, many of the early years of Saro are recorded to have been quite peaceful. Reservoirs were created, and roads and fortresses were constructed. Crafts were organized. The first queen organized weaving contests among the villages, which seems to imply either that weaving was a new skill which needed to be encouraged, or that new types of weaving were being introduced. From a census fragment we know that the number of mulberry trees in each village was counted, showing that silk was among the materials that were woven, in addition to hemp and ramie.

Geography and buildings

Attempts to locate the six villages have been various, but Jong Wook Lee (1998:18) reasonably points out that the locations of mountains and rivers conveniently divide the area that is now Gyeongju into six regions, each measuring about 10 kilometers in diameter. He estimates that each village would have had about 500 households, with a population of 2,500 in total.

The only building mentioned in the chronicles of the early stages of Saro is Namdang, the south hall, with a construction date of 249. The building was used as an assembly hall for the heads of households, who had previously alternated their meetings between the four sacred mountains surrounding Gyeongju. The first such assembly occurred on Mt. Namsan, "south mountain", suggesting the south hall connoted the importance of the south. The exact location of Namdang is unknown, but Adams (1979) reports that large pillar bases for what he calls a palace were found at the site of the Gyeongju museum. The museum is in the southern part of the city, not far from Wolseong-ro, so it seems to be a possible location, although it is also possible that the pillar bases were part of an early palace or later temple.

Leadership

The leaders of Saro are called kings and queens from the beginning of Saro. They were selected from among three families, Pak, Sok, and Kim. Rulership was passed among the three families, whose eligibility to rule was established by the fact that each had a founding ancestor with a miraculous appearance. The stories involve events such as being born from golden eggs, or found in a golden box, or attention was called to them by a neighing white horse, or a red bird. The traditional Korean tales thus emphasize the supernatural origins of the first rulers of the Pak, Sok, and Kim families. This folklore provides insights into the ways the royal families legitimized their right to rule, and the validation of their right to collect revenues and receive corvée labor. Another significant factor of these tales is that they highlight the importance to the ruling families of gold, white horses, and red birds, suggesting their origins in Xianbei and Xiongnu groups.

Sung Joo Lee (1998:25) relates that, "the royal household comprises the queens's family members and the queen's mother's family members and the King's kinsman." This emphasis on the female line is characteristic of Silla, but not the other kingdoms of Korea.

Saro was centered on the walled palace or castle known as Wolseong-ro, "Moon Fortress", where the leading Pak family of Saro is believed to have resided (although Lee S. J. 1998 says the Seok family lived there). The first king, Pak Hyeokkeose, was the head of the Pak clan, but there is an odd tale of his acquiring the area where this castle was built by trickery, claiming that the land had belonged to his grandfather, who was a blacksmith. He had buried iron slag in the area, and in this way he won his case. This story not only suggests the importance and antiquity of iron making in Silla, but also shows that some form of adjudication of disputes was in place. The palace of Wolseong-ro was destroyed long age, but its location on a low hill in a bend of the Namcheon River is known by remnant walls and a broken stone bridge over the South River.

30 *Saro/Silla and the historical record*

The Mounded Tomb period

Archaeology suggests that the Kim clan may have been latecomers to Saro. The rather sudden appearance of gold working and mound building at the same time, in the section of Gyeongju where the Kim clan lived, as well as a change in burial goods and evidence of trade through the Eurasian Steppes, imply a sudden and radical change. Although the first king from the Kim line was said to have miraculously appeared in a golden box, this was very likely a later fable interpolated into the history to legitimate the Kim rulership, making their line as old as that of Pak and Sok. Sung Joo Lee (1998:25) would put the time brackets around this period as from "the reign of King Naemul (356–402) . . . to the reign of Queen Seondeok (632–646)."

The mounded tombs began in Saro in the third or fourth century. The name Kim means gold or metal. As presumable goldsmiths, the Kim clan might well have been attracted to the location of the villages of Saro by the gold sand and gold nuggets found in the rivers of Gyeongju. Gold working of a very high standard suddenly appears in the Kim family cemetery. It seems likely that members of the clan who had the ability to make the astonishing gold crowns, jewelry, and other objects that began to appear at the time of King Michu, the first of the continuous Kim rulers, were among the important persons who had newly arrived. No prior evidence of gold or gold working exists anywhere in the southern part of the Korean peninsula.

The Kim clan occupied an area of trees known as Gyerim, "pheasant/chicken forest," where they had their stronghold and the family burial ground. Silla seems to have been known by the name of Gyerim in India, and perhaps elsewhere, stressing the importance of the Kim clan to Silla. Birds were thought to be messengers from the spirits, and long tails of birds were particularly prized.

Conquests

By the fifth century the central government in Gyeongju was strong enough to control surrounding polities. The *Samguk Sagi* records increasing numbers of conquests by Silla, (as well as increasing attacks on it). Bong Won Kang (2000b) indicates that Silla first conquered the nearer polities, and then reached out for conquests further afield. The names and dates of conquests are supplied in the *Samguk Yusa*: Apto-guk and Sabol-guk in Sangju, Somun-guk in Uiseong, and Iso-guk in Jingdo. Note that these were considered "states", each of them having "guk" in the name. One of these, Iso-guk, is recorded as having unsuccessfully attacked Gyeongju (Saro-guk). It was a "state-eat-state" world. Certainly, the polities in the rest of the peninsula and Manchuria were continually testing for dominance, perhaps an inheritance from their nomadic ancestors, whether Xianbei or Xiongnu.

The first set of recorded conquests by Saro occurred in the first and second centuries BCE. This group of polities was relatively near to Silla, not stretching its supply lines too far. Between 57 and 111, six states were brought under Saro's

Saro/Silla and the historical record   31

control, but in the second and third centuries Saro grew more ambitious, making war on seven cities to the north-east and south-east, all within Yongnam. By the fifth and sixth centuries Silla had raided and conquered all the states in Gaya. Silla may have been aided by the silting up of the Naktong River delta and the shifting of the southern shorelines, but the result was that Silla took over the trade with Japan that had previously been conducted by Gaya.

The maps of Saro's conquests compiled by Bong Won Kang (1984, 2000a), which he created from records in the *Samguk Sagi*, are worth examining closely to consider the battles that Silla carried out before it was strong enough to take on the other two Korean kingdoms. It is impressive that some expeditions required a mobilization of troops to battle quite far away from Gyeongju. For example, Hadong, situated near the south-western coast of the peninsula, is said to have been conquered in 294. Masan, in the south-central part of the peninsula, was conquered even earlier, in 158. Both distant expeditions must have strained Silla's resources, and yet Silla won these battles.

Kang (2000a) also made an important study of population size and warfare during the time that Saro was expanding. Kang estimated Saro's population at about 25,000 people in the second century BCE. He argues cogently that population pressure was not a cause of warfare, nor did it cause the formation of the state in the case of Saro/Silla. Battles were fought, he concludes, for workers and fighters more than territory. Skilled workers were needed, as well as farmers, builders, and fighters, which Silla could use more of for increasing conquests.

Although Mahan had more arable land than Pyonhan and Chinhan (Kang 2000a:875), "the battles were not basically about obtaining land. Considering all the historical and archaeological data available, Saro seems to have been one of the largest polities in the Jinhan region. It may have had 5,000 households." Kang concludes that the intent of warfare was to obtain manual laborers (p. 873), not to gain agricultural fields.

One must wonder where the labor power to pile up the enormous tombs of the Kim family graveyard came from. No one has yet estimated the labor cost of just the stone and earth mounds, not to mention the huge amounts of pottery, weapons, and jewelry within the tombs. Workers were needed to find the gold and iron ore as well, and to refine the iron, produce the molds, and create iron artifacts. Kang seems to have discovered an important point about reasons for Silla warfare, and the organization of labor. Agriculture was only a small part of the economy of Gyeongju.

The number of people who had to change their loyalty to another polity (or at least defer to a new recipient of their taxes) because of these battles is staggering, without considering the number of dead in the great battlefield cemeteries of Gaya. For example, in later wars when Silla conquered Baekje and Goguryeo, Kang cites the *Samguk Sagi* as recording that Jungto Yeon, a son of General Gaesomoon Yeon of Goguryeo kingdom, who surrendered to Silla in 666, ceded 12 forts, 763 households, and 3,543 people. Presumably the people were all welcomed into the Silla polity. But perhaps agriculturalists didn't much care what polity taxed them.

32 *Saro/Silla and the historical record*

Consolidation of conquests

Saro controlled its conquered polities with the same principles as were applied by Lelang, which doled out caps and seals to cooperating local chiefs of settlements. Silla seems to have bestowed gilt bronze crowns as objects of status, and allowed the former head to continue to control his or her people. Gilded crowns found in burials in the vicinity of Daegu and Busan suggest possible relatives of Silla or previous chiefs, being given the task of local governance. As will be seen in the following chapter, archaeology has revealed the use of iron armor and longswords by the fourth century. Horses, stirrups, and horse armor found in Silla graves, suggest that mounted warfare was increasingly important. By the mid sixth century Silla ruled over the whole Naktong valley, from Daegu to the southern coast. Whether new tactics or new materials for warfare (such as trained horses and/or armor) were brought to Silla by the Kim clan, giving them an advantage in more adept warfare, is an unsolved question.

As will be seen in the following chapter, archaeology in Gyeongju reveals the use of iron armor, iron swords, and stirrups by the fourth century, which probably gave soldiers an advantage in battles. Did Silla have a new weapon or a new tactic? Barbara Seyock (2014:99–116) shows that evidence of new riding equipment appears in graves in Gyeongju at the time of the battles with Gaya polities to the south. Was it battle steeds and stirrups that helped Silla's armies to victory?

Silla did not stop after conquering all the Gaya polities. The Three Kingdoms were almost continually at war, often making an alliance with a second at the expense of the third. In the fourth century Goguryeo pushed Baekje out of the Han River basin. Later, when Silla saw a chance, she in turn took the Han River region from Goguryeo in 553, creating an avenue to the Yellow Sea, and a direct route to China. Iseong Sanseong, a fortress on a hill 207 meters high, was built by Silla near Seoul to guard the Han River approach. It featured a nine-sided building, as well as a stone wall, and remnants of a possible palace with columns and large roof tiles (Kim and Lee 1987). A cache of horse-shaped belt buckles may have been made for the garrisons that manned the fort, although an alternative interpretation is that they were votive objects.

Silla also conquered polities on the east coast of the peninsula. King Sondok was so pleased with the success of his projects that he placed boundary stones at the extent of the conquests. Five of these boundary stones have been discovered so far, including one in the vicinity of Seoul, and two in what is now North Korea.

The Buddhist period

During the reign of King Pobhung, Buddhism came to Silla. The Buddhist period brought many new buildings to Gyeongju, including vast temple complexes, pagodas, monasteries, and schools of Buddhist thought. The *Samguk Yusa* is full of tales of miracles, but specific historical data is not easy to tease out of these tales. (Buddhism as a religion is treated in Chapter 8.) During this period Silla

Saro/Silla and the historical record   33

extended its reach, especially toward Baekje and Goguryeo. Roads were constructed and markets were established. Silla even created a navy to patrol the Yellow Sea.

Unified Silla

While Silla's forces were concentrated on enlarging their territory in the south, Goguryeo was raiding the towns in its neighborhood, and eventually turned its attention to the other two kingdoms of Baekje and Silla. Silla cagily helped Goguryeo push Baekje out of the Han River area, then appropriated the Han River corridor to the Yellow Sea for itself. Queen Jindeok built a navy, which controlled the Yellow Sea (Joe 1972:47). Silla then allied with Tang China to defeat both Baekje and Goguryeo in 668. Tang tried to use the victories for its own ends by setting up commanderies within the conquered states, but Silla successfully drove them off in three years, and for a while continued to prosper.

The city of Geumseong was known for its arts and culture, as well as its splendid royal residences. The *Samguk Yusa* supplies the number of 178,936 households in Geumseong at around the year 750. If one multiplies by five, a small average household, the total population would be more than 1.3 million. Calculating the area of the capital as 187 square kilometers, Bong Won Kang (2000a) suggests that this must be the number of the total population of the Silla polity, not just the capital of Geumseong. Kang concludes that the total number of households in the city itself was 35,787.

Markets were set up in Gyeongju to handle trade between villages as well as long-distance trade. Silla sent several kinds of goods to Tang: gold, silver, copper needles, fine cloth, horses, ginseng, dogs, skins, ornaments, and slaves. Silla received in return silk cloth, tea leaves, and books (Choi 1971:73). Queen Jindeok introduced Chinese fashions in court clothing.

Many villages had cottage industries, such as specialty weaving, metal working, lacquerware, or pottery. A tunnel kiln 25 meters long and about 7 meters wide for firing stoneware pottery was located near Gyeongju (Adams 1979:47). Some industries were supervised by the court, including: pure silk fabrics, silk for the lower classes, ramie fabrics, wool blankets and wool fabrics, leather products, leather shoes, tables, wooden chests, willow and bamboo objects such as mats and baskets, ceramics and tiles, clothes and embroideries, tents, lacquerware, and metal weapons and tools (Sohn et al. 1970:66).

Sumptuary laws, to be discussed in detail in Chapter 6, prescribed what each person was allowed to wear according to their rank and gender, as well as their horses, houses, and horse trappings. A new land system was declared in 689, which required a census of each village every three years. Each village specialized in a particular kind of nut or fruit tree, which belonged to the state. Mulberry trees, walnut trees, and pine trees, for example, were counted in the census. The number of cows and horses was recorded, as well as the age and sex of the villagers. Silla built roads to its harbors and to other towns, as well as to its naval base on the Han River. By this time, the city could brag that there were only tile-roofed houses all the way to the port.

When did Silla become a state?

This is a question that is of interest mainly to archaeologists, using archaeological criteria to define "statehood" with regard to prehistoric polities. But I agree with Bong Won Kang that the concept of "the state" is problematic for discussing Saro/Silla. He argues that the term "kingdom" is a better description than "state" for the Silla polity before it unified the Korean peninsula, because in Silla the selection of the ruler was still based on kinship. The problem I see with using the term "kingdom" is different from Kang's. Sometimes, Silla could have been called a "queendom," perhaps more often than the official list suggests. For example, Queen Seondeok and Queen Jindeok, the last of the Holy Bone rulers of Silla, both made fruitful contacts with the Tang dynasty that ultimately resulted in the Silla victories which united the Korean peninsula. As a united force, the region then resisted the attempts of Tang to establish itself there. However, I have been unable to find a satisfactory non-gendered term for this kind of rulership. As I discuss in Chapter 7, queens played important roles in increasing the power of Silla both early and late in the polity. I use the term "ruler" for the leader, and rulership to describe the polity, but they are not entirely satisfactory terms. Specific examples of early states show that this is not a problem unique to Korea (Kang 2005).

Kang makes another important point in noting that while chiefdoms were in competition with each other for "strategic resources, arable land, and populations for labor forces," they did not make war on each other so much for territory as for labor power. There is some evidence that farmers in Saro/Silla were conscripted for corvée labor, since an edict was passed in 144 exempting farmers from corvée duties during the growing season. I would conclude, however, that by the time of King Naemul, when giant tombs were erected and long-distance trade was flowering, Silla meets all criteria of statehood, including being multi-cultural.

Ju (2009:117) cautions, "In order to promote a systematic understanding of Sam Han society beyond matters of interpretation, we must inevitably depend on historical data for the specific details." However, archaeology can also provide specific details, as seen in the following chapter.

** Parts of this chapter are rewritten from a lecture by Nelson, S. M. (1995) "Tradition and Emulation, Urban Transformation in the City of Kyongju" presented at a symposium, "Forgotten Cities," organized by Professor Rita Wright at New York University in 1995.

3 Gyeongju archaeology

Many rich tombs have been explored in Gyeongju, of which the gold crown tombs under large mounds are the most celebrated (Lee H. 2012). However, bronze artifacts found under dolmens, and iron horse trappings in wooden coffins make the early graves interesting. Exotic glass beads in stone chamber tombs speak of long-distance trade even before the great mounded tombs. Archaeological discoveries also reveal evidence of manufacturing, fortresses, palaces, and temples.

The vast majority of archaeological excavations in Gyeongju have been the exploration of graves. These explorations have been the result of both research-oriented work and fortuitous finds, as well as salvage archaeology. Although several village sites have been located, and a foundry site has been excavated, systematic surveys specifically seeking many facets of the Gyeongju past, such as village settlements, production areas, mining, and agricultural areas, have only begun to be attempted. Important gaps in the knowledge of early Gyeongju will be filled during a long-term plan by the Korean National Research and Cultural Heritage Institute to survey and excavate the Wolseong-ro fortress area.

Archaeological sites in Gyeongju begin with a Paleolithic site in the eastern coastal region where deer herds might have attracted hunters passing through (Kim W. Y. 1982a), but the site is not near the city itself and it dates much earlier than the first permanent settlement of Gyeongju. Even evidence of the Jeulmun (Neolithic) period is spotty and scarce. It consists of scattered potsherds collected in Hwangseong-dong, and another area resembling the contents of a midden near the site of the National Museum of Gyeongju.

The nearest Jeulmun village sites that have been explored are west of Gyeongju. In addition, two Jeulmun sites were recorded in the vicinity of Daegu, and a rock shelter as well as ten Neolithic villages have been found in North Gyeongsang Province (Kim G. G. 2001).

The archaeology of central Gyeongju begins with dolmens in the Late Mumun period. The dolmens, placed over stone cist burials containing bronze artifacts, antedate the foundation of the Saro confederation. These burials demonstrate that the earliest settlers in the valley were accomplished farmers, probably growing rice and several other crops. Youn (1998:104) reports that the dolmens were found near current rice paddies and the edges of roads. The flat lands of Gyeongju, adjacent to the rivers and including marshy areas, would have been attractive

36 *Gyeongju archaeology*

to rice farmers. Unfortunately, radiocarbon dates are not available to confirm whether the dolmen burials had been abandoned before the wooden chamber burials came into the area, although it seems likely. These particular fields have not been studied, but research elsewhere in southern Korea would suggest that they grew barley and pulses as well as millets and rice.

Hou Han Shu descriptions of the Jinhan towns probably pertain to Gyeongju and the surrounding areas. Each village was said to have a leader and, indeed,

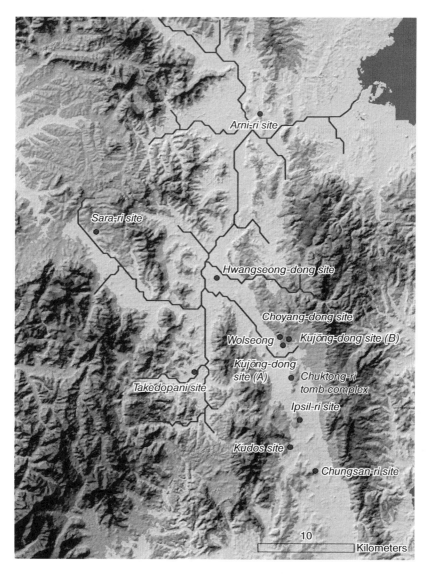

Map 3.1 Topological map of Bronze and Iron Age sites in and near Gyeongju. Redrawn from Yi Hyunhae, 2009, *Early Korea* Vol. 2. p. 38.

Gyeongju archaeology 37

Figure 3.1 Horse trappings from Silla tombs
Source: Harold Nelson

the Mumun burials in Gyeongju reflect a society with different levels of rank and authority, although ranks were less rigid than they would be later in the Mounded Tomb period. Dolmen burials are relatively few, although they existed in several groups of graves. Either this period did not last long in Gyeongju or the area was thinly populated at that time.

The Samhan period in Gyeongju is characterized by a soft pottery called *wajil togi*. Iron artifacts are plentiful in burials and are associated with well-crafted bronze weapons and other bronze artifacts such as horse gear, mirrors, and bells (Figure 3.1).

Buckles cast in the shapes of horses and tigers are of particular interest (Figure 3.2). Although the idea is ultimately derived from belt buckles of the Eurasian Steppes, the buckles were cast in local styles and made in the Korean peninsula, but probably not in Gyeongju (Kim Y. W. 2009). The Oundong site north of Gyeongju had particularly fine examples.

Rich pit burials with wooden coffins are sometimes found singly near the coast. These burials are likely not of members of the community, but traders or others passing through, since otherwise graves are grouped together in areas set aside for burials, presumably representing the inhabitants of a particular village (Yi 2009).

Figure 3.2 Horse buckle and tiger buckle excavated in North Gyeongsang Province
Source: Harold Nelson

A new type of burial appeared in the first century CE. It is similar to the wooden chamber burials but is more complex and surrounded by stone cobbles. Rows of these burials, each surrounded by stone cobble walls with wooden boards to keep the stones from rolling into the burial space, are dated to the first to third centuries and have mostly been excavated near villages.

Small mounded tombs may have been constructed as early as the third century. A wooden coffin lies beneath each mound often with an extra wooden chamber for burial goods that included lavish items such as complicated glass beads from South-East Asia. The mounds over the early graves are relatively small, but in plan they are similar to the later, larger grave mounds with wooden coffins. They have an extra chamber for grave goods and are covered with piles of cobbles topped with a thick layer of soil.

Huge burial mounds, now in a tomb park, represent burials in the fourth to fifth centuries. The contents of the gold crown tombs are particularly splendid. They are among a number of other elite tombs with gold artifacts that are thought to be those of members of the Kim ruling family. The most spectacular of these tombs not only have enormous mounds, but gold crowns, lavish gold jewelry, and piles of stoneware containers along with an arsenal of weapons.

Cremation became common with the advent of Buddhism in the sixth century, and elite tombs are fewer. However, a few stone-block tombs have been excavated in a variety of forms. Some have a passageway or other horizontal entrance. A few tombs have faint mural paintings that show influences from the other Korean kingdoms and beyond. Artifacts are rare— perhaps these tombs had been looted—but it is also possible that it was no longer customary to include rich burial goods, due to Buddhist influence.

Gyeongju archaeology   39

Some specific archaeological sites are discussed below to provide a sense of the differences through time as well as between tombs.

Archaeological sites

Possible Jeulmun site

An early site on the slopes of Wolseong-ro on the Namcheon River consisted of a scattering of artifacts and ecofacts: Kimhae pottery, bone arrowheads, deer horn daggers, carbonized seeds, fragments of iron, and seashells. The site bears similarities to shell middens near Busan and Daegu.

Mumun sites

At least a dozen of the sites in Gyeongju also have evidence of Mumun dwellings. These range from 2–20 house floors identified at a site, but the highly exceptional site of Eoil-ri had 345 dwellings. The most common location is on hill slopes and this includes Eoil-ri. Excavations at the site will help to understand the meaning of such a large village, at this time.

Hwangseong-dong dolmen site

The dolmen tombs in Hwangseong-dong appear to be the earliest burials in Gyeongju. The dolmens of this site are southern type dolmens—a large boulder placed atop a stone cist grave that was constructed from slabs of stone rather than the later cobbles that surrounded wooden coffin graves. Dolmens were spread over a large area, from the Liaodong peninsula to the entire Korean peninsula, extending to Japan. The dolmens represent the Bronze Age in Korea, but the bronze artifacts are largely in private collections. Reddish Mumun (plain) pottery was found in the graves, and a few stone tools, but little else. Most of the burials had been looted many times in the past, thus artifacts are scarce. No doubt the graves were attractive to robbers since such tombs are conveniently marked by a boulder and often contain polished stone daggers and stone necklaces, with an occasional bronze dagger or other very fine bronze workmanship of interest to collectors. Many bronze artifacts in southern Korea are known from collections rather than recorded excavations (e.g. Chin H. S. 1966). The artifacts were presumably collected before careful archaeological excavations were common, and before the importance of context was well understood; therefore, they are less useful for understanding the time period.

The presence of stone cists perhaps reflects one of the early migrations of people mentioned in the *Samguk Sagi*, which Kim Won Yong (1986:19) identifies as the Ye-Maek Tungus. These dolmens probably antedate by several centuries the establishment of the Lelang commandery in 108 BCE, so the Chinese documents discussed in Chapter 2 do not relate to this time period in Korea. Large cemeteries of stone cist burials (without dolmens) have been unearthed in the Xituanshan culture in Jilin Province in north-east China (Liu 1995), and cist

40 *Gyeongju archaeology*

graves are also common in northern Korea. Dolmens have been found throughout the Korean peninsula and Liaodong China. They are likely evidence of northern connections. Archaeology of other time periods, which also exists at Hwangnam-dong, will be described in chronological order.

Wooden chamber tombs

Ipsil-ri

At Ipsil-ri, a very rich burial was uncovered during the construction of a railroad along the east coast of Korea in 1920. The wooden chamber tomb was several meters below the ground surface. The burial contained bronze daggers, bronze spearheads, bronze halberds, many kinds of bells (some attached to unknown objects), and two geometric (Korean-style) bronze mirrors with multiple loops.

Also found were a fragment of an iron sword, an iron axe, and pottery (Samson 1929:14). Bronze buttons resemble those found around the feet in Liaoning burials, suggesting that they were attached to boots. Samson further notes that similar iron swords were found in North Korea with coins minted in 60 BCE, suggesting that this may be a site of the first century BCE.

Gujeong-dong

The Gujeong-dong site is a double burial of a man and woman. It consists of a square pit burial cut into a hill with two wooden coffins inside. It is dated by its pottery, both *wajil togi* (the soft decorative pottery of the early centuries CE), and early stoneware, suggesting a date later than Ipsil-ri. The very long (8 meters) coffin of the male on the north side contained many grave goods, including a dagger with a ring handle, a spear, and a halberd, all made of bronze, as well as iron axes, sickles, and knives. A double-headed bronze bell was also found. The woman's coffin was 6 meters long, and had many 30-centimeter-long spearheads in the bottom (Kim W. Y. 1975). It seems unlikely that she would have had no other grave goods, so perhaps her grave had been looted.

Other burials in this locality included wooden coffins placed in a circle. Armor, made with vertical iron pieces tied together with leather and decorated with glass beads was found (Park 2008).

Joyang-dong

Ten pit graves and ten jar burials were excavated at Joyang-dong in 1977 in a flat area that, according to Okauchi (1986), appears to contain the earliest wooden coffin cemetery in Gyeongju. The pit graves with wooden coffins are dated from 100 BCE to 100 CE on the basis of the pottery. This is the period in which the *Samguk Sagi* describes six villages gathering together to select a leader. These burials might represent the leadership of one of these villages.

The name of Joyang-dong (Choyangdong in McCune–Reischauer transliteration) seems to echo the site of Chaoyangdong in Liaoning Province, China.

It was a Xianbei site, but the name implies an association with Chaoxian, the name for Korea in Chinese. The name of the Korean Joseon (Chosun) dynasty is derived from it. The Chaoyangdong site is associated with the Murong Xianbei, where gold and gilt bronze artifacts such as saddlebows and belts have been found that closely resemble those of the Silla royal tombs (Leidy and Lee 2014) (see Figure 3.3). While the Chaoyangdong tomb in Liaoning is later than the burials in Joyang-dong, the area of Liaoning Province around Chaoyangdong has not been totally explored for earlier sites.

Grave 60 in Joyang-dong was a very rich burial, containing two horse-shaped bronze belt buckles. Such buckles frequently appear in elite graves from the Samhan period, but it is rare to find two buckles of this kind in the same grave. The horse and tiger buckles in the Gyeongju vicinity seem to have been cast in Korea, since they are similar in style and decoration to bronze mirrors, daggers, and bells that were cast in central Korea. Although belt buckles and plaques with zoomorphic themes are widely found in the Eurasian Steppes region (So and Bunker 1995), the numerous Korean examples are made with an entirely different type of belt fastener. Furthermore, there is a great variety of animals depicted on the steppe plaques and buckles. No animals other than horses and tigers are depicted on Silla belt buckles, whereas on those found in the Eurasian Steppes the belt buckles and plaques are much more varied (Bunker 2009).

Many fine bronze specimens of horse and tiger buckles (Figure 3.2) have been found in the vicinity of Gyeongju. Less carefully made horse buckles, probably made in molds, have been found in profusion at Iseong Sanseong, a fortress on the Han River with a Silla component. Unlike the early well-crafted bronze horse buckles, these later horse buckles seem to be emblems of a middle-rank soldier.

The wooden coffin tombs contained a profusion of bronze and iron grave goods, including iron weapons with lacquered sheaths, early Han mirrors with

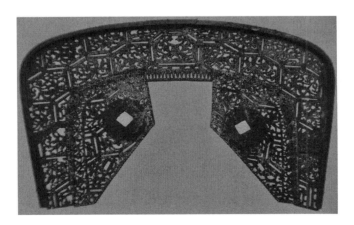

Figure 3.3 Gilded saddlebow from royal grave in Chaoyang
Source: Harold Nelson

42 Gyeongju archaeology

inscriptions, and bronze weapons. Four inscribed bronze mirrors of the former Han dynasty (206 BCE to 8 CE) were found in one grave, along with a great heap of iron weapons and ceramics. In Burial 38, Han-style mirrors were accompanied by a large reddish stoneware jar and other jars with horn handles, allowing the site to be dated to the first century CE. Burial 1 has wide-mouthed *wajil togi* vessels, polished black jars, iron daggers with attached handles, and bronze fine-line mirrors, products of southern Korea. In Tomb 5, a polished black-lacquered, long-necked jar has horn-shaped handles like those of some *wajil togi* pottery. An iron dagger axe, small bells with clappers, and a tiny 2-inch-diameter mirror were also present. This tomb is dated by its ceramics to the first century BCE.

Wooden chamber burials were found as well as wooden coffin burials. Iron artifacts in the tombs support the *Samguk Sagi* date of 57 BCE as the time of the founding of Silla. Horse gear and small bronze horse bells show that this was not only a horse-riding society, but also one that prized and decorated its horses. Jar burials were uncovered, but they contained no grave goods and are thought to be interments of children.

Sara-ri

Tomb 130 in Sara-ri is unusual because of its size and non-utilitarian, locally made artifacts. The wooden coffin was 3.32 meters long, 2.3 meters wide, and 100 centimeters deep, containing a Korean-style bronze mirror from the first century BCE, the oldest Korean-style mirror yet found. This large grave is dated to the first or second century CE.

The style of locally cast mirrors is characterized by geometric designs and handles having between two to four straps, while mirrors made in China have a single central boss and curvilinear designs. The style of Korean mirrors is ultimately related to the geometric mirrors of Liaoning. Korean and Northern Zone mirrors are very different from those made in Han China. Pieces of molds for geometric-patterned mirrors have been found in Korea, leaving no question that these mirrors were made in the southern Korean peninsula, although no foundry for casting them has yet been located.

Among the artifacts on the floor of Tomb 130 were four iron swords, the bronze mirror mentioned above, a long necklace with beads of crystal and other semi-precious stones, and flat, axe-shaped iron ingots paving the floor of the tomb. The 30 bronze pieces included a six-ring bracelet. The bronze sword had been placed in one corner, while another corner had four iron swords, the bronze mirror, and the long necklace. Two bronze tiger-shaped belt fasteners were each 20 centimeters long. Tiger belt buckles are much rarer than horse belt buckles and are always finely made. It seems likely that both denote rank, with the owners of tiger buckles outranking those wearing horse buckles.

Sara-ri (Sara village), the location of this tomb, linguistically seems to echo the location of Saro, one of the founding six villages which gave its name to the

Gyeongju archaeology 43

polity of Saro/Silla. Furthermore, the kind and quantity of the artifacts in this tomb imply a powerful leader, with the ability to command extensive goods and services. The length of the burial chamber has suggested to some that this might be the burial of Pak Hyeokkeose, the first king of Silla who, according to the *Silla Pon'gi*, was said to be very tall.

Hwangseong-dong

Another segment of the Hwangseong-dong site, from an era later than that of the dolmens, dates to the third century. It is located north of the North Stream, outside of the area of the early city. This segment is so large that three parts of Hwangseong-dong were excavated by different institutions. Altogether, 63 burials dating to the third to fourth centuries by ceramic chronology were excavated from this later segment. The Gyeongju University Museum excavated 24 features: 18 wooden chamber tombs, 4 jar coffins, and 4 other features. Although some very rich graves were excavated, they were not always the largest graves. Grave goods included pottery, iron spears, longswords, arrowheads, axes, and crystal and jade beads. No human remains were found.

Burial 8, a wooden chamber tomb, was particularly interesting because it seemed to belong to a member of the elite. Two large pots and four other ceramics were placed on the western side of the chamber, while on the eastern side many beads, probably from a strung necklace, lay in profusion. They included 31 crystal beads, many medium and small beads, and 3 *gogok*, the curved bead of leadership, suggesting that this was a person of particular importance.

A third area of this later segment of the site provided extensive evidence of iron production. The remains of a smelting furnace, iron slag, and a mold for an iron axe showed this to be a workshop for the production of iron tools. Seven round or oval house floors of the Late Bronze Age, and 20 house floors that were dated to the Proto-Three Kingdoms period were unearthed nearby (Kang 2003).

Wolseong-ro

A compact and interesting group of 31 tombs was found when archaeologists worked ahead of crews widening a street for a distance of 2 kilometers in the vicinity of Wolseong-ro, the former royal palace. These graves demonstrate the increasing wealth of the upper class, as well as extensive trading connections with distant lands.

The burials are dated in the fourth and fifth centuries by the extensive Gaya-style earthenware that included mounted cups, stands, and high-necked jars. These tombs appear to be transitional and are considered to be forerunners of the slightly later tombs with large cobble-and-earth mounds.

The tomb numbered Ga-13 has the earliest gold artifact found in Silla. It contains an elaborate pectoral or "chestlace" of blue and gold beads that is very similar to a necklace in the north mound of Tomb 98, which is thought by some

44 Gyeongju archaeology

to be the second earliest of the large mounded tombs. Gold earrings were found on either side of the place where presumably the head lay. Ten iron swords, and iron knives were found here, as well as longswords with a round pommel. It is interesting that horse equipment was included, especially stirrups and bits. These may be some of the earliest stirrups to be placed in tombs.

Tomb 29 contained plate armor in an ancient style, in which the vertical iron plates were tied with leather strips. The only earlier discovery of armor from the Silla region was at the Gujeong-dong site. This burial also has a stone bracelet of a style found in Japan. The date is estimated to the fourth century.

Hwango-dong

The mound of Tomb 3 at Hwango-dong marks this area as a cemetery, although not all of the graves had mounds remaining. Among the 31 tombs that were excavated, 23 wooden chamber tombs had stone cobble mounds. Unusually, food items were found in this site, including rice grains, clam shells, fish bones, and chicken bones. Clearly the deceased were being sent on their last journey with food (Kim and Yi 1975:79). Ito (1971:24) provides further information about other tombs with food remains: Tombs 109b and 122 in Hwangnam-dong, Tombs 1 and 6 in Songju, Tomb 2 in Chisan-dong, and in the backdirt(!) at Tap-ri.

Namsong-ri

At Namsong-ri, a long (2.8 meters) stone cist contained more than 100 bronze artifacts, some so far unmatched in other sites (Yoon 2012). Burial goods included 2 early mirrors, 10 daggers, and many bronze tools, as well as 106 tubular beads, a *gogok* (like the typical Bronze Age leader's necklace), and lacquer on birch bark.

Inwang-dong

This area contained looted but still interesting tombs. Tomb 19 consisted of a circle of stones 23 meters across, containing ten burial units marked off from each other with further lines of stones. It is interpreted as a family tomb, or as a sacrificial grave. Tomb 1 had a main burial chamber and a separate pit for burial goods. It had been looted, but a pair of gold earrings had been overlooked (Kim W. Y. 1978).

Hwangnam-dong

Hwangnam-dong is in the area around King Michu's tomb, which was cleared for the tomb park that includes the Heavenly Horse Tomb, Cheonmachong, and Tomb 98 (known as the Great Tomb), with two overlapping mounds. Dozens of small tombs with cobble-lined pits that date to the second and third centuries were unearthed, as well as tombs with earth and cobble mounds. Houses and walls had been built over and through these tombs, removing parts of their mounds but, surprisingly, many tombs had not been disturbed.

Gyeongju archaeology 45

The earliest burials are the stone chamber tombs. Some are small, only 1–2 meters long and 60 centimeters deep. Subsequent tombs are much larger, with stone cobble walls creating a rectangular space with boards inside to form a kind of coffin. Eight of these were excavated, averaging about 5 by 2 meters in size. River cobbles covered the top. These were of various types, with a single chamber or several chambers, or "gourd-shaped," with overlapping double mounds. Some unusual tombs had pottery structures in the shape of chimneys, and one was a burial of an entire horse surrounded by a circle of cobbles.

Two wooden chambers, including a large burial chamber (5 by 3.1 meters in size) and a subsidiary chamber for burial gifts, were placed in a line with a total length of over 9 meters. On the west side of the burial chamber, headdresses, earrings, necklaces, and belts were deposited. Swords and other weapons were beside the body. The accompanying wooden chamber held pottery, iron farming tools, and weapons, accompanied by horse gear. The additional chamber contained pottery and more horse trappings. It is estimated to be a fourth-century tomb (Kim and Yi 1975), and seems to be the forerunner of the royal mounded tombs such as Tomb 155 and Tomb 98 at Hwangnam-dong.

Burial 4 in Tomb Area C contained an extraordinary necklace, in particular a glass bead depicting a Western-looking face. There was much speculation about where it was made and how it came to Gyeongju. This bead will be described and discussed in Chapter 5. Among the many exotic objects found in the Wolseong-ro tombs are stone beads made of carnelian, jade, and crystal. Their varied shapes include *gogok*, hexagonal bicones, cylinders, and oblates.

Some important artifacts include a tortoise-shaped stoneware vessel, an imported cloisonné dagger, and a number of Jatim beads made in Indonesia (including the famous face bead).

The Mounded Tomb period

As local expressions of power and control, giant tombs visually dominated Gyeongju in the Mounded Tomb period. Even today, these enormous tombs constitute the most compelling sight in the central city. The largest tomb overall is a double mound measuring 123 meters long and 22 meters high (Kim and Pearson 1977), and not quite as tall as the highest mound, which reaches 25 meters. The tombs are so large that after the city ceased to be the capital, some of the mounds were treated as natural hills, with houses and streets along their flanks and trees growing from their sides (Adams 1979). As the city grew denser, the buildings and plantings that claimed this space were removed in the 1970s when the tomb park was created as a tourist attraction.

The large mounds cover several contiguous sections of the city. These areas are called Nodong-ri, Neoso-ri, Hwangnam-ri, and Hwango-ri, north-west of Wolseong-ro. King Michu (r. 262–284), the founder of the Kim dynasty, was the first to be buried in this area. A modest mound marks his tomb. Subsequent burials were on adjacent Kim family land. The precinct they inhabited is said to have included the area of the Gyerim Forest, a small part of which survives even

46 *Gyeongju archaeology*

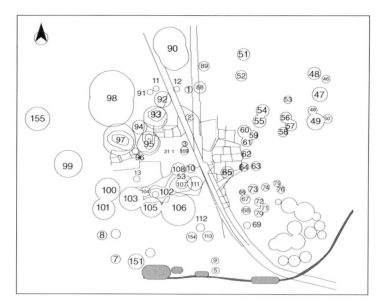

Map 3.2 Numbered tombs in Gyeongju

today, near the museum. The name refers to some kind of fowl; perhaps there were pheasants with long tails and/or crested heads. Exotic fowls and feathers are known to have existed in the Korean peninsula in ancient times, and perhaps this is the reason for the name of the forest. Korea was even known to Arab visitors much later as the Rooster Country. Red "phoenixes" were painted on an artifact made of birch bark in the Flying White Horse Tomb, and another tomb, nicknamed the Auspicious Phoenix Tomb, includes phoenix-like cut-out birds on a golden cap.

The huge mounded tombs were erected north of the earlier tombs on what might have been unused land or perhaps agricultural fields. Obviously, an impressive amount of the Kim clan property was used for tomb mounds, but the third-century tombs were not of epic size and were quite crowded together. It was not until the giant tomb building began that the tombs began to occupy so much space. What many scholars believe to be the first of the gold crown tombs, the gourd-shaped mound of Tomb 98, Hwangnam Daechong, was an entirely new phenomenon in Silla. Double mounds are those of a married couple so this mound is doubled in length, but even the circumference of each individual tomb is on another scale altogether, even from King Michu's tomb. This double mound was intended to make a very grand statement.

It is not merely size that makes these tombs important. They are crammed with golden jewelry and exotic imports. The most astounding features are the gold crowns and belts, seen as marks of rulership. Only five gold crown tombs have been excavated, and they are extraordinary (Lee H. 2012). They are known, in order of excavation, as the Gold Crown Tomb, the Auspicious Phoenix Tomb, the

Gold Bell Tomb, the Flying White Horse Tomb, and the north mound of the Great Tomb at Hwangnam-dong.

The Gold Crown tombs

The first Silla tomb with a gold crown to be discovered was dubbed the Gold Crown Tomb, "Geumgwanchong", because no other gold crown had yet been unearthed or even suspected. The gold crowns of Silla came as a complete surprise to the Japanese investigators in 1921, as well as to the inhabitants of Gyeongju.

The Gold Crown Tomb was found by accident in Neoso-ri, Gyeongju while an extension to a house was being constructed. The next two tombs to produce gold crowns were near the Gold Crown Tomb, on the east and west of it. Named the Gold Bell Tomb, excavated in 1924, and the Auspicious Phoenix Tomb, excavated in 1926, these tombs' mounds had been considerably eroded, although it appeared that they had not been broken into. The riches in these tombs had been totally forgotten over the centuries. Recently, in cleaning a sword at the National Museum of Korea, an inscription was found that reads, "Isaji." Although there is no recorded king of Silla by this name, the title for kings in this period (fourth century) was Isageum. This, of course, does not get us any closer to knowing which king it was.

Because the Gold Crown Tomb was broken into unexpectedly by construction workers, the exact location of the crown itself was not properly documented. It had been noticed that children were searching for glass beads in the construction hole (Kim and Kim 1966). However, archaeologists were called to document about 40,000 artifacts, including 20,000 glass beads that were subsequently unearthed. Many gold artifacts, bead necklaces, horse trappings, and weapons were cataloged (Yi 2010:6).

The crown in this tomb is simple compared to the other crowns excavated later, but it includes side dangles (as do all the gold crowns) of the sort that were characteristic of women's headgear among people of the Eurasian Steppes (Nelson 2008a). The tomb is thought to have been constructed in the second half of the fifth century. An unusual object called a "gold cap ornament" has "wings that spread upward and outward." It is delicately made with an openwork design, and has gold spangles attached (Lee H. 2012). A recent theory about these gold caps is that they were worn separately from the crown. Indeed, the headgear on the horse-rider from the Gold Bell Tomb could represent such a cap. In an attempt to learn more about the tomb construction, the Gold Crown Tomb was recently re-excavated, but very few artifacts had been overlooked in the original excavation.

For many years these were the only gold crown tombs known. However, in the 1970s, the South Korean government decided to create a park around the huge tombs near the mound that was called King Michu's grave. A careful and precise excavation of the Heavenly Horse Tomb was made in 1973, which turned up another gold crown. In 1975, both mounds of the double mound known as Hwangnam Daechong, the Great Tomb at Hwangnam-dong, were excavated, which produced a gold crown in the north mound and gilt bronze crowns in the south mound. The gold crown, it turned out, belonged to a queen. Her tomb has the largest mound of all, and the most exquisite tomb furnishings. This tomb and its meanings are further discussed in Chapter 7.

The next tomb to be excavated, the Gold Bell Tomb, has a typical wooden chamber which measures 1.5 by 0.6 meters in size, with the head toward the east. The gold crown had been placed in the vicinity of the head, and a sword lay near the waist. Among the most prized objects from this tomb are two ceramic vessels in the shape of horses with riders (see Figure 3.4). These are unusual water containers, with even spouts to pour from. The two represent a high-ranking officer and his servant (Kim and Kim 1966:38). The details of the horse trappings modeled in these two ceramics are valuable for showing how and where the various horse trappings were used, and where ornaments were placed. The stirrups are of particular interest, joined to saddlebows on both the front and back of the saddle. The riders' clothing offers a rare look into the garb of the period. A pair of boat-shaped vessels on high pedestals was also found, with a human figure holding a steering oar on each boat. These are valuable glimpses into the lives of Silla's elite.

In the Gold Bell Tomb, the wooden coffin is small, as are the objects placed in it. It is thought, therefore, that this tomb belonged to a young person who did not live to reign. The crown has a smaller circlet than other gold crowns and contains no *gogok*. It also has side dangles and, for that reason, the possibility of the occupant being a young woman could be entertained.

The excavation team of the Auspicious Phoenix Tomb included royalty: Prince Gustav VI Adolf of Sweden was privileged to join the excavation. Actually, the word that means "auspicious" is pronounced "so" and was meant to indicate "Swedish" in honor of the prince. The tomb was "gourd-shaped,"

Figure 3.4 Two clay vessels in the shape of horses with riders
Source: Harold Nelson

in other words, a tomb of a married pair. The north-eastern mound contained the gold crown. A wooden coffin was placed inside a wooden chamber. Inside the coffin were the accoutrements of royalty: gold crown, earrings, necklaces, bracelets, rings, and the royal gold belt. There were also glass bracelets, glass bowls, and many glass beads. An inner crown headdress was also in the coffin. Three phoenix birds with crests, perched as if in tree branches, grace the top of the inner cap (Lee H. 2012).

Lacquerware and horse trappings were placed outside the coffin. The two iron cauldrons placed on the floor of the eastern side among many ceramics are of particular note, since iron cauldrons are "epi-nomadic" artifacts associated with the Xiongnu (Seyock 2004). Another important find from the Auspicious Phoenix Tomb is a covered silver bowl from Goguryeo, which is not only remarkable in itself, but is inscribed with a manufacturing date that is 451 or 511. Most Korean scholars believe that the maker's date is equivalent to 451. Inscriptions are rare in these tombs and, so far, no Silla tomb has produced a name or date for the person interred in the tomb. Radiocarbon dates have proved to be of little help in dating, because the ranges of the tombs overlap considerably.

The Heavenly Horse Tomb has a mound 13 meters high and 47 meters in diameter. It was left open to display for visitors, with the dazzling artifacts more or less *in situ*. The name comes from a painting of a white horse on a mudguard made of birch bark (Figure 3.5). An extraordinary gold cap with a cut-out design is a unique object from this tomb.

Figure 3.5 Painted white horse from the Heavenly Horse Tomb
Source: Harold Nelson

50   *Gyeongju archaeology*

The body rested in a lacquered wooden coffin with the head pointed toward the east. A wooden chest contained burial gifts in three tiers. The wooden constructions were held together with iron clamps and nails. The heaviest objects, such as pottery and iron kettles, had been placed in the bottom of the chest. The middle layer held bronze vessels and decorated lacquerware, while on the top were placed four saddles, two sets of mudguards, and other horse trappings. Another chest contained 24 pieces of ox horn, a find that is unique. It may be related to the rhytons that came to Silla through the steppe route. Near the top of the mound, a harness and saddle had been placed. Kim Won Yong (1983) speculates, "It may be meant to symbolize the sacrifice of a living horse as a vehicle of the ascension of the buried royal person."

Other mounds that did not contain gold crowns were explored. The Ho-u (Washing Bowl) Tomb (No. 140a) produced a lacquered wooden mask with eyes of blue glass (McCune 1962:86). An inscription on a bronze bowl dates to 415 (Ito 1971). It was excavated by "the staff of the Korean National Museum and the U.S. Military Government" in the spring of 1946 (Chapin 1957:57). There was also a lotus ornament that suggests Buddhist influence, although the mask may be that of a shaman. Certainly, Buddhism was known in Gyeongju in the fifth century but it did not take hold until the sixth century.

Tomb 98 was a double tomb, the largest of all the Silla mounded tombs, measuring 22 meters high, 120 meters long and encompassing the mounds of both tombs. The south mound was the burial of the male, presumably the king, lying in a lacquered wooden coffin. His grave goods included many weapons—30 swords, 543 spears, 380 battle-axes, and more than a thousand arrows. But he did not lack for other grave goods. Several imported glass vessels were in a treasure chest at the foot of his coffin, and jars and other ceremonial jars were numerous. Earrings with thick rings had been placed on each of the three corners of his coffin (Lee I. 2012, Fig. 6.1).

The vast quantity of weapons and armor with the male (husband) in the south mound of Tomb 98 mark the king as the war leader (Nelson 1991, 1993a). It seems that these magnificent piles of weapons might have been the spoils of war rather than his private arsenal. This man was surely a warrior, a leader of the troops.

The north mound had been constructed several decades later than the south mound. It had presumably contained the body of the queen. She wore a crown made of sheet gold, covered with *gogok*, and a gold belt with dangles that bore an inscription, "belt for Milady." The crown was made of a circlet with uprights in the shape of antlers and squared-off trees, and many leaf-like *gogok* and gold dangles were attached to the uprights and the circlet with gold wire. Also in her coffin were five pairs of gold bracelets, two necklaces of glass beads, and multiple pairs of earrings. The amount of gold in the artifacts in her tomb came to almost 4 kilograms.

The placement of gold crowns and ceremonial belts with the queen in the north mound of Tomb 98 suggests that she was the spiritual ruler, probably

Gyeongju archaeology 51

with shamanistic duties (Nelson 1991, 1993a, and see Chapter 7). The crowns themselves furnish evidence of shamanic beliefs—trees and antlers are found on Manchurian and other shaman paraphernalia (Kim B. M. 1997; Nelson 2008b, and see Chapter 8). Dangling objects, especially the two long pendants that frame the face, are also found in Manchurian shaman costumes (Kim and Lee 1975). Thus, king and queen co-rulers may have occurred in Silla as they did in early Japan (Piggott 1997). Gender differences are not marked by any type of adornment. It has been suggested that gender is indicated only by the presence or absence of a sword by the side of the interred person (Ito 1971), but this, it turns out, is not an absolute difference either.

Related to shamanism, we read in the *Samguk Sagi* that mountains were sacred, and an early queen was the daughter of a mountain goddess. The sacredness of mountains may be expressed in the shape and size of the tombs. The large tombs create a virtual range of hills across the center of Gyeongju today, towering above the one-story houses. Chapter 6 contains further discussion of Silk Road artifacts that were found in these tombs.

Of the few inscriptions from the tombs, none seem to name the occupant. Thus, the exact order of the tombs is unknown, giving rise to intense speculation on the basis of small stylistic differences (Pearson 1985).

A multivariate study (Pearson et al. 1986) suggests that artifacts in the tombs support the existence of bone ranks, which will be discussed in Chapter 7. Gold crowns, belts, shoes, and other paraphernalia worn by rulers were found in the huge elaborate tombs, and lesser objects were found in small tombs. These are obvious displays of wealth and power. Sumptuary laws also upheld the endogamous bone ranks (Kim Chong Sun 1965). From the materials that could be used for hairpins to the number of horses and types of saddles allowed, conspicuous consumption was precisely defined by sex as well as by rank.

The temporal ordering of the large mounded tombs as well as their dates and the identity of their occupants are still matters of discussion and interpretation. The earliest acceptable date for the earliest of these tombs is the late fourth century. Consensus seems to be forming around Naemul (r. 356–402) being the king buried in the south mound of Tomb 98 (Leidy 2013).

Some unusual Silla pottery comes from private collections rather than excavations. One such stoneware jar bears incised drawing of animals around the rim, including nine horses, a deer, and a tiger. The drawings surround the shoulder of the vessel in two lines (Kim W. Y. 1973). Another Silla vessel of the same type had tiny pinched clay figures attached to the shoulder. They include a person playing a stringed instrument, an early representation of a kayagum.

Tombs of Unified Silla

Few tombs from Unified Silla have been excavated. Cremation became the mode of burial after the adoption of Buddhism but was not the only possible kind of burial. One royal tomb was made of stone blocks and contained small figurines,

52 *Gyeongju archaeology*

another had faded mural paintings. A tomb surrounded by large river cobbles had a side entrance with a burial platform. Apparently there was no consistent style.

A painted tomb near Daegu was built from irregular stone blocks that arched toward each other to form a dome. A narrow entrance led to a small chamber with two slabs for coffins. Some paintings were found on the walls. Although it had deteriorated, the lotus patterns could be seen (Keimyung University Museum 1984). The painted tombs are assumed to belong to Unified Silla.

Other archaeological sites

Some Buddhist sites have been excavated, including Hwangyongsa, the Imperial Dragon Temple. The size of its footprint is so large it is hard to comprehend. A sarira hole was excavated when a broken pagoda had to be moved, and the area of Donggung Palace with Wolji Pond (formerly known as Anapji) was cleared out, revealing roof tiles and end tiles with designs, as well as gilt bronze scissors and wooden dice.

A kiln for making house roof tiles was located in Hwagok-ri, and an area for the production of extra large and hard green-glazed roof tiles for Buddhist temples was found in Hwacheon-ri. This had the rising type of kiln that creates a very hot fire and allows very large ceramics to be fired. These will be discussed in Chapter 5.

Another new excavation is the unearthing of Jeongyang Sanseong. Silla had many fortresses guarding its approaches. First built in the sixth century, this fortress continued to be used and rebuilt through the Unified Silla period. It seems to have served as a warehouse as well as a fortress (Kim and Lee 1975).

Site No. 4 in the area of King Michu's tomb produced a segment of a castle wall under pine trees. Beneath this wall were two tombs of earlier style made of stone surrounding wooden chambers. Site No. 6 was crowded with tombs of various kinds. There were nine stone cobble tombs, two small stone chambers, and two large jar coffins. No mention is made of any artifacts within (Kim and Lee 1975).

Conclusion

Gyeongju is an important symbol in South Korea and extensive archaeological work has been done. More is being planned. The archaeological discoveries are important to balance the documentary record. Even so, archaeological materials can be interpreted in various ways, and debates still rage about dating, the order of the tombs, and the meanings that should be attached to them.

4 Production
Ceramics, bronze, iron, and gold

The economy of Gyeongju is thought to have been largely based on agriculture, but many products were needed locally for daily life as well as trade. It is likely that crops were grown within each of the original villages, but the houses and furnishings, clothing, and footwear were very likely made in each household or within specialized villages. Hemp and ramie were woven into cloth for daily wear and other uses. There were mulberry trees for fattening silk worms, and silk was spun and woven into brocades and other elaborate weaves. The paper mulberry tree was cultivated and made strong paper for floors and windows. Leather working was listed as a specialized occupation, but straw products such as shoes, mats, and roofs were probably local crafts, made within each village. Crafts that required special equipment or knowledge were no doubt products of different villages. The documents are rarely specific about production and the economy (Kim Chong Sun 2004), but in some cases archaeology can fill in the gaps.

Ceramics

No ancient area for making household pottery or firing it has yet been located in Gyeongju, but it seems likely that some pottery must have been molded and fired nearby. The two figures of men on horseback, master and servant, found in the Gold Bell Tomb (see Chapter 3, Figure 3.4, p. 48) must have been made locally, because they have so many attached details that some of them would have been likely to break off or at least crack if they had had to be carried very far. (I bought a copy of the master on horseback in Seoul, which was said to have been made using ancient techniques, but it has steadily shed its accoutrements over the years as I took it to show my classes). Some of the jars and stands in Silla graves were of Gaya style, and therefore very likely to have been imported, but others were a local style presumably locally formed and fired (Figure 4.1).

Virtually no pottery for daily use was found in graves. Pottery from the tombs seems to have been mostly created for ritual purposes. High stands have cut-out squares or rectangles, and are decorated with rows of wavy lines. One large jar is decorated with engraved horses and another has three-dimensional figures on the rim.

Figure 4.1 Silla pottery
Source: Harold Nelson

This hard-fired pottery is thought to be the prototype of the Sue ware in Japan. It was made on a wheel and fired to a vitreous state. In order to fire the pottery at a high enough temperature, "tunnel kilns" that rise up the side of a hill to allow a hotter fire were invented. Several of such kilns have been located in the western parts of Korea. The unfired vessels were placed along the slope, with the fire at the bottom. Air holes along the sides that could be plugged allowed the heat to rise and high temperatures to be reached in the tunnel kiln. Robert Sayers (1987) interviewed potters in villages near Gyeongju. He found excellent clay for making large pots, but only two potters in the region. His sketch of the layout of the work-site shows a tunnel kiln (p. 215). It is interesting that south of Ulsan there are many potters. Perhaps archaeologists should look there for the locations of Gyeongju's earlier pottery kilns. Buddhist-era kilns are known in Gyeongju. Tiles for both roofs and floors have been excavated at Hwacheong-ri in Gyeongju, notably some that are very large. Oversize decorative tiles were needed for the large temple buildings. Many of the end tiles were decorated with lotus flower and other patterns.

Many tiles were found when the Wolji Pond was drained. These may have been used on the roofs of palaces. On elite homes tiles were a sign of wealth. It is said that tile-roofed buildings in Gyeongju stretched all the way to the sea in Unified Silla.

Gyeongju cottage industries

Hochin Choi describes artifacts made by farmers for their own consumption, as well as court industries. Silla had numerous departments for overseeing this production. They included pure silk fabrics, silk and cotton fabrics, linen and ramie fabrics, wool blankets, leather products, leather shoes, tables and dining tables, wooden containers, willow and bamboo works, ceramics and tiles, clothes and embroideries, various tents, lacquerware, and weapons and metal implements. Each of these was a separate department (Choi 1971:66). Some workers were skilled in dyeing all the various colors that the robes for separate ranks demanded.

Leather is specifically mentioned as material for shoes in the *Hou Han Shu*. In Japan, where bone preservation is better than in Korea, horse skulls have been found with indications of having had their brains scraped out. This phenomenon is interpreted as the use of horse brains for tanning, a technique which may have come from Silla. Akira Matsui examined a horse skull from fifth-century Silla, and found the same marks on it. He concludes that, "archaeologically, it is also highly possible that the technique was introduced also from Silla, where it was frequently used." (Matsui 2009:132).

Bronze

When bronze appeared in southern Korea about 300 BCE, almost a millennium after it flourished in China, it was used for weapons, especially daggers and halberds, but also for non-utilitarian objects, such as mirrors and bells. The styles of the daggers and bells are clearly related to those of Liaoning Province in northeastern China around the seventh century BCE. The actual daggers and swords spread to northern Korea and finally to the south, but the geometric-style mirrors and bells were local Korean products. Far more of the Liaoning-style bronze daggers were found in the south-west of the peninsula than in the south-east, suggesting that the first impetus for creating bronzes locally lay in the south-west. Bronze weapons began to be phased out with the increasing use of iron. Some of the bronze daggers must have been highly treasured, having been carried in lacquered sheaths.

The first bronze daggers and mirrors made in southern Korea were based on Liaoning prototypes, but the styles became narrower and distinctly Korean. Among other differences, Korean bronze daggers used relatively more tin than the Liaoning daggers (Kim W. Y. 1986:99). It seems that these local styles must have been made somewhere in Korea, but "archaeological evidence of bronze production in the Korean Bronze Age is sparse, to say the least" (Cho and Lee 2013). No evidence so far of mining for copper ores or of bronze smelting in the Gyeongju area has come to light.

The evidence for local production of bronze daggers and mirrors is limited to talc and sandstone molds carved in the local styles. Daeyoun Cho and Donghee Lee (2013) used these molds to test for standardization of production, indicating production specialization.

In the Late Bronze Age, new implements such as pole-top bells and eight-branched bells began to be made. However, while Gyeongju was a consumer of these bronzes, the artifacts must have been made elsewhere and received in trade. Lead bronze is found in higher percentages in Chinese bronzes than in

56   *Production*

Korea. Korean bronze tends to have more zinc than lead. It has been suggested that the difference in alloy indicates production of the bronzes within Korea (Jeon 1974:247–254). Bronze weapons were replaced by iron weapons only when techniques of forging made steel superior to bronze.

Copper ores are widely distributed in Korea (Kim W. Y. 1986, Chapter 4). The widely admired bronze bells of Gyeongju were cast in Korea, probably near Gyeongju, so sources of copper must have been available. The famous Emille Bell that hangs in the museum comes with a tradition that the bronze and gold arrived on a mysterious ship from India, with a note saying "they" had been unsuccessful in casting bells. This does not help to solve the question of where the metals were mined and cast.

Iron mines and iron working

Many iron weapons but relatively few iron tools were found in Gyeongju graves. One might suppose that farmers who worked with hoes and pitchforks were buried more simply, and perhaps were not interred with their tools in any case. A few exceptions, however, are found in the Wolseong-ro burials, where agricultural tools were mixed with iron weapons and pottery.

An area of iron working in Gyeongju around the year 300 demonstrates that iron was probably mined and smelted in Gyeongju a bit earlier than the occurrence of gold mining, although iron had been produced in Gaya some two centuries earlier than in Gyeongju (Rhee et al. 2007). Rhee et al. (2007:424) state that iron body armor and helmets were produced by Silla as early as 300 and, indeed, these items have been found in Silla tombs, but direct evidence for the local casting of those artifacts is lacking. A mold for an axe in the iron smelting area of Hwangseong-dong suggests that tools rather than weapons were made at this site, although Kang (2000b) counts axes as possible weapons when separating iron tools from iron weapons. Iron axes were probably needed to make boards for the wooden coffins that were found in Gyeongju from the third century onwards. The wooden coffins were constructed with iron clamps holding the corners together.

The floor of an early burial in Sara-ri, Gyeongju, was covered with *cheol jeong*, the flat, axe-shaped iron articles that are believed to represent media of exchange in the early centuries CE (Rhee et al. 2007). After being traded they were presumably melted down and used to make new tools and weapons. A remarkable 1,332 *cheol jeong* paved the floor of the south mound of Tomb 98 in Hwangnam-dong. A huge number of iron weapons was also found in this tomb, clearly relating the occupant of this tomb to iron production as well as weaponry.

Studies of iron working in southern Korea by Yoon Dong Suk (1984) have concentrated on the Han River region and the Nakdong River valley. In the vicinity of Gyeongju, iron artifacts from Joyang-dong, Kujong-ri, and Ipsil-ri were examined. Yoon shows that all the sites he studied are in the vicinity of iron mines. It is interesting that cast iron implements could be made in very simple pits. Tuyeres and slag were sometimes found, suggesting somewhat more complex technology.

Gold

Silla was known as the country of gold (Ham 2014a:31). Gyeongju's reputation as a place abounding in gold lasted even beyond its time as capital of Unified Silla when it dominated the Korean peninsula (Koh 1958:60). Arab writers believed Silla's (or el Sila's, as it was known in the Arab world) streets were paved with gold. In the fourth and fifth centuries, significantly more gold was found in the mounded tombs of Silla than in any other polity of the time. Not only was gold used abundantly, but the objects made of gold were dazzling, sometimes further enhanced with precious stones and glass beads. Jewelry for necks, wrists, fingers, and toes was ornamented with a variety of techniques such as openwork, granulation, and pendant leaves or circles to shimmer as the wearer moved (see Figure 4.2). Beads were abundant, including the curved beads (*gogok*), which were attached with gold wire so that they could move with the wearer.

The origin of Silla's abundant gold is an unsolved problem. No gold mines have been located in Gyeongju, although gold is known to have been mined along Korea's east coast (Hulbert 1969:273) as late as the Japanese occupation (1910–1945). Patricia Bartz (1972:161) states that before World War II Korea was the fifth-largest producer of gold in the world (Bartz 1972:89). Homer Hulbert (1969:274) relates that placer mining took place in the south and shaft mining in the north. It would seem that if gold had been found in veins near Gyeongju, piles of slag near mined-out lodes in the mountains would still be conspicuous. No such slag piles have been recorded.

While it is widely thought that placer mining from the Gyeongju rivers provided Silla's gold, there has been no recognized evidence of it. In pondering the

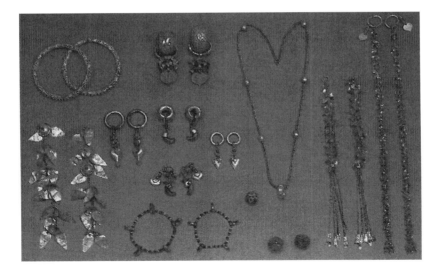

Figure 4.2 Jewelry from Silla tombs

Source: Harold Nelson

58 *Production*

origin of Silla's gold, it has occurred to me to wonder whether the enormous piles of cobbles that cover Silla graves constitute the missing evidence. If placer miners had been sifting the sands of the rivers, removing the cobbles and placing them in piles in order to pick up nuggets and sift the sands, one result would have been mounds of cobbles lining the streams which ran on three sides of the city. These accumulated stones would eventually turn into a considerable nuisance, especially in the center of the city where the mounded tombs were found. The rivers were the water source after all, and access to streams would have been paramount. The cobble piles would have to be moved away from the water sources. Compared to mountain streams in Colorado, for instance, where huge piles of cobbles are heaped beside streams that have been mined out, there are no jumbles of stream cobbles in Gyeongju. Thus, I suggest that the enormous piles of cobbles covering the gold crown tombs are telltale remnants from the search for gold in Gyeongju rivers.

The use of cobbles to make the walls of graves began in the third and fourth centuries, which coincides with the earliest appearance of gold artifacts in graves. At first, the cobbles were piled up against wooden boards to outline the graves, but later more cobbles were used for making low, circular walls around the graves. Korean archaeological reports incorrectly use the English word "block" to describe the composition of these stone walls, but photographs and drawings of the graves show that the walls around the wooden coffins are made of rounded river cobbles, not stone blocks.

Using the water-rounded stones from the river in this way was a creative use for the cobbles piled up inconveniently on the riverbanks. However, with increased extraction of gold from the rivers, the cobble pile increased, perhaps growing into hills.

In the fourth century, the Kim family graves in the area of Michu's tomb began to be covered with small piles of cobbles. By the fifth and sixth centuries, the number of stones that had been moved and washed in the process of placer mining must have become overwhelming. The person inhumed in the south mound of Tomb 98, the Great Tomb of Hwangnam-dong, or his kin, might have been either practical enough or megalomaniacal enough to perceive that he could have a magnificent mound by having the inconvenient stones piled on his grave, creating a huge hill, at the same time proclaiming the power of Silla for all citizens and visitors to admire. Later, when the queen was buried in the north mound of Tomb 98, her tomb received just as high a mound as the spouse who preceded her, and she was given even more magnificent burial goods than those of her husband. Further mounds were almost as high, but apparently a monarch's worth of river stones accumulated during each reign.

Another reason to understand the gold as local is that many of the Silla gold objects are unique, and recognizable as Silla objects, even though the techniques of working gold were the same as those used by the Murong Xianbei of Liaoning (Laursen 2014). The gold crowns and belts are two examples of Silla's unique style, unique in spite of being based on nomadic precedents (Figure 4.3). The broad necklaces of beads that cover the chests of royal burials are a unique

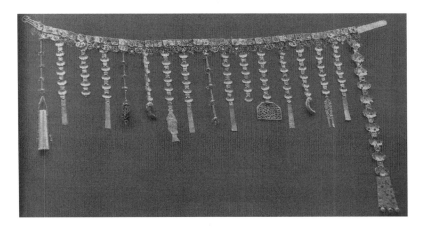

Figure 4.3 Gold belt from Tomb 98, north mound
Source: Harold Nelson

product of Silla gold working. Ham (2014a) calls this a "chestlace," because it is found over the chest rather than around the neck, but it is wide enough to call it a pectoral. In the mounded tombs this item of jewelry is always included as part of the [presumably] royal burial (Ham 2014a:60). In Wolseong-ro, Tomb Area C, Ga-13, where the earliest Silla gold was found, a pectoral made of blue glass beads was very similar to one in the north mound of Tomb 98.

Sarah Laursen (2014) notes that gold is not a difficult material with which to work: "Gold requires minimal tools, a limited workforce, and a relatively small quantity of raw material." This situation would suggest that, with a knowledge of gold working, even a small family of newcomers could have brought gold techniques to Silla, especially if they had discovered gold nuggets in the rivers for their raw material.

The gold crowns of Silla

The crowns of the Silla region are made in a variety of styles and materials. Those that were found outside of Gyeongju are thought to have been worn by local chiefs both before and after they were incorporated by Silla. Some may have been used for ritual purposes rather than marking a leader (Gu 2014). Therefore, gilt bronze crowns are not limited to Gyeongju, but the royal tombs of Gyeongju are the only place where almost pure gold crowns have been found.

The tombs in which the tall gold crowns have been found are known as the Gold Crown Tomb, "Geumgwanchong," Auspicious Phoenix Tomb, "Seobongchong," Gold Bell Tomb, "Kumnyeongchong," Heavenly Horse Tomb, "Cheonmachong," and the north mound of the Great Tomb at Hwangnam-dong (Hwangnam Daechong). The tall gold crowns are generally thought to have been

60   *Production*

worn only by rulers, and to have symbolized rulership. Each ruler with one or more gold crowns also wore a gold belt with streamers ending in symbolic objects, also made of almost pure gold (Figure 4.3). The crowns and belts together were exclusive to the ruler and defined him or her.

The similarities between ancient gold crowns in the Korean peninsula and those of the Eurasian Steppes are striking. Gold crowns of Silla have family resemblances to crowns as far away as Afghanistan. However, they have distinct differences from crowns from the Eurasian Steppes in being lavishly adorned with curved beads (*gogok*) made of jade or glass, and in being taller than most other crowns. Gilt bronze crowns similar in style have been excavated in other parts of South Korea, but Silla's crowns are the most lavishly decorated.

Gold across the Eurasian Steppes

Gold artifacts, especially crowns, have been found in burials across the Eurasian Steppes. Several authors have remarked on the similarity of the Tillya Tepe gold crown from Shibaragan, Afghanistan, encircling a woman's head, to the gold crowns of Silla (Nelson 2008a). Karen Rubinson (2008:58), comparing sites to the east with those of Tillya Tepe, notes similarities between the Tillya Tepe gold crown and that of a Xiongnu noblewoman from Xigoupan—both have dangles in front of the ears like Silla crowns, and both were worn by women. Another female burial with a gold crown was found at Kocklach on the north shore of the Black Sea, and a Liao "princess" also had a gold diadem. Gold crowns on female heads occur as late as the Liao dynasty of northern China.

Tillya Tepe had other similarities with artifacts from Gyeongju. It contained burial shoes with cut-out soles, a feature that is found not only in Silla and Paekche but also in the Pazyryk burials of southern Siberia (Rubinson 2008). Silver shoe soles with cut-out patterns were excavated at Shihuigou in the Ordos region (Linduff 1997:54). Metal shoes or shoes with metal soles for elite burials appear to be have been used widely by the steppe peoples.

Closer to Korea, the Xiongnu used gold lavishly and valued it highly (Bunker 2009:287). Immediately preceding the Saro period, mounded tombs containing a gold crown and belt very similar to those of Silla were unearthed in the vicinity of Chaoyang, in Liaoning Province, China. It is interesting, and perhaps relevant, that the Joyang-dong cemetery south-east of Gyeongju has a wood coffin burial dated to the first century containing four Han dynasty mirrors (Choe 1984). The relationship of the names seems potentially significant, since the dates are similar, closely linking the Silla elite to the Eurasian Steppes.

In Gyeongju itself, the earliest gold objects are those in Wolseong-ro, Tomb Area C, Ga-13, dated around 350 (Lee H. 2012:111). In 382 King Naemul was called ruler of Saro (an early Chinese transliteration of Silla) rather than king of the Jinhan, suggesting an important shift in perceptions of either the polity's power or that of the ruler (Yi 2009:51). Bodon Ju (2010:120) proposes that the middle of the fourth century should be considered the beginning of Silla. Regarding Silla and its gold crowns, he states: "As we enter the Fourth and Fifth Centuries, when

Most of Silla's gold crowns had many of the curved beads (*gogok*) attached with twisted gold wires. The *gogok* was an ancient symbol, used in the Eurasian Steppes (Watson 1971:131, 136; Park 2008:131; Lee I. 2012:131–135). In Korea it had been a symbol of leadership in the Mumun period, often found as the central piece of a necklace made of tubular stone beads.

The use of crowns is not known in Central China, but gold crowns have been excavated in Liaoning Province. Such crowns are restricted to the central Eurasian Steppes and north-eastern China, areas inhabited by a Tungusic-speaking people called the Murong Xianbei (Hong 2012; Laursen 2014). Central China did not use gold crowns to designate rank, and was far less lavish in the use of gold personal ornaments. Jade was valued more highly than gold in China, beginning in the Neolithic, with jade so prevalent in elite burials that the time period is sometimes called the Jade Age (Childs-Johnson 1988). With the beginning of Chinese state-level societies, in the Xia and Shang dynasties, bronze was the metal of choice for containers of food and drink offered to royal ancestors, not gold.

While Silla used both bronze and jade, gold was presumably selected by Silla as a reflection of a wider appreciation for gold among the steppe peoples where gold was an indication of leadership as well as the ability to contact spirits (Nelson 2008b).

The Silla gold crowns are not only stunning, but also full of significance. They were a marker of royalty, with the tall gold crowns belonging only to the rulers. The shamanistic characteristics of the crowns may have demonstrated that the rulers were uniquely able to be in touch with the spirits. The crowns were thus meaningful to their wearers and subjects in multiple ways.

Crowns of Gyeongju and its surrounding areas were unique in having gold in upright pieces in the shape of antlers. In this context it is relevant to mention the probable shamanistic meaning and derivation of the gold antler shapes. The relation to shaman crowns is obvious, and the curved jewels are another symbol of spiritual leadership (Nelson 2008b).

Silla's gold crowns, besides being well endowed with symbolism, are related to the lavish use of gold in burials rich in other precious objects in addition to those made of gold. Gold was highly valued among the peoples of the Eurasian Steppes. The earliest gold ornaments in Asia are found in a broad band across the central Eurasian Steppes, from the north-west of China to the north-east. In a study of the Eurasian Steppes, Katheryn Linduff (1994) concluded that, "Gold appears to be one of the earliest metals worked by the pastoral peoples in the northwest [of China]."

In the Eurasian Steppes, gold earrings have a gold tube that pierces the ear lobe and ends in a trumpet-shaped flare. The use of gold for ornamentation increases in the Bronze Age. Sarmatian burials of the Eurasian Steppes are also rich in gold. By the early centuries of the Common Era, gold was used lavishly and is found in burials such as the site of Shihuigou (Linduff 1997).

62   *Production*

Gold was possibly used for crowns in Goguryeo, but the easily re-entered Goguryeo tombs meant that virtually no artifacts from the mounded tombs of Goguryeo are known. Mural paintings depict many aspects of the lives of the Goguryeo elite, but no crowns appear in Goguryeo tomb murals, suggesting that such crowns were rare. The only crown attributed to Goguryeo is a gilt bronze crown, more like the crown from Tillya Tepe than those of Silla, which was found in an earthen wall at Cheongam-dong, near Pyongyang (McCune 1962; Kim B. M. 1997, Fig. 65). The only gold headgear that has been found in Paekche, where tombs were also looted, was from the intact tomb of King Munyong and his wife (Kim and Pearson 1977). These are floral forms that seem to have been attached to a cap of perishable material, for there is no suggestion of a metal circlet. Thus, it seems that the gold crowns of Silla are most closely related to peoples of the Eurasian Steppes, the Northern Zone of China, and only secondarily to the other Korean kingdoms.

It seems likely that Silla royalty used gold lavishly both as an extension of steppe culture and because gold was available in abundance. Whether the Kim clan were simply lucky to find gold in the sands of the rivers around Gyeongju, where they had settled, or whether they settled in that place because gold was found, is not recorded. Folklore, however, shows that gold was important in the founding legends of the kingdom. One of the early kings was found as a child in a gold box, and another emerged from a golden egg (Iryeon 1972).

Gold crowns in Central Asia

The antecedents of the crowns of Silla, and in fact the very notion of headgear based on a metal circlet, appear to have arisen in the central Eurasian Steppes concomitant with the use of gold. As has repeatedly been pointed out (e.g. Henze 1933; McCune 1962; Kim B. M. 1997; Nelson 2012), many shaman headdresses constructed on a circlet in the recent past have been collected by ethnographers. Although no ancient shaman crowns are known, it is presumed that the form of a circlet with uprights antedates the gold crowns of Silla.

Later kingdoms located in the Eurasian Steppes, for example the Liao dynasty, continued to use gold lavishly, including in gold crowns with dependent gold structures on either side of the face. Crowns appear on the heads of Buddhist statues and paintings at a slightly later time, from the Silk Road grottoes to Japan. The crowns on the heads of Bodhisattvas seem to represent divinity rather than royalty. Several Maitreya statues from Silla wear crowns, although they are not circlets with uprights like those of the Silla royal crowns. Buddhist crowns were often gilded, but although they did not have shamanistic connotations, connections among cultures which depicted gold crowns suggest that the crowns symbolized spirituality, which was not necessarily an idea separate from royalty.

The connections between the Silla crowns and other crowns found in the early centuries of the Common Era in the Japanese islands, the Korean peninsula, the valleys of Manchuria, and the peoples of the Eurasian Steppes extend to other characteristics besides gold and the use of crowns. The importance of horses is particularly notable in this regard (Nelson 2008a), as is the local manufacture of iron weaponry and bronze mirrors. Stylistic similarities across the broad band of the Eurasian Steppes are also important in perceiving connections in the cultures along this ancient highway of communication.

5 Silk roads and trade routes

The best-known trade route between western and eastern Eurasia has been named the Silk Road (see Map 5.1), connecting Chang'an, at that time the capital city of China, producer of the silk, and Rome, consumer of the silk, but this popular concept is no longer adequate to describe all the routes shown by recent archaeological discoveries and studies of material. The Silk Road has been shown to be not one continuous path of plodding camel caravans, but more like a "down-the-line" trade (Renfrew 1978) with various levels of trading at markets and oases along the way. In addition, while silk may have been the primary object of exchange from China on the route that led from Persia and through a sequence of oases south of the Tian Shan Mountains in what is now Xinjiang Province in China, other trade items were exchanged along this important route of contact between East and West, as well as along other routes. From a Korea-centric point of view, the famous Silk Road was not the main route through which goods traveled to and from southern Korean, nor was silk Silla's main export, although it was known for its exquisite brocades. Instead, artifacts and ideas reached Korea through a northern route.

For example, the silver bowls from Tomb 98 in Silla, and an earlier cloisonné dagger sheath, came to Silla across the northern Steppes from Central Asia and into the Korean peninsula through Manchuria. The Silk Road to Chang'an provided few artifacts to Silla, while the northern route through the Steppes was the source of most exotic items.

Based on both manufacturing techniques and compositional analysis, studies of the origins of exotic artifacts found in Silla reveal additional variations of well-traveled routes by which exotic goods made their way to Gyeongju, some requiring ships (the sea route) or perhaps horses (the Steppes route) instead of camel caravans plodding through the southern sands. Knowledge of these avenues of exchange provides important new insights into the Silla polity, insights which have not yet been entirely assimilated into the scholarly portrayal of the kingdom of Silla. The route through the Eurasian Steppes is just beginning to be appreciated, and the sea routes were only the stuff of folklore until recent chemical analyses revealed that such sea routes must have existed. From obsidian and beads to glass vessels, the origins of objects from distant places are being revealed through scientific analyses.

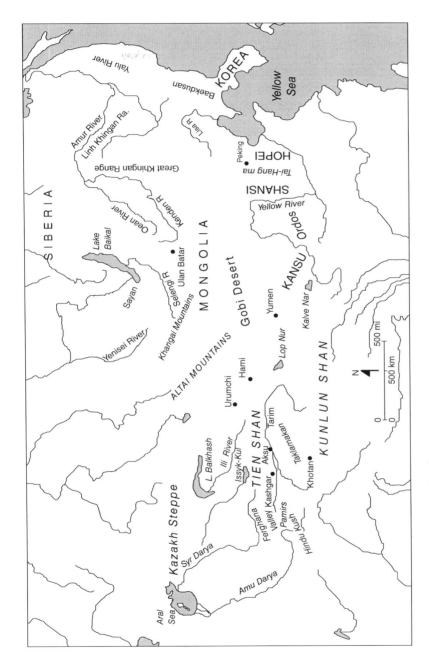

Map 5.1 "Highways" of the Eurasian Steppes

66 *Silk roads and trade routes*

Even in the Pleistocene era, populations in the Korean peninsula and its vicinity were not isolated from other societies and cultures. Travel by sea is implied in the Paleolithic era, as early as 16,000 years ago, from Japan to islands that could not be reached without boats (Ikawa-Smith 1986). In Neolithic times, the fact that similar artifact types have been found in the southern part of the Russian Far East, especially near Vladivostok, and on sites from the Tumen River and south along the Korean coast, also implies contact by sea. Similar pottery-making techniques, as well as decoration of the exterior of ceramic vessels, suggest close connections (Zhuschchikovskaya 2006).

The earliest evidence so far for trade in Korea is the movement of obsidian, which has been traced and found to cover a wide area, from the Korean peninsula to the Russian Far East to the islands of Sakhalin and the Kurile Islands in the Final Paleolithic (Kuzmin 2006a:169–172, 2006b). Especially prized was the high-quality obsidian from Baekdusan, a snowy volcanic mountain containing a large crater lake, Jeonji, the lake that straddles the North Korean/Chinese border. Obsidian from Baekdusan was found by geochemical studies to have been utilized in archaeological sites in the Russian Far East and possibly as far south as the south-eastern corner of the Korean peninsula at Dongsam-dong (Sample 1974).

Although the specific routes of the obsidian trade and the method of transport are unknown, it seems likely that the fishing peoples along the coasts of the East Sea would have been acquainted with the small settlements of people who lived along the coasts in the Paleolithic and Neolithic eras, and would have explored inland, especially up rivers. Major rivers flowing from Jeonji, (translated as "Heavenly Lake" in both Korean and Chinese) would have provided relatively easy ways to move obsidian blocks down to the coast of the East Sea, as well as north to the archaeological sites of the Russian Far East. Thus, long-distance trading was an old and well-established tradition within Korea, well before the time of the Samhan, when the town of Saro (Gyeongju) received its first beads from far away.

The bead trade

The obsidian trade was widespread and well established, but trade in decorative materials on the Korean peninsula seems to have begun with the bead trade (see Figure 5.1). The beads, found by the thousands in the southern part of the Korean peninsula as well as in south-western Japan, are now known to have originated in South-East Asia, where bead manufacture was a booming business (Francis 2002).

The beginning of the bead trade in India stems from the many kinds of colored stones quarried in the hills of Gujarat in western India. These attractive beads became part of the trade from India to Rome. Several types of gemstone were found in early Roman archaeological contexts in the Egyptian port of Berenike. "The abundance of Indian gemstones effectively closed off the Far Eastern Market" [from Egyptian stones] (Wendrich et al. 2006:36).

Hard stone beads came later to Korea, but glass beads arrived as early as the third century BCE (Lee I. 2012:115). Glass beads may have been created to rival

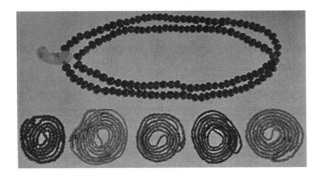

Figure 5.1 Early Indonesian beads found in Korean sites

the stone beads. They were made in Arikamedu, on the east coast of India, beginning in the first few centuries BCE. Roman artifacts are found at Arikimedu, and some of the glass beads created there have been found in the Roman world. The Indonesian islands of Java and Timur also became involved in glass making, perhaps because of their raw materials. The beads are known as Jatim beads, because they are impossible to tell apart. Glass making was exported to Oc-Eo in Thailand (Glover 1990; Glover and Henderson 1995), perhaps becoming a stepping stone to discovering enthusiastic buyers in southern Korea.

Korean beads

The trade in both glass and stone beads arrived in southern ports (or even on the beaches) of the Korean peninsula by the third century BCE (Lee I. 2012). The *Hou Han Shu* notes that the people of Mahan were very fond of stone beads and sewed them onto their clothes, or hung them from their necks and ears (Barnes and Byington 2014:108). The beads must have been transported in sailing ships to places where landing was possible and where there were settlements of an adequate size for sufficient potential buyers. Several beaches along the southern coast of the Korean peninsula (as it existed at that time) would answer this description, as well as bays along the south-eastern and eastern coasts.

The bead sellers were probably not the first contact by boat from peoples from the South Pacific. Two sites with head flattening, which is not a widespread local trait, have been excavated, one near the coast of South Korea (Kim J. H. 1978), the other in the Russian Far East (McKenzie and Popov 2015). Oddly enough, both featured a central burial of a mature woman.

Furthermore, a tradition among the Kims of Gaya is a tale of a princess from India, named Hwang-ok, "Yellow Jade," who arrived on the southern coast of Korea in a ship with red sails. The ship landed on the coast near Gimhae in 48 CE, with all her palace ladies and rich goods. King Suro happily took the princess as his bride. Her purported grave, a high-mounded, unexcavated tomb, is still

68   *Silk roads and trade routes*

locally revered. Kim Byeong Mo (1987) has researched how this ship might have come from Ayodhia, which is part of the legend (recounted in detail in English (Kim Choong Soon 2011:5–6)). With the evidence of the bead trade, we can be sure that ships arrived in Korea from the south and the tale seems less far-fetched than it once did.

The ships that brought colorful beads to Korea and Japan may have been ships from India, but ships from South-East Asia are more likely. Indian glass and stone beads dated between 50 BCE and 250 CE have been found in Oc-Eo in Thailand (Glover 1990:13–23). As Sunil Gupta notes, "Though material evidence for sea-going vessels of the Early Historic period is virtually non-existent, records of ancient boats and ships are prolific in textual sources, epigraphic and numismatic sources, sculptural representations, and cave paintings" (Gupta 1994:223). Ian Glover has described this as a "vast network of trade stretching from Western Europe, via the Mediterranean basin and the Red Sea to South China" (Glover 1990:10).

Archaeologically, the bead trade is first evident in the southern parts of the Korean peninsula and in Kyushu, Japan, in the third century BCE (Seyock 2004, 2015), but glass beads were also made quite early in Korea. Insook Lee (2012:115) describes the tubular beads often found in dolmen burials as the first glass beads in Korea to which a Chinese origin is ascribed because it is barium glass. Round glass beads were made in southern Korean in the Mahan polity, known through bead-making molds (Jeonju National Museum 2009:119, Fig. 102). Insook Lee (2012) also describes local glass production of beads on the site of Angyeri, north of Gyeongju.

Both stone and glass beads were found in Silla mounded burials; there were about 100,000 glass beads, mostly blue in color (Francis 2002:46–47). Some hard stone beads, as well as numerous beads made of amber and jet, and more than 10,000 Indo-Pacific glass beads were found in the tomb of King Muryong of Baekje and his wife (buried in 529) (Kim W. Y. 1983).

The placement of beads in Gyeongju graves does not always imply that necklaces were worn. For example, beads were left on the corners of the top of the burial chamber of the queen in Tomb 98. (Lee I. 2012:119, Fig. 6.3). What function did they have there? Were they a kind of talisman? A warning to thieves if they should get that far, digging through the pie of earth and stone? Did beads have supernatural abilities to protect the spirit of the deceased?

Studies of glass composition

Insook Lee (1989) was the first scholar to study the glass technology of early Korea. Her study of glass beads found in tombs in southern Korea was based on an analysis of the chemical composition of the beads. Lee distinguished three kinds of glass from Korean archaeological sites: soda glass, potash glass, and lead barium glass. She found that glass beads from the shell mounds of the southern coast, from the first century BCE to the first century CE, were made from soda glass. In contrast, potash glass was used in the second to third centuries. She believes it is very likely that these two types of glass were imported. Lead barium glass was commonly used in Korea in the Buddhist period, when beads were more often found in sarira containers rather than in tombs (Lee I. 1989). Silla tombs, even those of royalty, were less lavish in their grave goods than royal graves during the Mounded Tomb period.

In a subsequent study (Lankton and Lee 2006), glass beads from the Gimhae–Yangdong cemetery of the first to fourth centuries, and the Bokcheondong cemetery, an elite burial ground of the fourth to sixth centuries, were investigated. Both cemeteries served inhabitants of settlements near Pusan. These well-dated graves allowed the changes in the composition of the glass through time. The graves contained locally made pottery and iron artifacts, as well as ornamental objects of stone, glass, and metal, but no artifacts that originated in China.

The transition from potash glass to soda glass was confirmed by this chemical analysis. Another result of this study was the confirmation that from the first to the fifth centuries the glass beads in the study were brought to Korea already made, that is, they were not finished or refinished in this part of Korea. The bead composition and technology shows that the Jatim beads were produced in South and South-East Asia. Such beads were particularly notable in Silla tombs from the third and fourth centuries, where a famous face bead was found (see Figure 5.2). The techniques of drawing, winding, and making mosaic patterns, which appear on the beads in the cemeteries near Pusan, are all known with regard to Jatim beads.

A further bead study included beads from five locations in Gyeongju: Nosodong, Nodongni, Hwango-dong, Hwangam-dong, and Inwang-dong. The bead chosen for the study from Inwang-dong Tomb 6, dated to the fifth century, is a millefiori bead. The selection from Nosodong was a small glass bead with green and yellow stripes in a festoon pattern. Beads made of gemstones—cornelian, amber, and jasper—as well as monochrome glass beads, were found

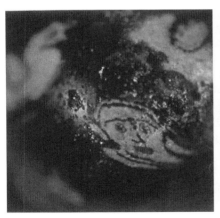 

Figure 5.2 Face bead from a tomb in Wolseong-ro, Gyeongju

70 *Silk roads and trade routes*

in the same grave in Nosodong. This burial is thought to have originally had a mound above it that had eroded over the years and, therefore, to be an early royal tomb. Two other beads selected for the study are from yet another tomb, the Ornamental Shoes Tomb, "Singnichong," and these are also millefiori glass beads. These beads are much more complicated than the early tiny beads apparently created by the millions.

The most famous and elaborate of the beads in the test is a face bead which was found in Wolseong-ro, Tomb Area C, Ga-13, near King Michu's tomb. The bead is quite astonishing, with what appears to be a European face embedded in its design. (see Figure 5.2). Designated as National Treasure No. 634, it is an unusual and remarkable bead. The bead is complex, with three different mosaic cane patterns, including a face with round eyes and a prominent nose, a white bird, and a tree or flower. Until this study, speculations had suggested Egypt, or Rome, or elsewhere in the Mediterranean world as its place of manufacture. However, this type of bead is definitely in the Jatim tradition, and provides firm evidence of trade between Korea and South-East Asia (Lankton et al. 2003).

A mega-study of 1,086 beads from South and East Asia included all the beads that had been analyzed for their chemical composition. The study found four broad compositional types. The commonest was high-alumina soda glass, which was present in Korea from the second century BCE to the sixth century CE. Potash glass in Korea is more restricted. It dates almost exclusively from the first century BCE to the first century CE (Lankton and Dussubieux 2006).

Beads in Japan

Early beads in southern Korea were tiny. While the first beads were almost certainly acquired in trade, later beads were made in the southern part of the Korean peninsula (Lee I. 1989). Molds for making glass beads have been found in south-eastern Korea in the Mahan region (Kim Y. W. 2009: [Jeonju National Museum 2009:119, Fig. 102]).

Presumably, the Indo-Pacific micro-beads uncovered in Yayoi sites in Japan were part of the same trade network as those found in southern Korea. Oga and Gupta (1995) cite the earliest Yayoi beads as dating to the third century BCE and mostly deposited in graves on Kyushu and Tsushima islands, those closest to Korea. While there were typically only a few beads together, one hoard of beads excavated on Tsushima island contained more than 9,000 micro-beads. The most common color of these beads was blue. Whether the color was especially selected in East Asia as having a spiritual meaning (as blue does in many cultures), or whether that was the most common color of bead available, is not known. Such micro-beads were being produced in Arikamedu, India, as well as Indonesia. Whichever their place of origin, they had a very long trip to southern Korea and the Japanese islands. One must wonder what trade commodities of Korea and Japan made it worth the trip.

It is worth noting that in the Oga and Gupta study noted above, only a total of five beads had been found in Early Yayoi sites, and rarely more than a single bead

Silk roads and trade routes   71

in each of the Middle Yayoi sites. Even by the Late Yayoi period, few sites had enough beads to make a necklace (Oga and Gupta, Table 1). Were some beads lost, or were they only used on clothing in the Yayoi period? Although micro-beads were transported to the Japanese islands as well as southern Korea, they seem to have been particularly prized in Korea.

On the other hand, the Fujinoki Tomb which, notably, contained Silla-style objects (see Chapter 9), astoundingly contained 16,000 micro-beads, presumably strung in necklaces or attached to clothing (Kidder 1987, 1989).

Local bead manufacture

By the fifth century the people of Silla had learned to make glass beads for them-selves. Clear evidence of bead making, consisting of a form for pouring the molten glass into small round concavities, along with waste glass, was found in Tokchon, Wolseong-ro, near the center of Gyeongju (Rhee et al. 2007).

Examples of beads made to the tastes of the customers are also found. Two such shapes are the *gogok* (curved bead), and tubular beads that had been used together to identify leaders in Korea and Manchuria since the seventh or eighth centuries BCE. Some tubular blue-green glass beads imitating the stone examples were found in the second century BCE. This is lead-barium-silica glass, similar to Chinese glass, but made in specifically Korean and North-East Asian shapes (Lankton et al. 2009). These shapes were parts of necklaces that were emblems of leadership in Bronze Age Manchuria. They are also found in Korea in southern dolmens, often with a *gogok* in the center of the string of tubular green beads. Another glass shape that was even more made specifically to suit the customer is the *gogok*. The glass *gogok* on some of the Silla royal crowns could have been locally made, but there is no evidence suggesting that they were.

Imports to Gyeongju from Lelang and Han China

Beads, however, as numerous as they were, did not constitute the only kind of trade, although they may have traveled the longest distance. Metal artifacts were traded as well. Many types of bronze weapons, horse trappings, jingle bells, and mirrors, as noted in Chapter 3, were among items brought into Gyeongju and its vicinity and buried with the distinguished dead. Also included in the burial goods were Han Chinese objects such as lacquerware and chariot parts, and some epi-nomadic items such as iron helmets and kettles. These artifacts were mixed in with pottery, and iron tools and weapons that are believed to have been locally produced.

Objects that must have originated in China, such as lacquered sheaths for daggers and lacquered fans, probably came to south-eastern Korea through the Lelang colony, even though they were made much farther away. Many elaborate Chinese goods were imported to Lelang for the use of the Chinese overlords of the commandery, with expensive materials such as lacquer, silk, tortoiseshell, silver, gold, and exotic stones such as turquoise and amber. Mirrors, chariots, and horse trappings have been found in Lelang graves, along with personal adornments and wooden implements, and wooden coffins too. Very few of these found their way to graves in Gyeongju.

Glass vessels

In the fourth century, after the demise of the Lelang commandery, new classes of exotic items began to appear in the tombs of Gyeongju. Notably, glass vessels were added to the artifacts reaching Gyeongju from afar. These were deposited in the royal tombs (see Figure 5.3). Although it has not always been clear exactly where the glass beads, silver bowls, and dagger sheaths found in Korean graves originated from, or through what paths and mechanisms they ended up in Korean tombs, many of them were guessed to have been Roman by comparing the shapes and styles. These artifacts have been briefly mentioned in Chapter 3 in the context of their find spots, but a closer look at the technology of manufacture helps to trace their origin.

The glass cups, bowls, and pitchers that had been carefully placed in Silla mounded tombs posed a different set of questions from those of the beads (see Figure 5.3). Glass vessels were obviously prestigious, and perhaps a little mysterious, an article of wealth that was suitable for display (An 2004). Glass has been discovered in several tombs in China, but it is most conspicuous in Manchurian tombs. The Murong Xianbei of the Northern Yan (406–436) and

Figure 5.3 Glass vessels from Silla tombs

Source: Harold Nelson

the Tuoba Xianbei of the Northern Wei (386–535) placed many glass vessels in noble tombs.

In particular, the Xianbei of Manchuria used glass vessels as items of conspicuous consumption. "One of the special treasures was glassware imported from the west," Jiayao An (2004:59) reports, with reference to a particular nobleman who showed off his treasures of wine glasses, bowls, and cups. An also notes that the beauty of glass was celebrated in poetry. Owning glass was a sign of true refinement of taste, as well as wealth.

When the glass vessels of Silla royal graves were first excavated it was assumed that these were articles of Roman glass. The styles were similar, as were the techniques of glass making. However, once again, analysis of the composition of the glass helped to solve the question of origin.

Twenty-five glass vessels that had been excavated from nine Korean royal tombs in Gyeongju were used in the compositional study. Pieces of broken glass found in the graves or left over from reconstructions were selected, rather than destroying even a tiny bit of any of the whole vessels. Tests of the chemical composition of the glass found that the greatest compositional resemblance to the Korean glass artifacts were glass vessels from Bactria/Tokharistan. The location is described by that term because of changing names through the centuries (Lankton et al. 2006).

A glass vessel from the Feng Sufu Tomb of the Northern Yan, dated 415, was tested with the same techniques, and found to match glass from Bactria in its chemical composition. This result is particularly interesting because it tends to reinforce the area across which the glass was carried, north of the Altai Mountains and across the Eurasian Steppes to Liaoning. The presence of glass vessels in Manchuria clearly shows that not only were glass vessels and glass beads from very different origins, but also the route of travel was not at all the same. These have been shown to be two separate glass making traditions.

Glassware imported from the West was rare and beautiful, and therefore a special treasure. One way to appreciate the reverence for such glass is that a glass pitcher in the south mound of Tomb 98 in Gyeongju had a broken handle that had been mended by winding a gold cord around the broken pieces to hold them together.

Glass bowls and pitchers have not yet been found in Baekje or Gaya graves. One way this might be explained is to note the close relationships of the Silla leadership to the leaders in the north-east. The glass vessels in Silla tombs, after being created in Central Asia, could have gone directly from Northern Yan or Northern Wei to Silla. One Central Asian glass vessel was even found in the Gobi Desert (Honeychurch 2015:2882).

Metal artifacts

Some of the imports into Gyeongju clearly belonged to Han Chinese traditions, items such as parts of chariots, canopy ribs and points, for example, and Han dynasty mirrors. They probably came to Gyeongju through the Lelang commandery near Pyongyang. The value of these objects to the Gyeongju people must have been their foreignness, for there were no whole chariots, but pieces of chariots, and sometimes pieces of broken mirrors, which must have been valued for being exotic, rather than having any use value (Seyock 2014). Presumably, they were actually detritus from the Lelang colony, perhaps being peddled as magical artifacts.

Other artifacts came from the "epi-nomadic" tradition, (a useful expression coined by Barbara Seyock to indicate that these objects were similar to those used in the north-east Asian Steppes, but were used by a population that was not nomadic). These objects mostly consisted of horse gear, such as bits and stirrups, the nomadic type of belt buckles, and an occasional bronze or iron cauldron or helmet.

Which iron artifacts were received in trade, and which manufactured either in Gyeongju or elsewhere on the Korean peninsula are not questions that can yet be answered definitively. Outcrops of iron were available near Gyeongju, and local evidence of iron smelting has been found. However, evidence of tool molds would be necessary to know exactly which tools were made locally. To make some informed guesses, axe forms, at least, must have been local since they were intended as trade goods. Agricultural tools are likely to have been forged in Gyeongju as well. Local blacksmiths probably knew how to make horse bits and stirrups. But these are questions the next generation of archaeologists will have to solve.

As for bronze, the bronze mirrors and bronze swords have been studied minutely in order to arrange them in typological order, which is presumably related to the chronology of the times in which they were made. Geometric mirror styles are related to mirrors in Liaoning Province, and are an entirely different style from the mirrors that were made in central China. A few imitation Han mirrors have appeared, but they are usually very small, and crudely made, making them easy to distinguish from genuine Han mirrors. Bronze daggers made in Korea also have distinctive styles, being descended from the Liaoning dagger with its bracket-shaped edges. The daggers gradually became narrower and the edges less pointed, so they can be serrated. However, there is still some disagreement about the exact order of the types, therefore they are rarely used to date a particular burial or hoard.

Artifacts of precious metals

One of the most spectacular of the metal objects found in the sixth-century graves of Silla is a dagger sheath found in Gyerim-ro, Tomb 14. It is unlike anything else found in Korea, but has analogies in a dagger sheath from Kazakhstan in the Hermitage Museum in St. Petersburg, Russia. Another such dagger sheath is depicted on a mural painting of the fourth to fifth century in Kizil Cave 69, Kucha kingdom, in Xinjiang. (Yoon 2012). The dagger inside is made of wood, and would not have been an effective weapon, so it was clearly simply for show.

The sheath is decorated with gold outlining designs inlaid with glass and garnet. The style indicates that it is an import, but the gold is also distinctly different from the gold of Silla, with much more copper than is found in Silla gold.

A small silver bowl found in Tomb 98 (Figure 5.4) may also have had Central Asian origins (Bush 1984). The bowl is decorated with repoussé technique, quite unlike any art of Silla and, thus, are certainly imports. An article by James Lankton et al. (2009) shows that silverwork from Bactria/Tokharistan is similar to the rare silver items in Silla mounded graves. It is also interesting that shapes of metal containers echo those of glass and pottery. Furthermore, analyses of bronze artifacts and "stylistic and weave studies of tapestry fragments recovered from Noyon Uul suggest a Bactrian origin in Central Asia" (Honeychurch and Amartuvshin 2006:265).

While the fifth-century Steppe Road was probably the source of the silver vessels as well as the glassware that ended their journeys in Silla tombs, other precious objects were made in Silla. In particular, the gold artifacts are likely to have been locally made. That said, it is not difficult to find the forerunners of Silla's gold art among the Northern Wei. Openwork and inlaid gems were typical of art of the Steppes. "Hat ornaments" with dangles, antlers with leaf shapes and

Figure 5.4 Silver bowl from Hwangnam Daechong, south mound
Source: Harold Nelson

76 *Silk roads and trade routes*

spangles dangling from them, and so forth, bear a strong relationship to dangles on Silla jewelry and crowns (Pak 1988; Laursen 2014).

Young Sook Pak singles out the leaf-shaped gold ornaments common on Silla earrings and crowns, noting that "an almost identical pendant consisting of several leaves hanging from a tiny parasol is used in a Xiongnu tomb at Aluchaideng in Inner Mongolia" (Pak 1988:51). This gold has recently been studied in a dissertation (Laursen 2014). Pak speculates about the relationship between these two cultures, asking, "Would it be too far-fetched to assume that those nomads and horse riders dwelling in the vast Eurasian Steppes did move eastward settling in various places, and finally reached the Korean peninsula, at the far end of the Steppes?" (Pak 1988:47). There is much to recommend this speculation in more recent discoveries in Manchuria.

Gold is found among the Xianbei at the beginning of the fourth century (Watt 2004:38), perhaps reflecting unworked gold from Silla reaching them as raw material. Shared techniques suggest common uses of gold. The technique of granulation, so beautifully applied to the earrings in the northern mound of Tomb 98, was presumably brought by Xianbei artisans to Silla after gold nuggets were discovered to be plentiful in Gyeongju's rivers. Cut-out sheet gold is another technique common to both areas, along with dangling round or leaf-shaped objects attached with gold wire, and edges outlined with dots.

Perishable luxury goods

The sumptuary laws of Silla (see Chapter 6) allow an insight into perishable luxury goods imported into the kingdom. Among the many goods prohibited for one rank or another, but presumably not only allowed but actually available to the highest rank, the Sacred Bone, are such materials as reindeer leather and various kinds of fur, brocade and raw silk, gems, jade and ivory, and even types of fragrant or colored wood, such as purple sandalwood and Chinese juniper. It must have been a very lively market.

Silla's side of the trade

The distances from which objects and materials came to Gyeongju are remarkable. The extensive trade of Silla, and its participation in the wider world of Asia, is becoming better known through excavations of tombs. But what did Silla provide in exchange? Trade objects from the Korean peninsula are known to include iron in the form of ingots shaped like flat axes, and probably gold was traded as well, perhaps as gold dust or nuggets rather than in the form of finished products. As we have seen in Chapter 4, gold was plentiful in Gyeongju, and exquisite gold and gilt bronze objects were created there. But Silla gold objects have not so far appeared in Chinese, Manchurian, or Xiongnu graves (although they have turned up in tombs in Japan, see Chapter 9). Similar gold artifacts in Manchurian graves are probably the inspiration for Silla gold artifacts, rather than the other way around. Thus, it is more likely that gold nuggets or bars were the medium of exchange from Gyeongju, rather than finished objects such as rings, bracelets, and necklaces.

As for clothing materials, Silla had its own mulberry trees, silk cocoon unraveling and weaving, as well as ramie and hemp for everyday clothes, so only elaborate items of clothing or fabrics for display would have been welcomed in Gyeongju, more likely as gifts from one royal house to another than as items of trade. A tale about one gift from China is told to illustrate the keen intelligence of Queen Seondeok. She received an embroidered image of peonies from the Tang ruler, and remarked that they were very pretty, but had no scent. When asked how she knew such a thing, she replied that there were no bees in the picture.

To summarize, objects found in archaeological sites can be tested to discover which of them are locally made and which of foreign origin. They can be compared by style and manufacture to similar artifacts found elsewhere, and reasonable guesses can be made about their place of origin. However, a newer tool of compositional analysis has proved that it can solve questions of place of manufacture beyond doubt. The studies of obsidian, glass beads, and glass vessels discussed in this chapter open up a new window of understanding of the economies of ancient cultures. Knowledge of the sources of materials and the methods of manufacture, as well as the place of manufacture, opens up new ways of understanding these cultures.

6** Ranking and sumptuary rules

Silla was a ranked society from the start. According to the *Samguk Sagi*, families were differentiated even before the six villages had joined together to create the polity of Saro, because each village had a leader and a leading family. The decision to make common cause against perceived enemies of the villages was made by the leading families of each of the six villages. The leaders and their families went to the top of a mountain to create the polity of Saro, but the farmers, artisans, and other workers are not mentioned, and presumably had no choice in the matter.

A leader was selected, but decisions had to be agreed upon by the six village heads. Eventually, the governmental function needed to expand, and to create posts with duties differentiated. Officers began to be appointed for many facets of government. These are reflected in the burials. When the Mounded Tomb period began, differences in tomb sizes and the quality and amount of grave goods suggest very great inequalities in rank and status. By the time Silla unified the peninsula, offices were thoroughly codified, even to the colors of robes designated for particular officers, much of it adapted from Chinese protocols.

Even when the grave mounds were still relatively small, riches could be buried within. For example, this chestlace (see Figure 6.1) was excavated from a tomb in Wolseong-ro. Gold jewelry made with exquisite techniques was found in high-mounded tombs that were not in the Kim family tomb park. Even gilded shoes or shoe soles were placed in the tombs of the high elite.

The sumptuary rules

The sumptuary rules of Silla were based on a system of endogamous ranks of people who were expected to marry within their own group (Kim Chong Sun 1977). This was known as the *golbeum* system, or bone ranks (Yi 1984). The bone rank system mandated endogamous groups with specific rights and privileges in every level of Silla society. These groups were named, from the top down, as Holy Bone (or Sacred Bone), True Bone, and the Head ranks, Six, Five, and Four, below which were commoners. The ranks described what offices a holder of that rank would be eligible to occupy, as well as details of their lifestyle.

Bone is the Korean metaphor for genetic relationships, instead of blood, as in English one would speak of "blood" kinship. In Ancient Silla (Go Silla) the

Figure 6.1 Large chest ornament of gold and glass from Tomb 155 (Heavenly Horse Tomb)

highest rank was called *Song'gol*, "Holy Bone" or "Sacred Bone," and only those whose parents were both Holy Bone were eligible to be kings and queens (Grayson 1976; Kim Chong Sun 1977). It is important to note that, "The holders of the highest status, *Song'gol*, were eligible for the throne, regardless of sex" (Kim Chong Sun 1977:47), which made Silla distinct from other Korean polities of the time, but with similarities to Yamato in the Kogun Period (Piggott 1997).

The bone ranks were at the same time social, economic, and political (Grayson 1976; Kim Chong Sun 1977; Nelson 1991, 1993a, 2003; Sasse 2001). The highest rank of *Song'gol* conferred eligibility to rule. Birth into the Sacred Bone rank did not specifically confer the rulership, it only allowed a person to be in the pool from which rulers could be chosen. The ruler was selected by a council of Sacred Bone (Kim Chong Sun 1969) from among its own rank.

A rule of hypodescent has been inferred from the list of rulers, which includes the names of the ruler's parents, their spouses, and their spouses' parents. It seems that no one could belong to the rank of Holy Bone unless both parents were from that rank, and a person took the rank of the lower ranking parent (Grayson 1976; Sasse 2001). In their official roles, people of the Holy Bone rank were distinguished by purple robes. This seems relevant to some otherwise mysterious prohibition of purple clothing or objects. Even the True Bone were not allowed to display anything purple or even purplish.

The second rank was *Chin'gol*, "True Bone." True Bone were high nobles, but True Bone persons only became eligible to rule after the pure *Song'gol* rank had died out. Two successive queens were the last survivors of the Holy Bone rank. Below the two highest noble ranks were the *Ryuktupum*, the *Odupum*, and

80 *Ranking and sumptuary rules*

the *Sadupum* ("Sixth," "Fifth," and "Fourth" Head ranks, respectively). Everyone below the Sixth to Fourth Head ranks was a commoner, ineligible to serve in the court. The Fourth Head rank was sometimes grouped with commoners in the list of rules.

Beginnings of the bone ranks

Much scholarly discussion has been directed to the question of whether the *golbeum* system began as early as the fourth century, in the Mounded Tomb period during which the gold crown tombs were erected. A few scholars have used the absence of any mention of Holy Bone in the sumptuary rules to assert that the rules were written after 668 when the kingdom of Silla united the peninsula by conquering the other Korean kingdoms of Baekje and Goguryeo.

However, they have the argument backward. The rules imply the existence of Holy Bone, a group which are not mentioned presumably because they could flaunt their wealth and position without limits. True Bone persons, on the other hand, were not allowed to wear clothing or decorate houses or horses with precious materials, and they especially were required to avoid purple. Furthermore, the *Samguk Sagi* describes the reinstatement of the rules according to ancient tradition, demonstrating that these were not new rules (Kim Chong Sun 1965). Far from showing that the Holy Bone no longer existed when the rules were written, the restriction for True Bone demonstrated that the higher rank, Holy Bone, was still present to keep watch on those who had no right to the same privileges they had.

The main information regarding the system is derived from a document that lists and describes in detail how the sumptuary laws apply to each rank (Kim Chong Sun 1977). Many aspects of clothing, housing, horses, and horse equipment are prescribed by rank. Some examples of the restrictions to which the True Bone rank was subjected follow.

Sumptuary laws specify what people of different ranks in a particular society may own or wear or otherwise display. The rules cover everything relating to a person's self-representation in public. When there is a danger of any non-royal group trying to rise to the level of royalty, sumptuary laws may be enacted. The rules are intended to keep traders, for example, who may become rich, or artisans who create particularly desired wares, from profiting to the extent of appearing to be, and perhaps being mistaken for a higher class than they were born into. The basic intent is to keep everyone firmly locked into the place in society into which they were born (Kim W. Y. 1975).

Restrictions of clothing

With regard to clothing, the True Bone were not permitted to wear "wrinkled purple reindeer leather boots" (Kim Chong Sun 1977:59), perhaps because purple was a color allowed only to the Holy Bone, but perhaps also because of the rarity or sacredness of reindeer leather, since reindeer must have been an import into the southern Korean peninsula from at least as far away as Manchuria. Other restrictions for male True Bone, *Chin'gol*, are "embroidered trousers made of fur, brocade, or raw silk." Female *Chin'gol* were not permitted to wear hairpins that were engraved and inlaid with gems and jade and of course were not permitted to wear crowns. They could not hang carved wooden fish from the eaves of their houses or polish their front steps. They were forbidden to use purple sandalwood for their carts or their saddles (Kim Chong Sun 1977:59–69).

Details of the clothing restrictions are particularly interesting and useful to archaeologists and historians since clothes were mostly constructed from perishable materials. In terms of clothing it is interesting to note that both boots and trousers are mentioned in the sumptuary laws, along with headgear and underwear. For example, True Bone men could wear a headcloth but not a crown. The True Bone men were not permitted to sport embroidered trousers made of fur, brocade, or silk.

Male Sixth Head rank could wear headcloths of coarsely woven wool, but they were forbidden to wear boots made of wrinkled purple reindeer leather. Women of the Sixth Head rank were prohibited from wearing combs with gold inlay, or hairpins of pure gold or silver decorated with gems and jades. They were allowed to cover their hair only with gauze-like materials such as raw or thin silk.

Fourth Head rank men likewise were permitted only lesser materials for their headcloths, and were restricted to hemp underwear. Their female counterparts could dress their hair only with hairpins of silver or lesser material, and could not wear crowns. Women of the lowest nobility were not allowed to wear underskirts, but they could wear combs of ivory, antler, or wood. Commoners' hairpins were required to be made of bronze, stone, or lesser materials.

Horses

The number of horses was not directly regulated, but is implied by the size of the stables permitted to each rank. No restrictions in stable size are recorded for True Bone, who were at liberty to keep as many horses as they liked. However, the *Ryuktupum* could have a stable big enough for five horses, *Odupum* were limited to three horses, and *Sadupum* and commoners could stable only two horses.

The section of the rules pertaining to horse-riding equipment begins with saddles for both genders and all ranks. Horse-riding and the horse decorations were clearly part of the daily pageantry of the elite. Also subject to restrictions by rank were saddlecloths and pillows, mudguards, bits, stirrups, and reins. For example, even True Bone men were not permitted to use saddles made of imported wood, especially purple sandalwood and Chinese juniper. Their saddlecloths were forbidden to be made of fur, raw silk, or brocade. Bits and stirrups could not be decorated with gold, bronze, gems, or jade. The reins were not to be braided or

82   *Ranking and sumptuary rules*

finely knit, nor could they be dyed purple. Mudguards had to be dyed with hemp oil. This last restriction would be inexplicable were it not for the fact that a few artifacts identified as mudguards have been found in royal tombs. These have been made of birch bark and painted with images of white horses. Perhaps the intended restriction was any images on mudguards.

Even True Bone ladies were prohibited from using saddles inlaid with jewels. Women's saddlecloths and cushions reflect those of the men of their rank, and could not be made of fur or raw silk. Bits and stirrups could not be plated with gold, and the reins could not have gold and silver threaded into them.

The Sixth Head rank were further limited in the wood from which saddles could be constructed for, in addition to the restrictions for True Bone, they were not allowed to use alder, locust, or silkworm oak wood for their saddles, nor decorate them with precious metals, gems, or jade. The saddlecloth had to be leather, but for their saddle cushions they were permitted padded silk, finely woven ramie cloth, hemp, or leather. No embellishments of bits or stirrups were permitted, and reins had to be made only of leather or hemp rope.

Women of the Sixth Head rank interestingly have fewer restrictions on the type of wood that could be used for their saddles than men of their rank, but like men they were restricted to plain bits, stirrups, and leather mudguards.

Men of the Fifth Head rank had the same restrictions on the types of wood that could be used for saddles as the rank above them, but they were also specifically forbidden from applying silver or gold inlays or plating to their bits and stirrups. Women of the same rank had similar restrictions, except that tiger skins are also specifically forbidden for their saddlecloths, as is dusting purple powder on the reins.

Fourth Head and commoner men were required to use mudguards of poplar or bamboo. Bits could only be made of iron, and stirrups of wood and iron. The reins were required to be made of hemp rope. The restrictions on women are fewer, but similar. Women seem to have been allowed a bit more splendor in each rank, but it is impossible to tease out any gender implications from this fact alone.

It is clear that both women and men owned horses and rode them. One might expect that horses would be restricted to upper-class men, but it turns out that horses were a major means of transportation for everyone. The horse culture, inherited from the Steppes, included women as well as men on horseback. Women on the Steppes were expert riders, and could use a bow with accuracy from the saddle. The gender and rank parity allowed everyone to ride horses, using the splendor of the horse trappings to distinguish primarily by rank rather than gender.

Houses

Sizes of houses went along with sizes of stables, becoming progressively smaller and less ornamented for each lower rank. Sacred Bone could build palaces of any size, but True Bone, as previously stated, could not build houses larger than 24 *cheok*. The exact length of the *cheok* at that time is unknown, but a sense of

Ranking and sumptuary rules 83

it can be gained from the fact that the height of fences was restricted for the Sixth Head rank to eight *cheok*, reducing to six *cheok* for commoners' fences, which suggests a linear dimension of about one meter. House length restrictions down the line from True Bone were 21 *cheok*, 18 *cheok*, and 15 *cheok*—each three *cheok* smaller than the rank above, making a visible difference in house sizes.

Other limitations regarding housing related to the costliness of house construction materials. Only the Sacred Bone could roof their houses with Chinese tiles, or build high eaves. Their houses could be decorated with gold, silver, bronze, gems, and the "five colors." Hanging carved wooden fish from the eaves of the house was likewise a privilege of only the highest rank. This apparently odd restriction on wooden fish may indicate that these carved objects were gongs to call the spirits. Gongs such as this can be seen in the Bulguksa Buddhist temple to this day. Korean Buddhism adapted many traits of earlier religious traditions, so a spirit-calling gong might predate the establishment of Buddhism in Silla.

The height of the house platform was also important, being restricted in lesser ranks to two steps or fewer. The steps of True Bone and lower ranks' houses had to be unpolished, and could not be made of stones from the mountains. Perhaps the Sacred Bone were connected with mountain spirits, regarded as very important in pre-Buddhist Korea (Lee K. 2004:53). The Sacred Bone alone could build fences with a beam and a pillar, which I understand to refer to a gate like a torii, marking off sacred space. Inside the properties, the screens of Sacred Bone houses could be embroidered, and furniture constructed from Chinese juniper inlaid with tortoiseshell was permitted. The richness of the houses was intended to dazzle, inside and out, and no other rank could rival the Sacred Bone.

The sumptuary rules of Silla demonstrate, among other things, that women riding horses was taken for granted. The severity of the restrictions was based on rank rather than sex. While differences in clothing marked gender, differences in wealth display marked rank. All had access to horses. The upper ranks that formed the Silla nobility in south-eastern Korea used many items of material culture that relates them closely to the Tuoba Wei in Chaoyang, Liaoning Province.

A statistical study of the royal tombs

Archaeological confirmation of the *golbeum* system was sought by a group from the University of British Columbia (Pearson et al. 1989). The research began with 131 burials from the Old Silla kingdom in Gyeongju. The first attempt of the research group was to use "burial types, orientation, method of construction, and relationship of tomb typology to sex the deceased," given the lack of bodies and inscriptions to provide this information (Pearson et al. 1989:1).

In the first segment of the study they found three groupings, relating to the size of the burial. The stone-surrounded wooden chamber burials were found not only to be the largest, but also to contain a significantly larger number and variety of artifacts than the other two categories of graves. Apparently, within each group the sexes were treated equally.

84 *Ranking and sumptuary rules*

The second analysis by the Pearson group is more relevant to the question of the existence of sumptuary rules during Ancient Silla. For this study, the group used only the stone-surrounded wooden chamber type of tombs, in other words, mounded tombs. There were 62 tombs and 96 types of artifacts in the original analysis. A cluster analysis of the artifacts in the tombs resulted in five groupings of tombs, which could be surmised to represent the five highest ranks. The cluster numbers are simply random. Only two clusters contained gold crowns and gold belts with pendants, artifacts thought to be symbols of rulership. These were numbered Cluster 5 and Cluster 3. Those who were buried with gold crowns are believed to have been actual rulers, or kings and queens (Kim 1997). One might surmise that the occupants of these tombs belonged to the *Song'gol* class, and that some were rulers—those named in the king lists of the *Samguk Sagi* and the *Samguk Yusa*.

Although Pearson et al. (1989) make no such speculation, other considerations might lead one to suppose that burials without tall gold crowns were *Song'gol* individuals who did not become ruler.

The streets of Gyeongju

The sumptuary rules of Silla allow us to imagine the Sacred Bone men and women riding their horses on the streets of Geumseong. A Sacred Bone man could have ridden on a purple sandalwood saddle, with a fur saddlecloth and an embroidered brocade saddle cushion. Mudguards bearing a painting of a heavenly white horse declared the sacredness of the rider as well as the horse. The metal parts of the horse trappings were embellished with gold and jade, and purple reins also declared that his rank was Sacred Bone. On official occasions he might have worn a gold crown, perched carefully on his head. His long-sleeved jacket was made of silk brocade, encircled by a belt decorated with white jade, and he wore this above embroidered and fur-trimmed trousers. His boots of purple reindeer leather carried through the purple theme of his exalted rank.

The lady of the Sacred Bone wore an embroidered silk robe over long-sleeved undergarments of silk. Her socks were embroidered, and her boots were made of fur. Over her whole outfit she wore a fur cape, embellished with gold and silver threads, as well as with feathers from peacocks and kingfishers. Colored combs in her hair were made of rare tortoiseshell and her hairpins were inlaid with gold and jade. To top off her coiffeur, she wore a gold crown shaped like flowers. Her horse was decked out at least as splendidly as that of her male companion, with jewels inlaid into her sandalwood saddle. Her saddlecloth and cushions were made of fur and silk, or even tiger skin. Bits and stirrups were plated with gold and decorated with jade, and the reins were braided with gold and silver threads.

The noble ladies and gentlemen were almost as gloriously attired. However, in spite of all this splendor displayed by those of the highest rank, even the lowliest village woman could ride on a horse, even if she could only do so in plain clothing and with simple horse trappings. Neither gender nor rank deprived a person of the right to ride a horse.

Silla held on to its nomadic past and became sinicized more slowly than Baekje and Goguryeo. Both of the latter kingdoms adopted Buddhism at least two centuries earlier than Silla. However, Silla had adopted China's written language very early, and by the fifth century much of China's system of governance too. Queen Seondeok began making overtures to the Sui and later the Tang dynasties, and adopted many Chinese traits. Eventually, the bone ranks and their sumptuary rules faded away.

** Parts of this chapter are rewritten from: Nelson, S. M. (2008a) Horses and Gender in Korea: The Legacy of the Steppe on the Edge of Asia. In K. Linduff and K. Rubinson (eds), *Are All Warriors Male?* Walnut Creek, CA: AltaMira Press.

7** Rulership in Silla

The fact that it was a queen who was buried in the north mound of Tomb 98, the largest of the mounded tombs, wearing one of the finest of the golden crowns, has created a difficult question of historiography for the Silla polity. The problem is not that this woman could not have been a ruling queen, for there are three ruling queens in the lists of Silla rulers. The problem is that there is no ruling queen in the historical king lists during the Mounded Tomb period.

In researching this question, I have broadened my search from the local Silla data (Nelson 1991, 1993a) to comparisons with queens and empresses in Japan (Nelson 2014), further to the regional level including Manchuria and Mongolia (Nelson 2008b), and recently to queens in China. The search for a solution to the question of women rulers in Asia reaches beyond Gyeongju, but sheds light on the identity of the queen in Tomb 98.

With regard to understanding the Silla polity, the testimonies of the *Samguk Sagi* and the *Samguk Yusa* are relevant, if possibly somewhat skewed by the interpretations of their authors. Each of the two documents offers a list of the kings and queens that differ from each other only slightly. An interesting feature of these lists is that, although rulership is attributed to a king, in many cases queens are also listed by name, as are their relatives and antecedents, as well as some members of the kings' families. This attention to familial details suggests that the queens' families are equally important, and that descendants were eager to claim their heritage from these illustrious ancestors. Yung Chung Kim (1977:37) explains that, "the matrilineal system had existed side by side with the patrilineal system in limited areas nearly until the unification of the peninsula. Consequently, Silla women had more legal rights and a relatively high status in the society."

Ruling queens of Silla

The *Samguk Yusa* story of the formation of the polity of Saro concerns heads of six clans *and their families*, (surnamed Yi, Cheong, Seo, Choe, and Bae) all of which "claimed to have a divine progenitor" (Iryeon 1972:77). These families came together in a sacred place and made decisions as a group, because of encroaching enemies. To parse the statement about exactly who made the

Rulership in Silla 87

decision to unite, we need to know who would be eligible to head a family, and what other members besides the leaders could have been included in the decision-making.

Magical births were ascribed to both the first queen and the first king, suggesting that they may have arrived from elsewhere, perhaps with skills and knowledge that were new and useful. Queen Aryong was born from a dragon, a very powerful ancestor, while King Hyeokkeose burst out of a golden egg. Together, they went through the kingdom encouraging the women in their weaving efforts, a tour disapproved of by a much later commentator, because women, even the queen, should have remained at home!

The next queen was the daughter of a mountain goddess, giving her very high status, perhaps higher than that of the king, whose pedigree is less impressive. These queens were leaders with supernatural powers, born to interact with spirits. The supernatural ancestry of queens was as important as that of kings.

Chong Sun Kim discusses the rights of maternal lines as well as paternal lines. Regarding families he writes,

> It seems that same emphasis on maternal lines was practiced among the commoners. In Silla, a woman's right to head the family was acknowledged. Unmarried daughters were allowed to head the family, though in the case of a married daughter, the son-in-law was to be its head.
>
> (Kim Chong Sun 1977:39)

Yung Chung Kim (1977) explains that, "The matrilineal system had existed side by side with the patrilineal system in limited areas until the unification of the peninsula by Silla. Consequently, women had legal rights and a relatively high position in society."

The process of decision-making that led to the selection of a central leader is not described, but it seems that the decision, once it was made, was honored by all, at least before Silla began to self-destruct in its last years. It is not known who made final decisions, or how they were arrived at. There is no information about whether this position entailed making decisions about any kind of group efforts, such as extending agricultural fields by creating reservoirs, building protective forts on behalf of all the clans, contacting the spirits and leading rituals, deciding to raid other polities, or leading soldiers to battle. It seems that any of these decisions would have had to have been made by a centralized authority. A consensus would have been an unwieldy method. Eventually, there were overlords of each of these areas, as well as of others, but it is not recorded when and how this occurred.

The only thing we can be sure about is that leadership was invested in families or clans, rather than individuals. Further emphasizing clans, the king lists are careful to include the clan of each king, selected from one of three clans: Pak, Seok, and Kim. Oddly, none of these are among the families named in the original village groups, a discrepancy that is never explained. These three royal clans may have entered Gyeongju at separate times, taking over the leadership and inventing

88 *Rulership in Silla*

a divine ancestor to equal (or surpass) those of the original six families. However it occurred, the leadership is said to have changed peacefully from one of three royal clans to another.

The title of the ruler changed through time, possibly reflecting changing responsibilities. One title means shaman, which is discussed in Chapter 8. Some recorded accomplishments attributed to the early rulers include building a very large pond in 330, presumably for irrigation, and on another occasion the king opened his storerooms to the people because of a famine. The main events recorded are battles and disasters. No doubt much was edited out by the authors of the histories.

Assigning sex to the burials

Silla tombs rarely contain human remains, so discovering the sex of the burial depends on identifying artifacts that belong to males versus females. While this process is always fraught with uncertainty, it is even less secure for Silla, which seems to have unisex burial objects. The particular difficulty of sexing Silla tombs is brought out in an extensive study by Akio Ito (1971), in which he includes all the Silla tombs that had been excavated at that time. Ito found that earrings, necklaces, rings, bracelets, belts, and headgear could belong to either sex, and that styles of artifact could not be separated according to gender either. Approximately half the burials in his sample lacked a sword, so Ito postulated on this basis that men were buried with swords and women were not. However, in some *bubu* (husband and wife tombs), both graves have swords.

Anazawa and Manome (1987) suggest that it is not the *presence* of a sword but the *placement* of a sword that indicates sex. They assert that swords in men's graves are placed in the coffin by the side of the deceased, but the sword is deposited elsewhere in the case of a woman. This proposition is not testable as a general rule without additional data, but as an absolute it is negated by examples.

The north mound of the Great Tomb at Hwangnam-dong (Tomb 98) is assigned to a woman by inscription (a belt has a scratched phrase, "belt for Milady.") The south mound of Tomb 98, with a plethora of weapons, actually lacks some of the types of weapons found in the woman's tomb, all of which are listed in the Pearson study (Pearson et al. 1989:40, Appendix 1). What can be made of that? If gender is related to weaponry, what is the connection?

Considering the selection of rulers by the Silla elite, it appears that gender was not an issue when choosing a ruler. There were ruling queens as well as ruling kings. Queen Seondeok (r. 632–646) was the ruler who introduced Chinese customs and culture to Silla, and supported Buddhism. She was considered to be very wise, and several examples of her cleverness are cited in the histories.

Queen Jindeok (647–653), the last of the Holy Bone line, built up Silla's navy, commanding control of the Yellow Sea (Joe 1972:62). She "sent costly presents to the Tang emperor including a belt of silk into which was woven a special ode to the emperor" (Kim Y. C. 1977:27). In this way, she established solid relations with the Tang dynasty in China, creating the foundation for the eventual alliance

Rulership in Silla 89

between Silla and Tang that ultimately defeated Baekje and Goguryeo and gave Silla control of most of the Korean peninsula. Queen Jinseong (r. 887–896) continued to send ambassadors to Tang and encouraged trade, but she ruled at a tumultuous time in Silla's history, and was effectively the last ruler of Unified Silla (Joe 1972) as factionalism grew rampant. She was unable to stop the factional struggles which caused the disintegration of the Silla state.

Not all ruling queens were acknowledged in the official histories, however. The wife of King Gyeongdeok assumed the regency over their son, King Hyogong (r. 765–780) (Kim Y. C. 1977), but she is not named in the list of rulers. Bear in mind that these lists as they now exist may have been edited by their twelfth- and thirteenth-century authors to conform to Chinese Confucian attitudes, which the elite were anxious to emulate (Deuchler 1992). Two other regents are acknowledged, but not included as rulers in the king lists. The wife of King Peopheung became regent for their son, during which time the territory of Silla expanded, the Buddhist temple of Heungyun-sa was completed, and reform measures were enacted (Kim Y. C. 1977:29). Lady Manweol was another regent, who ruled in the eighth century. She was not so successful, and the Silla state began to disintegrate during her time in office due to factional fighting.

The queen in Tomb 98 must have been another such unmentionable queen. We know that women were literate (as they were also in Japan and China), for "Kim Yusa was taught and instructed by his mother" (Kim Chong Sun 1977).

Most scholars agree that in the kingdom of Old Silla gender relations were less hierarchical than in later Confucian-influenced regimes in Korea (Grayson 1976; Kim Chong Sun 1977; Kim Y. C. 1977; Deuchler 1992; Sasse 2001). On the basis of a combination of archaeological and historical evidence, it is possible to go further, and to argue that women and men in Old Silla enjoyed social equality.

The evidence of the sumptuary laws (Chapter 6) shows that women were not confined to the house because they owned and rode horses. Boys were not favored over girls, male and female restrictions on dress and other possessions were equal according to rank, and a woman could achieve anything, including the rulership, as long as her aspirations were permissible within her social class.

Furthermore, Yamato Japan offers several examples of co-rulership of a male–female pair (Piggott 1997, 1999). Although the historical documents, written long after the events recounted, describe a single ruler for Silla, usually male, it is consistent with the archaeological and ethnographic evidence to posit that, like Yamato, in the early years Silla may have been ruled by a male–female pair, with a woman of the *Song'gol* (Holy Bone) as the ceremonial and secular ruler, while her husband (also *Song'gol*) served as the war leader, in a pattern similar to the leaders of early Japan, or the war chiefs and peace chiefs of the Cherokees (Trocolli 2002). The *Hou Han Shu* reports that each village of the Samhan had a chief, and a person to negotiate with the spirits, gender unspecified. Even those villages may have had co-rulers with different responsibilities.

The hypothesis of co-rulership derives from several sources. First, it is necessary to consider the archaeology of the Old Silla period—both the contents of the discoveries and the underlying assumptions used to evaluate the data from the excavations.

90   *Rulership in Silla*

A number of assumptions are built into the common interpretations of Silla burials, of which the most important for this chapter are: 1) gold crowns and gold belts indicate rulers; 2) preferentially, rulers were men; and 3) double mounds contained the graves of a husband and wife, separately interred.

As we have seen in Chapter 3, in the city of Gyeongju, several large, impressive crowns made of sheet gold and covered with *gogok* and gold dangles have been excavated from Silla tumuli. These gold crowns, along with gold belts with multiple pendants, have been assumed to be royal regalia due to the elaboration of their designs, the costliness of the material, their relative scarcity, their placement in the largest tombs, and the quantity, quality, and character of the goods found with them.

Another important assumption has been that the rulers of Old Silla, as listed in the *Samguk Sagi* and *Samguk Yusa,* were men (kings), with the exception of Queen Seondeok (r. 632–646) and Queen Jindeok (r. 647–653), the two final *Song'gol* rulers, and Queen Jinseong (r. 887–896) of Unified Silla, who were called "female kings" (although the English language literature calls them queens), distinguishing between the king's consort and a ruler with intrinsic power. We do not know if such a distinction was made at the time of their reigns.

Finally, double burials are interpreted as those of wife and husband. Although there are separate interments, the second burial is spatially close enough to the first to cause the second mound to overlap the first, producing a gourd-shaped mound. This configuration is not common, but it is found sporadically in both the Silla and Gaya regions, suggesting co-equals, if not necessarily co-rulers.

The results of the excavation of Hwangnam Daechong (Tomb 98), the largest of the Silla tombs, in Hwangnam-dong, in Gyeongju, violated at least one of these assumptions. Since this was an example of two burials related by the second mound overlapping the first, it was expected that a male would have been buried in one mound and a female in the other. No human bones were found in the north mound, but a few teeth and a partial mandible, described as belonging to an elderly male, remained in the south mound. To the excavators' surprise, the north mound in Tomb 98 contained the gold crown and belt of rulership, rather than the south mound, known to be a male. It may have been tempting to think of the north mound as another male grave (violating the assumption of a husband–wife pair), but the discovery of a ceremonial belt with the inscription, "belt for Milady" scratched on it was what definitely confirmed the north mound as being the tumulus of a queen.

Furthermore, the woman's burial gifts seem to be of higher quality than the man's. Although the southern burial boasted gilt bronze crowns and a silver crown, in the north tumulus the amount of gold jewelry was dazzling—not only the sheet gold crown and belt already noted, but also necklaces, rings, earrings, and bracelets, amounting to several kilograms of gold. Exotic imports, including precious glass vessels from the Western world, probably originating from as far away as Central Asia (see Chapter 5), accompanied the queen (Kim and Yi 1975; Kim and Pearson 1977). It would be interesting to excavate another *pubu* mound in Gyeongju in order to explore whether it represents another incidence of the queen outliving the king, and perhaps ruling as regent or in her own right.

Rulership in Silla 91

The quantity of equipment for warfare in the south mound of Tomb 98—the king's burial—was spectacular in a different way. More than 1,000 projectile points, 543 spears, 380 battle axes, and 30 swords accompanied him, as well as armor with silver leggings, and a pavement of iron axe money. In the largest mound of Silla, however, the quantity seems appropriate. Surely, this man was a successful war leader. In addition, this king was buried with imported glass vessels, and a pair of silver bowls, as well as gold and gilded objects; he was clearly a person of importance. The fact that his queen outlived him does not diminish his accomplishments, as implied by the quantity of weaponry.

As noted above, ruling queens are recorded for Silla; thus a woman buried with a crown could reasonably be interpreted as a ruler. But Tomb 98 cannot be the grave of Queen Jindeok or Queen Seondeok, because the tomb is dated to the late fourth or early fifth century and these known queens both died in the sixth century. If we are to believe the histories, the north tomb must be earlier than 502, when human sacrifice in tombs was outlawed, because the bones of a teenage girl were found outside the burial chamber of the south mound, as if thrown in for a sacrifice (Kim W. Y. 1983). The queen in Tomb 98 was buried a few decades later than her husband.

Ch'oe (1981), who divided the Silla tombs into six periods based on the structure of the burial chamber and associated grave goods chamber, places the south mound in the 350–400 period and the north mound in the 400–450 period. This would make the burials King Naemul (r. 356–402) and Queen Poban, the daughter of King Michu, who seems to have established the Kim clan in Gyeongju.

A study by Richard Pearson et al. (1989) referred to in Chapter 3, uses cluster analysis on the contents of excavated Silla burials of the Mounded Tomb period in an attempt to identify social ranks. One result is that a group of artifacts, including gold crowns and belts, delineate a group of royal tombs. Exotic imports were also found with this cluster in addition to lavish numbers of gold artifacts. This finding lends weight to the assumption that gold crowns and belts were symbols of rulership.

In the study, the tombs with the highest status appeared to be those of women, but this was glossed over in the conclusions:

> While a few female burials *give the impression* [emphasis mine] of being larger and richer than those of males, we are reluctant to base any firm conclusion on such a small sample. It does seem clear that females are not inferior to males on present evidence.
>
> (Pearson et al. 1989:22)

Kinship and kingship in Silla

Some scholars infer that, instead of patrilineal clans, corporate kinship groups existed in Silla. Both parents were required to be *Song'gol* for the offspring to retain that status (Grayson 1976). Thus, the queens were important, and their identities are preserved in the lists of kings, along with their fathers' names and, sometimes, their mothers' names. Partial kinship charts can be created from these

92   Rulership in Silla

lists (see Figure 7.1 on p. 96, Figure 7.2 and Figure 7.3 on p. 97). Between the third and fifth centuries the king's daughter's husband, not the king's son, was the most likely to succeed as king. It seems that the queen's heritage was more important than that of the king.

Werner Sasse (2001) examines the succession patterns for Silla kings listed in the *Samguk Sagi*, which "pose a number of riddles and are complicated enough to have been interpreted in light of many other societies' rules and regulations, one of the most convincing of which is the Tungusic dual organization." This confirms my own reading of the king lists.

He goes on to say that, "there is strong evidence for gender complementarity in early Silla," and concludes that, "the importance of women in the Silla political structure has probably not yet been described correctly" (Sasse 2001:242).

Evelyn McCune (1962:35) believes that the Silla family name Pak, "seems to have applied to Neolithic populations who still had matrilinear social structure and shamanistic religions." Martina Deuchler (1992:228) notes that "Most conspicuous was the continued strength of the maternal line of descent in reproducing elite status . . . For the elite the reproduction remained bilateral."

However, Korean archaeologists have commented little on this apparent anomaly. Perhaps it introduces awkward questions, challenging the ancient documents in a basic way, or perhaps the problem is simply considered uninteresting. But, in the light of both the attempt of some Western archaeologists to engender the archaeological record (Conkey and Spector 1985; Gero 1985; Conkey and Gero 1991), and the interest in the process of state formation (Patterson and Gailey 1987; Barnes 2001), the mystery of Tomb 98 presents an important opportunity to probe further, not only to discover its probable occupant, but also for whatever light this tomb may shed on the development of gender roles within states. Even as late as the Goryeo dynasty bilateral descent was the rule (Deuchler 1992).

The history of Silla according to ancient documents was discussed in Chapter 2. Documents include the *Samguk Yusa* written by a Buddhist monk (Iryeon 1972), the *Samguk Sagi* written in 1145 by Kim Pusik, a Confucian scholar, some brief notes in Chinese histories, and a fragment of an eighth-century census. Of these, the partial census can be considered to be unbiased with regard to gender relations, along with the disapproving Chinese observations. However, in the light of Chinese attitudes at the time the histories were written, it is likely that both Buddhist and Confucian authors would suppress or distort historic gender equality in Silla in early times, if it existed.

The fragment of a census document, which must be accepted as unbiased, does throw some light on gender in Silla. The census figures are divided into six age levels. Land was allocated to each adult, male or female (Kim Chong Sun 1965), rather than being assigned by household, or to a male head of a household. This in itself demonstrates that women were considered to be full adult members of the society. According to the census, more women than men inhabited these villages, by a wide margin (194 adult males to 248 adult females in three villages). Although undercounting of males is possible (able-bodied men might have hidden to avoid corvée or military service, for example, or men might have been killed

Rulership in Silla 93

in battles or become monks, leaving women to run the villages), the discrepancy is so great that it must indicate at a minimum that a preference for sons over daughters had not yet arisen; the social system did not yet favor males. The *Wei Zhi* relates disapprovingly that the people of Jinhan, predecessors of Silla, "drew no distinctions of sex and age" (Parker 1890:209), framing the times both before and after the rise of Old Silla as lacking gender inequality.

More circumstantial evidence of gender equality can be found in folklore and in anecdotes regarding the early rulers. Many local deities, especially mountain spirits, which apparently were at the top of the pantheon, were female. Aro, a sister of King Namhae, is recorded as having directed the ceremonies for his post mortem worship (Kim Chong Sun 1965:273). Even today, village ceremonies are performed by women (*mudang*), and the carved village guardians were traditionally a pair, a male and a female. This configuration is congruent with Karen Sacks' (1979) argument that when women's place in the society is defined primarily as part of a kin group, gender equality is more likely than when women are considered primarily as wives.

Martina Deuchler (1992) documented the slow change in women's status in Korea, from the Goryeo to the Yi dynasty, resulting in a strongly patriarchal society no earlier than the middle of the Joseon dynasty (1392–1910). Deuchler shows that even in the Goryeo kingdom (918–1392), bilateral descent was the rule, with a balance between matrilineal and patrilineal kin (Deuchler 1992:37). Uxorilocal residence was still the rule even in the early Yi dynasty. It is, therefore, exceedingly anachronistic to interpret the Silla period as patrilineal.

Women rulers among the non-Chinese peoples of East Asia, relatives of Silla

"[Nomadic] women rode horses, traveled long distances, and participated in military decisions," Keith McMahon (2013:112) points out, drawing a distinction between nomadic and Chinese women. Some of those differences are reflected in the archaeology of the Steppes. McMahon shows that two Northern Wei (386–534) empresses were the real rulers of this non-Chinese dynasty (p. 134). The Empress Feng (442–490) was bi-cultural in Xianbei and Chinese ways and fluent in both languages. She was literate and knew mathematics, and was entirely capable of running the government (McMahon 2013:139). She became regent twice. A second regency allowed her to consolidate her reign.

The next Feng empress was the sister of the first, but it appears she was not as competent. Another great empress lauded by McMahon is the Empress Dowager Ling, who also was regent twice. The account of her regime shows her as sound, strong, and adept, but not necessarily a good ruler, depending on one's place in the empire.

Women buried with the trappings of power are found throughout the Steppes. In a possible antecedent culture in the eastern part of the Northern Zone of China, the two female graves excavated at Nanshangen, "are much richer in artifacts than those of the three male graves" (Shelach 2008:101). In the cemetery of Maqingou,

94 *Rulership in Silla*

gender and wealth or prestige do not seen to be related, since belt plaques and ornaments are equally distributed between men and women; however, one of the richest graves belonged to a woman whose burial goods included horse gear. In Tomb 4 of Xigou, in the Ordos region of Inner Mongolia, gold necklaces decorated with semi-precious stones as well as carved jade and gold earrings are believed to imply an elite female leader. In Daodunzi cemetery, four of the six catacomb burials, presumed to indicate status, were females. Plaques decorated with animals and cowrie shells were found in the largest numbers in female graves of the second century BCE (Shelach 2008). Furthermore, crowns found archaeologically in North-East Asia are almost always on the heads of women (Pak 1988; Nelson 2008a).

In Japanese records we find that, "women ruled frequently in prehistoric, proto-historic and early historic Japan." Although sometimes women in Japan ruled alone, they might also rule as half of a "gender complementary chieftain pair" (Piggott 1999:17). The Empress Suiko of Yamato (r. 539–571) was a member of the Soga family of Korean descent through her mother. She was a legitimate ruler, like the women of Silla in the same time period.

Attitudes toward women in China

Where did the Chinese abhorrence of women rulers come from? It seems that the problem was built into the system of patrilineal descent, which often left a widow able to control the government through her young son who had been named emperor. By appointing her own family members to posts of power, she could effectively become the ruler and control the government.

In *Women Shall Not Rule*, Keith McMahon discusses the queens who did rule in "Chinese" dynasties that are roughly contemporary with Silla. The perceived problems caused by an empress favoring her family with court jobs seem to have become a great difficulty with regard to the orderly running of the country. Another part of the problem was that the ruling males were allowed concubines, whose sons were equally eligible to rule with sons of his wife, causing much intrigue and murder in the inner court, as women tried to promote and protect their own sons.

Under the nomadic custom of choosing a capable ruler from any member of the royal family, women could and did rule in their own right. Even as late as the empire of Genghis Khan, his daughters were given territory to rule (Weatherford 2010), which they did very capably. "Four of Genghis Khan's daughters became ruling queens of their own countries and commanded regiments of soldiers" (Weatherford 2010:xiv).

In the Liao dynasty, women participated in both military and civil affairs. Aboji, the first ruler, became khan in 907. His wife was Empress Yingtian, who accompanied her husband to battles and was described as "austere and imposing, resolute and decisive, and a brave strategist" (quoted in McMahon 2013:258). Another Liao empress led an army and defeated the Song, as well as running the government when her husband was away. After his death she was known as Empress Dowager Chen-tian (954–1009).

Rulership in Silla   95

According to McMahon, the last woman to rule in her own right in China was Empress Wu of Tang, who presided over a flowering of the arts and trade, as well as military aggression against Korea. Her name was Wu Zetian. She began her career in court as a concubine and was recommended to her husband by the emperor's wife as a rival for his favored concubine. But the plan backfired, and Wu Zetian became the empress in 655. She ruled with her husband until his death in 683 but, as his health grew poorer, she took on more and more of the governing. She used the symbolism of titles, among other tactics, to gain control of the government, awarding herself a title that had never before been granted to a woman.

Ruling in her own right, Wu Zetian used rituals to demonstrate her position. She wanted to be seen as a cosmic ruler, linking herself to Nü Wa, the primordial goddess of China. She also used Buddhism to claim her place as a Bodhisattva. Wu Zetian built grandiose buildings to demonstrate her power and as a constant reminder of it.

Bret Hinsch (2002:21) sees succession to power in a somewhat different way. She finds that the early reign of Empress Lü (d. 180 BCE), the wife of the first emperor and mother of the second emperor, was "especially important in the history of Chinese women." The son officially ruled while his mother controlled the government. This process established a line of dowager empresses. The "usurper" Wang Mang, whose coins are found in many Korean archaeological sites, was the son of the Empress Dowager Wang (45 BCE to 23 CE).

Although Silla was the last of the Korean kingdoms to become sinicized, some movement in this direction occurred even during the era of gold crowns in Silla. The first Chinese mention of Silla is in the *Nanshu*, reporting that in Wei times (220–264) there was a state in Korea called Sillu (Parker 1890:221). Naemul (r. 356–402) was the first Silla ruler whose name is found in Chinese annals. Very slowly, Silla adopted Chinese culture. In 375 the custom of posthumous names for kings was instituted (Kim C. S. 1965:80). By 528 Silla used the Chinese term *wang* for king, adopted the Chinese calendar, and allowed Buddhism to flourish. Thus, a gradual change from gender complementarity to male dominance may have begun as early as the fifth century, under China's influence, but it took many centuries to complete. The acceptance of a Confucian ideal gradually eroded women's ability to influence public policy.

In Silla, women were accepted as rulers or co-rulers, but by the end of United Silla, the Confucian ideal of dependent women was increasingly embraced by the men of the fragmenting polity. The archaeology of Tomb 98 is a useful corrective to documents which were written long after the events they describe, showing a powerful queen.

Conclusion

Discovering gender equality in Ancient Silla (Go Silla) allows a new perspective on the generalization that women's status becomes subordinate in all state-level societies, a premise underlying much of the feminist literature on state origins (e.g. Rohrlich 1980; Lerner 1986, and see a critique of this perspective in Nelson 1993a:297–299).

96 Rulership in Silla

In Silla, constraints on women may have existed, but restrictions were by rank, mirroring those on men. Chapter 6 discussed the caste-like system called *golbeum* (bone ranks), that discriminates by rank rather than by gender. *Golbeum* are inferred to be kin-based groups stringently enforced with a rule of hypodescent—a child belonging to the *golbeum* of the lower-ranked parent (Kim Chong Sun 1977).

The census fragment discussed above also suggests gender equality. This document is a bit later than Old Silla but, since in terms of gender equality the trend through time was toward increasing domination by men, any equality still existing in the eighth century could be assumed to have been the same or more favorable to women in an earlier time period. Thus, the census document has some applicability to understanding earlier times.

To return to Silla royalty, according to the king lists, the succession was unpredictable by any rule of linearity. Figure 7.1 shows the kinship among the rulers before Naemul. The only obvious rule that can be deduced from this chart is the necessity for the ruler to be *Song'gol*. Beginning with Naemul, a father-to-son sequence can be extracted (see Figure 7.2), although one of the intervening rulers appears to be an unrelated man. Somehow, a person who was not of the Kim clan ruled.

More importantly, a mother-to-daughter pattern of queens can be isolated from the chart, reaching from Sullye's mother to Aro (see Figure 7.3). In fact, the

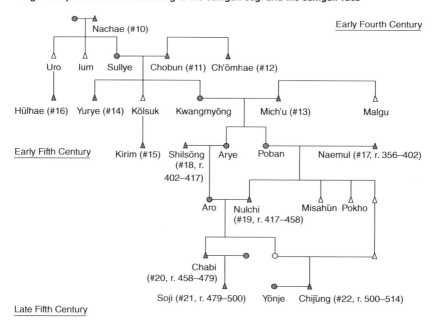

Figure 7.1 Kinship chart showing early kings and queens of Silla

Source: Nelson 1991

Rulership in Silla 97

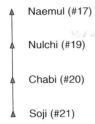

Figure 7.2 Kinship chart showing lineage of male kings of early Silla
Source: Nelson 1991

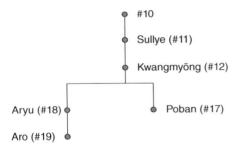

Figure 7.3 Kinship chart showing only queens of early Silla
Source: Nelson 1991

husband of the previous queen's daughter was the most likely person to become the next king, which suggests a line of ruling queens, or married pairs who were co-rulers, but based on the queen's status.

Cross-cousin marriage, of course, allows both of these patterns to be found at once, but a shift from mother-to-daughter toward father-to-son seems to have occurred during the Mounded Tomb period. The unnamed queen ruler in the north mound of Tomb 98 may have been the pivot of this change.

The assumption of the husband/wife double burial appears to be correct for Tomb 98. All evidence suggests that the gold crowns and belts are indeed markers of rulership status. Thus, the third assumption, that the rulers were necessarily men, needs to be modified. Since the crown in the woman's grave suggests rulership, women rulers would probably have been suppressed where possible by later historians, whether Confucian or Buddhist.

It may be our Western unstated assumption of a single ruler that requires modification. I suggest that the burials in Tomb 98 represent a married pair who ruled jointly, the man as the military head and the woman as the secular (and perhaps spiritual

98 *Rulership in Silla*

and ceremonial) leader. Whether she was Poban or some other queen, she outlived her husband and granted herself an equally resplendent burial, but was excluded from the later compilation of kings. Complementarity of men and women, and of male and female roles, is implied in other evidence regarding Go Silla, such as the sumptuary rules, making this hypothesis seem all the more likely.

** Parts of this chapter were rewritten from Nelson, S. M. (2014) The Statuses of Women in Ko-Shilla: Evidence from Archaeology and Historic Documents. *Korea Journal* 31(2):101–106, and Nelson, S. M. (2014) Women Rulers in Ancient East Asia, a paper delivered at the Korean session of the Society for American Archaeology, 2014, in Honolulu, Hawaii.

8** Religions in Gyeongju

The religions of Silla are cumulative rather than sequential, but it is quite likely that the elite and commoners had different beliefs and rituals. The earliest religion was animistic. Animism was basic, an underlying sense of the spirituality of rocks and mountains, streams and wells, trees and birds, and tigers. Each new belief system kept or absorbed some of the previous spiritual beliefs. For the early settlers in Gyeongju, the environment was full of spirits who resided in rocks, trees, mountains, and streams. The spirits needed attention, both with household rituals and public ceremonies. Good spirits could be called with bells and drums, and bad spirits could be driven away by those with special abilities.

Shamanism, brought with the elite from the northern forests (Xianbei) and the Steppes (Xiongnu), coexists easily with animism, and is similarly based on belief in unseen spirits who can be reached by gifted practitioners. Although the beliefs are similar, shamanism adds both rituals through which to contact the spirits and a variety of symbols as well as symbolic acts to remind people of the spirits and to manipulate them. The Gyeongju version of shamanism in particular is understood through symbolism manifested in the gold crowns of the rulers, reflecting the shamanism of the forests with reindeer antlers and birch trees. Melded with these beliefs was the reverence for white horses and gold from the Xiongnu, and red birds, symbol of queens.

Buddhism was another introduced religion. It arrived in Gyeongju from northeastern China fully formed, with scriptures, forms of architecture, sculpture, and other arts. Buddhism had a long journey to Gyeongju from India, through the mountains of Afghanistan and the Central Asian Steppes, before being accepted by some of the Xianbei groups north of China. People of the Steppes preferred Lamaism, so it was through the Xianbei relatives that Buddhism reached Silla.

Buddhism is not an exclusive religion. It tended to adopt earlier beliefs, and encode them into the local Buddhist ones. According to Jonathan Best (2006), in the Three Kingdoms of Korea, Buddhism was chiefly a religion of the elite. One effect of this division was that shamanistic activities could continue without sanction among the non-elite ranks. Active elements of both shamanism and animism exist in Korea to this day, and of course Buddhism still exists as well, alongside Christianity.

Animism

Animism has come to mean the belief that all things, animate and inanimate, have spirits with which humans may interact for good or ill. Spiritual beings are held to affect or control the events of the material world (Tylor 1871:427). Although animistic beliefs are not usually recoverable by archaeology, documents do supply some suggestions of animism.

The earliest settlers in Gyeongju worshipped mountains and streams, and thus chose to conduct their important meetings in those places. The mountains were sacred, the abode of capricious goddesses, who could bring rain or withhold it. The *Samguk Yusa* might not be expected to contain any overt references to animistic beliefs since it was written by a Buddhist monk, yet in that document two of the early queens were said to be daughters of mountain goddesses. Lady Unje even bore the name of Mt. Unje, where her mother reigned. It is also recorded that the revered Silla general, Kim Yusin, was aided by the female spirits of three sacred mountains. The founding fathers of Silla were said to have "climbed a high mountain, where they worshipped and prayed to heaven," after which they held a meeting to decide that they should unite and elect a leader (Iryeon 1972:49). Changboh Chee (1974) connects the mountain spirits with the piles of stones found on the tops of passes through the mountains in Korea, where wayfarers each added a stone as they passed. Chee also declares that the "worship of mountains is a North Asian trait" (Chee 1974:144). Evelyn McCune (1962:30) suggests that these rock piles are "points of contact between the spiritual and human worlds." Queen Seondeok (r. 632–646) chose to be buried on an auspicious mountain with Buddhist meanings (Rhi 2012).

Bodies of water, especially streams, were animated by other spirits. The first prince and princess of Silla were bathed in streams after they were miraculously discovered—the boy in the East River and the girl in the North River (Iryeon 1972:50). Another early queen, Queen Aryong, was associated with the waters of a healing well. She must have been considered numinous, for she was appointed keeper of the shrine to Hyeokkeose, the first king. Thus, in the *Samguk Yusa* we have statements about the importance of mountains and rivers in Silla cosmology. Presumably, Iryeon retained these references to animistic beliefs because they were too well known to be omitted, or perhaps he was satisfied that they were compatible with Buddhism. Even the Confucian author of the *Samguk Sagi* relates that in 109 CE the Silla rulers made sacrifices to mountains and rivers because of calamities which had befallen the country (Kim Chong Sun 1965:131).

Gregory Henderson (1959:15) points out that the *Samguk Sagi* suppresses much information related to the native beliefs of Silla because they were an embarrassment to his Confucian mindset. Although much did remain, even in Kim Pusik's work the gender of the mountain goddess mysteriously underwent a sex change at some unknown time. The old man with a tiger, who occupies a shrine in many Buddhist temples, is the mountain goddess transformed by Buddhism into an old man (see Figure 8.1).

Figure 8.1 The Mountain Spirit and his tiger, a common image in Buddhist temples in Korea

Source: Photo of painting bought in shop on Chongno in Seoul in 1970 by the author, photo by Harold Nelson

Later water goddesses/spirits are found in protectors of sea travel. Silla objects have been found at sea goddess shrines in both Korea and Japan. At Jungmak-dong, a site on a narrow peninsula jutting far into the Yellow Sea, where trading ships landed from the fourth to sixth centuries, offerings to the sea goddess have been excavated. The offerings include gilt bronze horse trappings, iron weapons, beads, and pottery. An imitation Chinese mirror and *gogok* show that some artifacts were deposited here, beginning in the third century. Similar shrines on Okinoshima island celebrate three sea goddesses, where even more offerings have been found, including a ring almost identical to a group of rings found in Tomb 98 (Im 2010). These rings were trade items from far to the west, and must have been very precious. Shaman ceremonies are still conducted in the Jungmak-dong location.

Birds were considered to be messengers from the spirits. A crown in the Lucky Phoenix Tomb has cut-out gold birds on one headdress (see Figure 8.2), and a painting on birch bark in the Flying White Horse Tomb depicts a red bird. The red bird is, of course, the phoenix. Other birds must have figured in the belief system of early Silla, since there is a bird in the name of Gyerim Forest (rim means forest), variously translated as rooster or chicken, but which may originally have been an undomesticated bird with a long tail. Long feathers are said to have been placed in tombs so that the occupant could fly to heaven. Pottery representations of birds also occur. Kim W. Y. (1986:240) notes that Silla people worshipped the sun, white horses, and red birds.

Gregory Henderson (1959:150) suggests that Kim Pusik, the author of the *Samguk Sagi*, suppressed mention of both animism and shamanism, "because of the intolerance he [Kim Pusik] apparently possessed, as a strict Confucianist, of the

Figure 8.2 Crown from the Lucky Phoenix Tomb, with gold cut-out birds
Source: Harold Nelson

Religions in Gyeongju   103

native religions and beliefs of his own country." By this same token, for example, he seems to have omitted much material relating to shamanism in his discussion of Silla history. Shamanism might have been particularly shunned because "shamanism . . . symbolizes complementarity and equality. Women are given cosmic and ritual importance in the eyes of the gods and ancestors" (McCune 1962:112).

Shamanism

The shamanism of Gyeongju probably arrived with some of the settlers from the forests of Manchuria (Xianbei) or the Steppes north of China (Xiongnu), where somewhat different types of shamanism were practiced. Shamanism tends to use more non-perishable artifacts than animism. Beginning in the Korean Bronze Age artifacts that might be ritual objects were placed in Bronze Age graves. For example, a bronze, trumpet-shaped object from Dongso-ri is assigned to the third century BCE. Bronze bells and mirrors, of which many were found in Gyeongju, probably had functions in shamanistic rituals (Kim W. Y. 1986:169). Some oddly shaped bronze artifacts with decorative motifs comprised of short, slanted lines characteristic of the Late Bronze Age (the motif is also present on Korean mirrors) have been interpreted as shamanic implements, although they do not precisely match any objects used in current shamanism.

Shamanism was present in the early culture of Gyeongju, when the ruler may have performed the functions of head shaman. The title of an early Silla ruler, *chachaung* (Iryeon 1972), is translated as shaman. This title was used for rulers of Saro before the third century. The close connection between the archaeological remains of southern Korea and Manchuria, especially Liaoning Province, support the likelihood of shamanistic interpretations of the gold crowns of Silla, a correlation that has often been observed (Henze 1933; Kim W. Y. 1986).

Silla is known for a youth association called Hwarang (Rutt 1961). Its members consisted of sons of the nobility who were taught to sing and dance for the spirits. The group of boys traveled to mountains and rivers where spirits dwelled. Surely these are shamanistic activities? These outings were considered training for warriors (Rutt 1961) but, nevertheless, the Hwarang institution seems to have had a shamanistic as well as an animistic basis.

Before the Hwarang society was established, a girls' association called *wonhua* had existed, in which elite girls learned to dance and appreciate nature (Rutt 1961). The change from training girls to training boys perhaps suggests a shift from gender equality to a patriarchal bent because of the need to train warriors, but the shamanism of the training is clear. On the other hand, it is possible that the girls' association did continue, but mention of the *wonhua* was suppressed by the Confucian perspective of the writer of the *Samguk Sagi*.

Shamanism is specifically mentioned in the *Samguk Sagi* in connection with rituals of song and dance, not to mention drinking rice wine, associated with many different groups in the Korean peninsula. Chinese documents describe early

104   *Religions in Gyeongju*

Koreans as performing rituals with singing, dancing, and strong drink (Parker 1890), which is not only compatible with shamanism, but can describe some shamanic rituals in the present called *kut.*

As to the gender of the shamans, Kim Y. C. (1977:21) asserts that shamanism was organized around women as "active ritual leaders." This leadership was not confined to the village and family levels, as it is today, nor were the shamans considered lower class. Upper-class women who became shamans had a special name, *son'gwan* (Kim Y. C. 1977).

Other evidence that shamanism was not limited to farmers is found in the royal crowns, which imply shamanic beliefs, and echo rituals that have been recorded in Manchuria and Siberia. An early exploration of this theme by Carl Henze (1933) regarded virtually everything about the gold crowns of the mounded tombs as being related to shamanism. The crowns are constructed on a circlet, a form used by shamans even today. One shape of uprights on the crowns obviously represents deer antlers, with references to the sacred reindeer of the north. Another shape of squared-off upright is said to represent stylized trees, with the branches having gold, leaf-like finials and other leaf-shaped ornaments attached to them by gold wires. This is said to reproduce the shamanistic tree of life. Antlers and trees together reinforce the suggestion of shamanistic beliefs. The side pendants as illustrated by Yung Chung Kim (1997:33, Fig. 12), are also found on some headdresses belonging to women shamans in Manchuria and Siberia. After Henze pointed out the similarities of crowns in Siberia, this theme has been repeated many times (e.g. Nelson 1993; Kim Y. C. 1997).

It has been suggested that the *gogok* (curved beads) on the crowns resemble the teeth or the claws of wild animals, such as tigers or bears. Although both animals appear in Korean folk tales, there is no direct evidence connecting the *gogok* to either animal. However, the *gogok* do appear in large numbers in Silla tombs that are clearly those of royalty. They were used to indicate spiritual power since the Early Bronze Age. The earliest date for a *gogok* is eighth or seventh century BCE (Lee I. 1987:368–369). The crowns make an emphatic statement of spiritual power, presumably intended to impress the populace.

Kidong Lee (2004:50) describes the shamans of early Silla: "In the early records of the Silla annals, shamans frequently appear as old women or mothers, sorceresses who possessed the ability to see the future, foretelling both fortune and misfortune." This observation underscores the importance of women shamans, and shows that they were not a late invention in Korea. Chinese documents describe early Koreans as performing rituals with singing, dancing, and strong drink. This is not only compatible with shamanism but can also describe some shaman rituals called *kut.*

The ruler was said to foretell the future by looking at the wind and clouds, and knew in advance if there would be calamity from flood or fire or if the harvest would be bountiful or poor. Queens were particularly recorded as prognosticators. Queen Seondeok was famous for reading portents, and it was she who ordered the construction of the astronomical tower from which the configurations of the stars and planets could be viewed.

Shamanism in the Steppes and forests

White horses were worshipped in the Steppes as part of shamanistic religion there (Humphrey 1996). Ideology relating the Silla kingdoms to the Steppes includes reverence for the horse, especially white horses, as noted above. A horse of unknown color was given a burial of its own in an elite Iron Age burial ground in Gyeongju, as noted in Chapter 3. Silla and Baekje sealed a peace agreement with the sacrifice of a white horse under the direction of Tang.

Furthermore, horses were caparisoned in style. Royal tombs feature saddlebows made of gilded bronze in cut-out patterns. Horses were adorned with bronze bells and ornaments as well as painted saddle blankets. The members of the Sacred Bone rank were not only displaying their wealth and elite status, but with such pomp they were also honoring the horse. A saddle was placed near the top of the south mound of Hwangnam Daechong, bringing to mind the suggestion in the *Samguk Sagi* that the spirits of Sacred Bone people departed to heaven on a heavenly horse (Kim and Pearson 1977).

Shamanistic ideas did not disappear with the advent of Buddhism. It is said that a shrine for the first king was erected in the seventh century in which sacrifices for spirits of the four seasons were held. "The king's sister Aro was appointed to officiate at these ceremonies; one may generally recognize the spiritual predominance of females in Silla society" (Lee K. 2004:52). Shamanism continues to be active in Korea to this day (e.g. Kendall 1985), thus it is not at all surprising to find indications of shamanism in the Silla kingdom.

The Chinese goddess Xiwangmu, the Queen Mother of the West, also had a shrine in Seondosan, Gyeongju (Rhi 2012:28). She was connected with Daoism and was depicted on Han Chinese mirrors, which must have had magical properties.

Buddhism

Buddhism came to the Korean peninsula through north-east China. The leaders of Baekje and Goguryeo both allowed Buddhist monks to come and preach, and eventually accepted Buddhism, Goguryeo in 372 and Baekje in 384. Monks from the north-west brought sutras and Buddhist images (Kim Lena 2006). Marananda, who preached in Silla, was a prominent monk who came from the Donghu barbarians, also called the Xiongnu.

Buddhist monks appeared in Silla several times, according to the *Samguk Sagi*. Visits from the first three monks were unsuccessful. Monk Sundo came from a Xianbei group in Liaoning in 372, bringing sutras and images, and Marananda came from the Xiongnu to preach in Gyeongju in 384, but was rejected by the elite. Mukhoza, a monk from Goguryeo, made a visit to Gyeongju sometime in the mid fifth century but there was still resistance and even hostility in the essentially animistic and shamanistic Silla society. Preaching Buddhism was declared a capital crime in Silla. The rulers may have feared to risk offending local spirits by bringing in other gods.

106 Religions in Gyeongju

The successful establishment of Buddhism in Silla did not occur until 527, when a Buddhist monk, Ichadon, arrived to preach in Gyeongju once more. The king declared that the monk must be punished. Ichadon was decapitated according to Silla laws, but it was said that white fluid flowed from his neck instead of blood, and he was declared to be a Buddhist martyr (*Samguk Yusa*). According to the historian Jonathan Best (2006:24), the beheading was actually a scheme between the king and his devoted Buddhist subject to further the acceptance of Buddhism. The elite of Silla withdrew their objections to Buddhism due to this martyrdom and the accompanying miracle.

Buddhism was also willing to compromise, "bringing the gods of the native religion under its influence" (Joe 1972:117).

Buddhist monuments were constructed under governmental auspices. Goguryeo even built a school in which literacy was taught. However, Silla was resistant to Buddhism. Gyeongju became a location for several schools of Buddhism, as well as enormous and well-endowed temples, once the elite had decided to take Buddhism to its heart with enthusiasm. The city became replete with Buddhist temples and monuments. Best (2006) suggests that the "magico-religious element" in Korean Buddhism affected the way it was manifested in art. Correct ritual, including correct performance, had to be carried out "in the proper artistic and architectural environment."

Not only new types of art, architecture, and literature arrived with Buddhism. but also new ways to think about the present and the future. In terms of material culture, incense, large bells, and colorful temples were introduced. Buddhism was a religion for the senses.

Hwangyongsa, the Temple of the Imperial Dragon, was begun in 553 as a "great imperial temple" (Chapin 1957). It was 9,000 square meters in area. Although it was destroyed in a Mongol invasion of 1238, when it was excavated more than 20,000 relics were found, including tiles with dragon relief carving and a gilt bronze Buddha image (Kim B. M. 1987:41).

Helen Chapin describes the temples of the time, "Temples were small cities in themselves—centers of production, learning, and worship. Each large temple had its own school and very often college or university with professors learned in Chinese and Sanscrit." She describes workshops to make images of wood, stone, and bronze, as well as mementos for pilgrims, shrines, ritual vessels, and textiles for monks' clothing and textile hangings.

According to Myung Dae Mun (1998), the Hwangyongsa temple prominently featured a bronze Buddha image cast with 21,000 kilograms of bronze and about 6,000 kilograms of gold. These quantities of precious materials are evidence of the enthusiasm with which the elite of Silla embraced Buddhism. But the purpose wasn't so much to become one with Buddha as to accrue worldly benefits (Best 2006:20).

The most popular figure in Buddhism in sixth-century Silla was the Maitreya, (known as the Miruk in Korean) (McCune 1962). While standing Miruks seem to have been preferred in Baekje, in Silla the Maitreya's pose of meditation, with one leg across the other just above the knee, was the most popular (see National Treasure No. 83).

In the mid seventh century, a Silla monk named Chajang received a message from a dragon king that Silla must build a nine-story pagoda in the grounds of the Hwangyongsa temple in order to win battles over Baekje and Goguryeo. This building was accomplished in 645, and the prediction came true a quarter of a century later. That pagoda was burned in a Mongol raid, but another lovely stone pagoda graces the Bulguksa monastery.

A Buddhist monk named Hejo made a pilgrimage to India and Pakistan in the eighth century, bringing back sutras. Many other Buddhist monks went to India by sea or by land. Korean monks also went to teach in Japan and they traveled to north-east China to bring back new learning. Gyeongju was seen as the center of the arts and learning.

At the time of the unification of the Korean peninsula, Buddhism played a part in the acceptance of Unified Silla with the defeat of Baekje and Goguryeo. King Munmu (r. 661–681) declared that his wish was to become a great dragon in the East Sea so that he could guard the Buddhist *dharma* (way of living) and the kingdom. His ashes were scattered on a large rock off the coast, and a monastery was erected from which the rock could be seen. Six more monasteries were constructed in Gyeongju in the Unified Silla period, and the Sokkuram grotto guards Gyeongju from the sea. (The finds of portable Buddhist art are numerous. Namsan is full of Buddhist images carved on rocks.)

Even in Buddhism, Silla women were important. Apparently, they were seen to make far more positive efforts than men with regard to social activities centered on Buddhist temples. This was related to the spiritual–magical abilities that women were said to possess.

Buddhist monuments in Gyeongju

Time and invasions have left only traces of many of the magnificent temples and schools that once existed in Gyeongju. The most-visited Buddhist constructions in Gyeongju include the Bulguksa monastery and the Sokkuram artificial grotto. Both are on Mt. Tohamsansa, on the west side of the city, and both were restored in the twentieth century. Great pains were taken to follow the original plans as much as possible, and the results are pleasing to the eye.

Bulguksa, the Temple of the Pure Land, is Historic and Scenic Place No. 1 in South Korea. It was begun in the early sixth century and was built along one of several rivers flowing from the surrounding mountains through the city of Gyeongju. The monastery has a pair of graceful stone bridges that lead up to a platform where a bell tower graces one side and a drum tower is on the other. Two stone pagodas, quite different in style, have survived. One is severe but elegant, the other ornate, almost baroque.

The monastery had more than 80 buildings when it was established in 774, and is said to have been the largest Buddhist complex in all of East Asia at the time. The wooden buildings were totally destroyed by invading Japanese armies in 1593, but the stone bridges and pagodas remained from the original monastery. Reconstructed wooden buildings stand on some of the original stone platforms.

108 *Religions in Gyeongju*

Two quite different stone pagodas were also left mostly intact. Some of the wooden buildings were reconstructed. The temples are painted with designs in shades of coral and aqua, the usual colors of Buddhist temples in Korea, which contrast strongly with the lack of color in most Japanese Buddhist temples.

The best-known and most-admired Buddhist monument in Korea is the Sokkuram grotto, National Treasure No. 24, which was constructed in 751 in the Unified Silla period, during the reign of King Taesong. The central feature is a large seated Buddha, carved from granite and 3.26 meters high, who looks out placidly toward the East Sea. The Buddha sits on a lotus table at the back of the grotto. He is guarded by the eleven-headed Goddess of Mercy, among other guardian statues. The rising sun hits the third eye (which is thought to have contained a large jewel, no longer present, to reflect the sun).

Many Buddhist monuments that once existed in Gyeongju are little more than traces now, or even only words in a book. One of the ways to appreciate the fervor and extent of Buddhism in Gyeongju is to hike around Mt. Namsan, because this contains a feast for the eyes for hikers interested in Buddhist art. Around virtually every bend in the path some artistic hand has created representations of Buddhas and Bodhisattvas.

Some temples are being recreated as a result of archaeological excavations, Hwangyongsa, for example, the Imperial Dragon Temple, three miles south-east of the center of Gyeongju. The extent of this very large Buddhist temple can be appreciated only by walking through and around the field in which it once stood because very little of the temple actually remains. Excavations revealed square bases for columns, making a corridor surrounding the building that was 189 meters by 162 meters. There were also foundation stones for an intermediate gate, a wooden pagoda, three shrines, and a lecture hall (Mun 1998). It was completed in 553. Invading Mongol armies destroyed it in 1248. The nine-story pagoda was made of wood and was 68 meters tall (Mun 1998).

Although many have vanished, pagodas are still plentiful in Gyeongju and it is said there are over a thousand of them (Chung 1998). The earliest pagodas were made of wood when Buddhism was first introduced, but none of them have survived. The earliest brick pagoda was erected in the time of Queen Seondeok in 634.

Sarira containers, or reliquaries, hold Buddhist relics. They have been found in a number of pagodas in Gyeongju. A sarira hole below a pagoda at Hwangyongsa temple was excavated when the base of the pagoda had to be moved. It contained no objects of interest other than a circular disk, but other reliquaries that have been discovered are made of precious materials and contain various Buddhist relics. One container held a silver needle, suggesting that "some of these objects belonged to a Silla queen" (Ch'oe 1998:152).

Buddhist Silla was renowned for the size and resonance of its bronze bells. The Emille Bell is the best known and is 3.33 meters tall, weighing 25 tons. It has graceful relief carving of Buddhist angels, among other decorations that are cast into it. It was a remarkable feat of bronze casting, which had to be repeated several times before it was successful. The bell was cast for the Bongdeok-sa temple, but can now be seen at the National Museum of Gyeongju.

Religions in Gyeongju 109

Buddhist art from Silla is quite remarkable. Perhaps the most famous is a seated, gilt bronze Maitreya. The figure is elegant in proportions and dates from the late sixth to the early seventh century. The Maitreya wears a simple headdress, but another similar Maitreya, also from seventh-century Silla, wears a hat that appears to be adorned with rosettes (Leidy 2013).

Many Buddhist buildings were destroyed by fanatical Confucians in the Joseon dynasty, but many Korean museums have statues and other mementos of Buddhism on display.

** Parts of this chapter were rewritten from: Nelson, S. M. (1995) Roots of Animism in Korea: From the Earliest Inhabitants to the Silla Kingdom. In H. Y. Kwon (ed), *Korean Cultural Root: Religion and Social Thoughts*, pp. 19–30. Chicago, IL: North Park College and Theological Seminary.

9** Gyeongju and Japan

Although the written record says little about Silla's relationships with Japan, archaeology can provide some clues. Silla artifacts in Japanese tombs are solid evidence of contact (Kidder 1987, 1989). Myths and tales provide an approximate context. Perhaps most important, some similarities of social structure between Silla and Yamato that are unlike China but resemble those of the Steppes, also suggest extensive contact between Silla and Japan. In this chapter I will argue that the "land-pulling myth" of Japan (Carlqvist 2010), in which Izumo, a land across the East Sea from Silla, is said to have pulled land from Silla to make a peninsula in Izumo, suggests a memory of the hegemony of Silla in Izumo.

Connections are notoriously difficult to demonstrate. What can be inferred about migration of people or diffusion of ideas, about trade, warfare, or other contact between polities, when similarities in artifacts are found? The big picture may escape us if the hypothesis is based on archaeology alone, and documents are usually open to various interpretations. Tales are often dismissed as only myth. There is considerable ambiguity in the case of Silla and Japan, but the fact that some kinds of connections existed is solidly based on Silla artifacts in Japanese tombs.

Silla's relationship to Japan has not been the subject of much scholarship in Western languages. It has been assumed that the relationship between Silla and Japan was mostly hostile, because Yamato was allied with Baekje, and the introduction of Buddhism to Japan came largely through Baekje and their (Korean) Soga relatives, who were influential in Yamato and sometimes even occupied the Yamato throne. Buddhism itself was an instrument of Soga aggrandizement, removing the native gods or at least making them less effective.

While interactions between Japan and Baekje have been discussed in book-length format (Covell and Covell 1984; Hong 1994), and groups of immigrants from Japan have recently been the subject of a book (Como 2009), there is little about Silla and Japan. Only J. Edward Kidder, writing about the Silla objects in the Fujinoki Tomb, has brought Silla into the picture.

The (largely discredited) "horse-rider" theory, which posits "nomads" from the Manchurian polity of Buyeo bringing horses to Japan by way of Baekje (Egami 1964; Ledyard 1975) was an interesting although flawed attempt to explain facets of archaeological discoveries in Japan, especially the appearance of horses from "the continent," which I perceive as a way of not saying Korea. Much of

Gyeongju and Japan   111

the problem was that, while there were many arguments about the archaeology in Japan, the theory did not attend to the archaeology of the supposed antecedents in those polities on "the continent," meaning the Korean peninsula, where the supposed nomads lived in cities (Pak 1996; Byington 1997), and had little cause to gallop to Japan (by-passing most Korean polities), and create a horse-riding aristocracy.

However, while there is general agreement that the concept of horse-riding nomads from Buyeo taking over Japan is an exceedingly simplistic and unlikely way to explain the explosion of amounts of horse equipment (and presumably also horses) in the Japanese islands, influences or immigrants from the Korean peninsula are nevertheless usually implicated in the arrival of large numbers of horses used by the elite in the Japanese islands.

Newer archaeological discoveries allow glimpses into the complexities of population movements in East Asia which alleviate the Buyeo/Baekje problem, but they add few new perspectives on the shifting polities within the Korean peninsula or between Silla and Japan. The horse-rider theory should have opened a dialog about the peopling of Japan from Korea, but the Japanese belief that their society was created *de novo* within the Japanese islands defeated any such outcome at the time.

Michael Como (2009) pursues a different kind of connection between the Korean peninsula and the Japanese islands. His interest is in the Hata family from Goguryeo, especially the influence of that family on the textile industry in Yamato, and the implications for women of the ideology presumably brought by the Hata family to the Japanese islands.

Gina Barnes (2007) has offered another perspective on the ideology of the Yamato state, noting the popularity of the Han Chinese deity, the Queen Mother of the West, especially as this deity is figured on mirrors found in Japan. Both Como and Barnes remark on the correlation of goddesses, shamans, and women, and note that women were not viewed in Japan as they were in China, where "women shall not rule" became the watchword (McMahon 2013).

Joan Piggott (1997, 1999) concentrates on the queens and empresses of Yamato, and has arrived at similar conclusions about the relative equality of women among the elite. My research into early Silla shows that rank was more important than gender in selecting a ruler (Nelson 1991, 1993a), which is a related finding.

Archaeology, documents, and a similar social structure in the ruling classes of Yamato and Silla thus are the basis of my argument about Silla's temporary rule in Izumo, the part of Japan on the East Sea, closest to Silla. Particularly telling, I believe, is social structure, suggesting that the family structures of ruling elites who migrated into both the Korean peninsula and the Japanese islands are similar and probably related.

The elites from Korea brought characteristics from cultures farther north: shamanism, sun worship, horse-riding, and categories of artifacts and materials established by elites to distinguish themselves from commoners, who were perhaps villagers already living and farming in the locations into which the elites intruded. These characteristics are common to Silla and Yamato.

112   *Gyeongju and Japan*

Evidence for Silla in the Japanese islands is fragmentary, but both folklore and artifacts suggest that Silla had a strong relationship with the polity of Izumo on the western side of Honshu, the major island of Japan. This is not a new idea, but it is not generally accepted. However, Hong (2012:22) states boldly that Izumo was understood to be a colony of Silla. Kidder (2007:30) writes of Yamato's "obsession with Izumo," which suggests that Izumo was not yet in Yamato's grasp. Kidder points out that the huge caches of swords and bells discovered in Izumo, including 39 bronze bells and 358 bronze swords, may have been a source of envy, or an indication of the wealth of Izumo. It is clear that folklore and archaeology meet to demonstrate that Izumo was once the seat of a powerful leader, but the connection with Silla requires yet other evidence.

Artifacts

The observation that the mounded tombs of Korea and Japan are distantly related to the kurgans of the Steppes, through the peoples who inhabited the north-eastern Steppes as well as forested Manchuria, has been made so often it hardly needs to be documented further (e.g. Okauchi 1986). Additional characteristics of steppe society, such as horse-riding, the worship of white horses, archery, and shamanism, are often cited as they appear in Korea and Japan as well. It is not necessary to insist that each of these traits exists in every case, but the similar origins of much culture of early Korea and Japan are evident. But why insist on Silla, rather than Baekje and Goguryeo, or particularly Gaya?

One obvious difference between Silla and the other Korean kingdoms is the quantity of gold at Silla's command. Artifacts found in Japan and identified as Silla are mostly gold or gilded objects, created by artisans with a high degree of refinement. This lavish use of gold can be traced to cultures of North-East Asia, and gold crowns and belts have their origin there as well. This alone suggests Silla as the source of the gold objects in Japanese burials, and perhaps the transmitter of other North-East Asian characteristics as well.

As already noted in previous chapters, Silla's gold crowns are among the most striking of artifacts which, along with gold belts, have been understood among Koreanists as objects symbolizing not merely royalty, but rulership. Five tombs with gold crowns have been excavated from the Silla "kingdom," and altogether 155 mounded tombs have been described in Gyeongju, most of them unexcavated and apparently intact. So far, only five of these large mounds have been found with tall gold crowns and gold belts (Ju 2010).

In Chapter 3 we have seen that immediately preceding the Saro period mounded tombs containing a gold crown and belt very similar to those of Silla were unearthed in the vicinity of Chaoyang, in Liaoning Province, China. It is interesting, and perhaps relevant, that the Joyang-dong cemetery south-east of Gyeongju has a wood coffin burial dated to the first century CE containing four Han dynasty mirrors (Choe 1984). The relationship of the names seems potentially significant, since the dates are similar, closely linking the early Silla

Gyeongju and Japan 113

elite to the Steppes. These are the Pak kings and queens, probably the first outsiders to insert themselves at the top of the Saro hierarchy, and get selected as rulers.

In Gyeongju itself the gold objects in Wolseong-ro Ga-13 are the earliest-known gold in Silla. They are dated around 350 (Lee H. 2012:111). In 382 Naemul Maripgan was called ruler of Saro (an early Chinese transliteration of Silla) rather than king of the Jinhan, suggesting an important shift in perceptions of power (Yi 2009:51). Bodon Ju (2010:120) proposes that the middle of the fourth century should be considered the beginning of the Silla polity. Regarding Silla and its gold crowns, he states:

> As we enter the Fourth and Fifth Centuries, when the centralization and stratification of power had been established, the tombs of the highest order in terms of both quality and quantity are concentrated . . . in the downtown area of Gyeongju.
>
> (Ju 2010:121)

These, of course, are the Kim tombs, representing the third-century clan intrusion into Gyeongju.

Gold jewelry is lavish in Silla, often made of pure gold and embellished with colored stones and glass. More utilitarian types of objects were gilded rather than being made of pure gold, which is too soft to be used without small amounts of other metals. The gilded artifacts include saddlebows and ceremonial shoes, both of which were made with openwork decorative patterns. Horse trappings, such as bells, ornaments, and stirrups, are also frequently gilded. The ruling family and associated nobility can be easily imagined, shining in their gold accoutrements and riding horses similarly resplendent in gilt bronze trappings.

An early book in English on Japanese archaeology contains a drawing of Silla style earrings from the National Museum in Japan (Munro 1911:436). Tsunoda Ryusakyu is quoted by the Covells (1984:36) when he describes objects from Nintoku's tomb in Naniwa near the Inland Sea as containing, "Korean objects uncovered by storm damage in 1872." Could the earrings in the museum be among such objects? They are very similar to jewelry in Silla tombs, and are easily recognizable as the style of Silla.

Kidder (2007:30) reports gold and gilt objects from the Inariyama–Sakitama Tomb in Gyoda City, Japan. Artifacts included a gold crown, a pair of gilt bronze shoes, iron armor, horse trappings, and six bronze mirrors. This tomb is associated with a prince named Yuryaku, to be discussed later.

The Fujinoki Tomb is the best known of Silla artifacts in Japan. J. E. Kidder has described it in detail. There are many reasons to associate this tomb with Silla, including the gilded horse trappings and the style of the saddlebows. There are also metal soles for burial shoes. Thus, some Japanese archaeologists associate the burial with the Mononobe clan, who sided with Silla, rather than the Soga clan, who originated in Baekje. Kidder concludes that the artifacts came from

114 *Gyeongju and Japan*

both Silla and Baekje (p. 84). However, the crown that was excavated later is obviously from Silla, and is likely to represent a person from Silla who was given a splendid burial in Japan.

Other elite Koreans in Japan

In locating an area called Kibi in ancient times, Michael Gorman (1999) notes many artifacts that he believes point to a "Korean" origin of the early elite. These objects include necklaces, earrings, and wrist bells. In this context it is interesting that while one edge of Kibi abutted the northern side of the Inland Sea of Japan, it apparently adjoined Izumo on its northern side. Several horse-shaped buckles from the Sakakiyama Tomb in Kibi (possibly that of a retainer) are similar to the buckles widely found in southern Korea, and are particularly numerous in Iseong Sanseong, the Silla fortress near Seoul (Kim et al. 1988). Thus, the mysterious Kibi, suppressed in the official Yamato annals, may also have had connections with Silla.

The opening of the Fujinoki Tomb (Kidder 1987, 1989) caused great excitement in the Korean press. The objects were much like Silla ones: saddlebows, ornamental shoe soles, and many horse trappings. The grave occupant is seen by some to be a Mononobe, a clan related to Silla. The Mononobes were defeated by the Soga clan, related to Baekje. Other Japanese archaeologists believe this is a Soga grave, but the artifacts are more closely related to Silla. Kidder (1987:453) supports the idea that the person buried in the Fujinoki Tomb is the Emperor Sushun, who was also an enemy of the Soga family.

Shamans and *gogok*

Silla was also connected to polities in the Japanese islands by a particular kind of shamanism. Shamans are often depicted in the round on *haniwa* (figures placed around the outside of *kofun* (mounded tombs of Japan)) found on or near the *kofun*. The clay shamans often wear a *gogok* in the center of a chain of tubular beads, or a necklace with several such curved beads, which originated in the Central Asian Steppes as an emblem of rulership, and was taken up with enthusiasm by Silla, which covered its crowns with *gogok*. These representations offer similarities with shamanism in the Korean peninsula (Nelson 2008b). Joan Piggott suggests that the women of dual-gender pairs functioned as shamans, and that their duty was in part sacerdotal.

Gold and crowns in Central Asia

Gold artifacts, especially crowns, have been found in burials all across the Steppes. We have seen in Chapter 5 that gold crowns were found on women's heads through both time and distance. Gold crowns on female heads occur as late as the Liao dynasty of northern China. Tubular beads and comma-shaped beads (*gogok*) were found together in dolmens in Manchuria, most often a string of green or white tubular beads having a *gogok* in the middle of the front, giving the curved bead prominence (Watson 1971:131, 136; Lee I. 1987:133–135). Won Yong Kim states that the Korean *gogok* have been tested and shown to be of different stone than that found in Japan (Kim W. Y. 1986:376, fn. 9, citing Eun Ju Choi 1986. He suggests that raw jadeite was once mined near Gyeongju (Kim W. Y. 1986:350).

An elite burial in the Tsukuriyama Tomb group in the Izumo region contains a stone spindle whorl, suggesting a female occupant. One of the earliest mounded tombs in the Izumo region, it contains three bronze mirrors, more than any other tomb in the complex, as well as iron swords and a knife. Beads are also notable, since they were locally made from a material known as Izumo stone. Bead shapes included both tubular beads and *gokok* (Kidder 2007:105). A tomb in Himanoyama contains tubular beads that seem to form a diadem, leading to the suggestion that it was the tomb of a female shaman. I have argued extensively elsewhere for women shaman as leaders (Nelson 2008b), and will not repeat that extensive evidence here.

Simple trade with Silla in gold items seems unlikely. These were symbols of rulership. However, gold crowns and burial shoes closely associated with the elite seem particularly inappropriate as trade items. Their presence implies instead the burial of rulers allied to Silla. It is worth considering whether the region called Izumo in Yamato times was related to Silla, or perhaps actually functioned as a colony of Silla.

Myths and folktales

A more intriguing possibility of understanding the presence of Silla in the Japanese islands is the land-pulling myth. Anders Carlqvist (2010) discusses the story found in Japan's histories of the origin of the area on the western side of Honshu called Izumo. The tale declares that some of Izumo's land was "pulled" from Silla. Carlqvist interprets the tale from an Izumo perspective, while I find it useful to consider this from the Silla side, thus demonstrating Silla's influence, and probably presence, in the Japanese islands. The myth can be seen as explaining why Izumo belonged to Silla, rather than why land was taken from Silla. It suggests that Silla nobility once ruled in Izumo. Carlqvist says that "as far back as the Yayoi period the area nurtured its own unique culture" (p. 186).

Perhaps echoing the land-pulling myth, a tale of a Silla man, Yeonorang, who was magically taken to Japan to become king, is recorded in the *Samguk Yusa*. In their comment on this point, Ha and Mintz (1972:57) write, "Ilyon points out that Japanese records contain no mention of a person from Silla becoming king. He speculates that perhaps Yeonorang became a daimyo, a Japanese nobleman on the coast of Japan facing Korea." But could Yeonorang have been Yuryaku? Linguistically, it seems possible. The Japanese chroniclers would have been motivated to omit Yuryaku's Silla connections if he had them, as his artifacts suggest he did.

Other folklore connects Sosano-o, reported as the first ruler of Izumo, with Silla. The sacred treasures of Japan—the curved jewel, the sun mirror, and short

116 *Gyeongju and Japan*

sword—are credited to Silla prince Ama no Hihoko (Sun Spear of Heaven). Indeed, the divine treasures are all found earlier in the Korean peninsula, and since they are related to both royalty and communication with spirits, at least those ideas must be related in the two regions. The sacred treasures of Japan originated in Korea, suggesting an early and close connection between the rulers of the various chiefdoms in both regions.

Shrines

The possession of lands on either side of the East Sea would have been an enormous advantage to Silla for trade and shipping. Various commodities were made in Izumo that could have been shipped as trade objects. The placement of shrines on coasts and islands suggests that trade was particularly important and in need of supernatural protection. The Great Shrine at Izumo is one of the earliest and largest shrines in Japan. It was and is an important shrine for all of Japan. All *kami* (local spirits) in Japan are required to appear at the Izumo shrine every year in October, emphasizing its primacy.

Three shrines to sea goddesses are found on islands near Izumo. One offering to a sea goddess at the Okinoshima site is a Silla gilded saddlebow, and another is a ring in the style found in Tomb 98. Silla is implicated in the movement of artifacts with leadership symbolism. According to the *Kojiki* (translated as "Records of Ancient Matters" or "An Account of Ancient Matters"), the oldest extant chronicle in Japan, dating from the early eighth century, the protohistoric Jingu was descended from a Silla king (Hong 2012:243). This is particularly relevant because Jingu was also associated with the sea goddesses (Kidder 2007).

The three shrines of Manakata are dedicated to sea goddesses. Although women are traditionally not allowed on the island of Okinoshima, a gold ring similar to one found in the grave of a Silla king was found in the shrine. The three shrines to sea goddesses were clearly related to seafaring, and presumably to trade. Another such shrine has been excavated at Jungmak-dong, Buan-do, in Jeonbuk do, South Korea, where activities of women shamans continue to this day (Im 2010). This series of seafaring-linked shrines demonstrates the importance of trade and movement around the region.

A nine-meter difference in the tide creates the crash of the waves at Jungmak-dong. Many islands in the vicinity contribute to making navigating to this peninsula, and landing there, hazardous. In spite of the difficult seas, the archaeological deposits show that through the centuries landings were made and rituals were held. Such ceremonies must have occurred again and again during at least five centuries, for this is an archaeological site as well as a place where current rituals are held. People came to these sites largely for good luck on their journeys, especially desiring calm seas.

Jungmak-dong was excavated in 1992 by the Chonju National Museum. The excavation covers an area 20 by 10 meters, which is 20 to 30 centimeters thick. About 800 artifacts were unearthed, including gilt bronze horse ornaments in the style of Daegaya, iron weapons, beads, and pottery. Miniature copies of objects

Gyeongju and Japan 117

in stone, representing iron axes, knives, and armor, each had a perforation for hanging, possibly from trees. The miniatures were mixed together in the artifact layer, along with pottery identifiable to time and place. For example, Chinese porcelain jars were made at a kiln established in 479 in Nan Chao in southern China, providing a date for some of the deposits. An imitation of a Chinese mirror shows its power, even in a copy. Korean-style curved jade ornaments (*gogok*), of the sort which cover Korean crowns in profusion, gleam among the other offerings, and fragments of gilt bronze saddlebows lie among the broken pots.

A few of these remarkable discoveries at Jungmak-dong date back as far as the third or fourth century, but the bulk of them relate to the fifth century when Silla was flourishing. Dating of the artifacts allows a kind of stratigraphy, although the thin deposit layer was not recorded in stratigraphic levels. The earliest rituals at Jungmak-dong seem to have been conducted only with pottery and perishable materials. In the second stage, jars and pots presumably contained food and drink for offering to the gods. Horse-shaped clay figures may have been dedicated specifically to sea gods. Large pots contain iron spearheads and bronze bells.

Relationships among the polities of Korea and Japan can clearly be appreciated at Jungmak-dong. Early sea traffic hugged the coasts, in spite of the huge tidal swells and rugged coastline of the western Korean peninsula. Jungmak-dong was one of the stops on the trade route between China and Japan.

Powerful women

Women buried with the trappings of power are found throughout the Steppes. Several with gold crowns have been noted in previous chapters. In graves of a possible antecedent of Silla in the eastern part of the Northern Zone of China, the two female graves excavated here at Nanshangen "are much richer in artifacts than the three male graves" (Shelach 2008:101). In the cemetery at Maoqinggou, gender, and wealth or prestige do not seem to be related, since belt ornaments and plaques are equally distributed between men and women. However, one of the richest graves at Maoqinggou belonged to a female whose burial goods included horse gear. In Tomb 4 of Xigou, in the Ordos region of Inner Mongolia, gold headdresses encrusted with semi-precious stones and necklaces as well as gold and carved jade earrings are believed to constitute evidence of an elite female leader. In the Daodunzi cemetery, four of the six catacomb burials (presumed to indicate status) were females. Animal plaques and cowrie shells were found in the highest numbers in female graves in the second century BCE (Shelach 2008).

In Japanese records we find that "women ruled frequently in prehistoric, protohistoric, and early historical Japan" (Piggott 1999:17). Although sometimes women ruled alone, they might rule as half of a "gender complementary chieftain pair." In trying to tease out relations between Yamato and Silla, it is important to point out that the Empress Suiko (r. 539–571) of Yamato was a member of the Korean Soga family through her mother. She was a legitimate ruler, who ruled in

118   *Gyeongju and Japan*

her own right, like those of Silla in the same time period. Joan Piggott (1999:20) points out that "insular rulership was frequently gender complementary and contrapuntal, with the female partner charged with sacral duties," which may be relevant to some of the non-ruling queens of Silla who are named in the *Samguk Sagi* and *Samguk Yusa*.

Not only with regard to rulership, but in terms of nobility, being a member of the elite was more important than being male or female. In short, rank trumped gender. In Silla, women were eligible to rule because of their place in the kinship structure, which set them above all non-elite men. The bone rank system (Chapter 7) ensured that women were the equal of men within their own rank. Piggott tells us that a "strategy of rank consolidation by royal endogamy" allowed the family of Great King Kimmei to dominate the succession. Empress Suiko was Kimmei's daughter by a Soga consort. Suiko was a "double royal" female, who performed sacral duties as well as those of rulership, but the Soga family prominence ended with her reign.

Conclusion

While the relationship between Silla and Izumo remains speculative, and the further relationship with Kibi is another question mark on a string of inferences, it is nevertheless intriguing that queens could rule in Yamato as well as Silla, and Suiko was called an empress until the demise of the last of the Soga family in Yamato. In Silla, queens continued to be occasionally selected to rule even after the Silla conquest of the peninsula. It is clear that the sense of family was more important than gender. Families were the building blocks of "kingdoms," rather than individual leaders coming to power by their abilities only and representing the entire population. The leadership of women reveals the importance of kinfolk in jockeying for power in the forming of pen/insular state.

** Parts of this chapter are rewritten from: Nelson, S. M. (2015) Relationships between Silla and Japan. In B. Seyock and A. Schottenheimer (eds), *Crossroads, Trade and Interaction in Ancient Northeast Asia: Reassessing Archaeological and Documentary Sources.* Special Issue of *Crossroads* 9:83–96.

10 Gyeongju in an East-Asian perspective

A summary

Chapters in this book have presented ways to view the city of Gyeongju and the Silla kingdom that balance archaeological evidence with the historical documents, but give preference to archaeology when the two present differing interpretations of the past. Korean archaeologists have not only created new knowledge with excavations in Gyeongju, they have pondered and discussed what that new evidence, produced by excavations, means in terms of understanding both the details of Silla's history and the development of states in general (Lee S. J. 1998, 2016).

My conceptual framework is anthropological archaeology, but within that rubric I equally emphasize the view from Korea and the importance of women in Gyeongju history. My research suggests that both the Korean peninsula and the women of Korea have been understudied and undervalued in the history of East Asia. Archaeologists, in coming to any sort of conclusions, are constrained to consider multiple lines of evidence, "evidence that depends on background knowledge derived from a number of different sources" (Wylie 2002:192). I have relied on various kinds of technical expertise in this book, but I also refer to historians with additional background knowledge to offer evidence that converges directly with the question of ethnicity, and the roles of women, especially women with power. I have shown that history and archaeology point to the fact that women rulers were important in Silla, as well as important in the social structure of their likely relatives in Manchuria and Japan, and even among the people of the Steppes.

Identities and ethnicities

For the time period of the rise of Silla, from the first century BCE to the sixth century CE, it is more appropriate to invoke ethnic groups than identities, although for earlier periods identities have been emphasized (Shelach 2009b). In the case of the early centuries BCE, groups appear with names in written documents. While ethnicity can be assumed, even if it is fictitious, such fiction emphasizes the importance of family and clan. For later periods of Chinese history, Evelyn Rawski (1981) rejects a Sinocentric perspective on the peoples and states of what is now north-east China.

120   *Gyeongju in an East-Asian perspective*

In terms of society (rather than culture), my perspective on Gyeongju has been twofold (Di Cosmo 2002): looking at women's lives in the history of Gyeongju; and focusing on social structure as a means of understanding cultural continuity and change. I emphasize Gyeongju as a player in the politics of East Asia, where ethnicity is a driving force. In that time and place, ethnicities did matter, as indeed they do now (Bennett and Standen 2011). Different ways of seeing the world, and different assumptions about the world elicit different behaviors, and when the world is a place where every other group is either a potential enemy or a potential ally, the politics of family and clan are prominent.

The changing ethnicity of rulers in China and Manchuria is particularly relevant for understanding how the Silla kingdom came to be, and why it developed as it did. Some of the contemporaneous rulers of dynasties that were adopted into the history of China were distantly related to the rulers of Silla. In Manchuria, the Xianbei peoples probably spoke languages mutually intelligible with those spoken in the Korean peninsula, and had languages and cultures that were so unlike those of China that Chinese historians called them barbarians. These "barbarians," however, not only shared many traits with splendid Silla, they became rulers of central China from their vantage point in the north for several hundred years. The dynastic clans of the Wei, Sui, and Tang all had roots in cultures that were related to Silla.

Although there is little in written history about their shared ethnicity, archaeology demonstrates connections between Silla and both the Xiongnu and the Xianbei in material culture, from the style of burials to artifact forms, to materials such as gold and birch bark. Gyeongju was the heir to many aspects of Manchurian material culture. Links can also be seen in similarities of social structure and ideology, suggesting stronger relationships than trade in objects or the borrowing of technology (Lee I. 2012).

> The ruling elite of the Northern Yan dynasty, who were of mixed ethnicity, had strong ties to the Murong Xianbei, a branch of the nomadi pastoralists who first appeared as an independent confederation based in Inner Mongolia and Jilin and Liaoning provinces in the mid first century BCE and rose to prominence in the second century CE. Different branches of the Xianbei confederation continued to play an important role on the Steppes and within China during the tumultuous third and fourth centuries when the Murong Xianbei controlled states such as the Former Yan (337–370), the Later Yan (384–409), and the Northern Yan. Based in the northeast next to the Korean peninsula, the Xianbei also had access to the Steppes . . . It is possible that the horse riders traveling along this route, who may originally have reached the southern part of the Korean peninsula while presumably searching for gold, may also have contributed to the flowering of the Silla kingdom.
>
> (Lee I. 2012:128–131)

Certainly, the Xianbei, to whom the earliest stirrups found appeared to belong (Hong 2012:26; Tian 2014), were consummate horsemen and formidable foes in

Gyeongju in an East-Asian perspective   121

battle. It has already been noted that the co-occurrence of gold working, along with mounded tombs, and horses with horse gear suggest an influx of an actual group, and many researchers have suggested that these characteristics mark the arrival of the ruling Kim clan in Gyeongju.

Several researchers have commented on the similarities between Silla's gold technology and horse culture with, specifically, the Tuoba Wei of Liaoning Province. (Pak 1988; Lee I. 2012; Laursen 2014). While it is not necessary to posit horse-riders galloping into Gyeongju and taking charge, it is compatible with the archaeological evidence, although some of Gari Ledyard's details need to be refined, as he himself is well aware (Ledyard 1983).

Gyeongju's connections to Manchuria and the Steppes

This summary draws together the various strands of connections, both material and non-material, and shows their relevance for understanding the development and decline of Silla. The archaeology demonstrates that different groups arrived at different times. Even the tales of the *Sanguk Sagi* tell of people appearing suddenly, often becoming "king."

Some of the last immigrants to Gyeongju brought with them the tradition of mounded burials, a reverence for white horses, and a preference for gold, all of which are related to steppe cultures. Just as important are shamanism, and a belief that women were capable and equal to men. It is useful to recapitulate the similarities in artifacts, designs and technology, symbolism, materials, and ideology to note again the enduring heritage of the Steppes and forests of Manchuria for the people of Gyeongju.

Artifacts related to the Steppes

Bronze artifacts that herald the Bronze Age in Korea include weapons and mirrors that echo those of the Northern Zone of China (Lin 1986) without being exact copies. However, the earliest daggers in Korea are indeed identical to those found in Liaoning, China, and are most likely imports. In Liaoning, these daggers are found in association with horse trappings, and on one occasion with a depiction of a horse-drawn chariot, as at the site of Nanshangen (Guo 1995; Liu 1995; Tan et al. 1995). In the Korean peninsula, the shape of daggers gradually changed from a wide-bladed weapon with edges like curly brackets—{}—into slender daggers with vestigial pointed edges. The changes in shape can be charted in small steps through time, so the ancestry of the Korean dagger is undisputed.

In addition to Korean daggers, other objects such as knives, belts, mirrors, horse equipment, personal ornaments, and clothing all display affinities to the Steppes. Mirrors with geometric motifs are another artifact found widely in the Northern Zone of China, a region that crosses the steppe zone of Inner Mongolia and includes Liaoning Province and southern Jilin Province (Lin 1986). Ornamentation consists of hatched triangles and rows of slanted, short, straight lines. Korean mirrors tend to have two strap handles rather than a single one but,

122 *Gyeongju in an East-Asian perspective*

otherwise, the mirrors are echoes of Northern Zone examples. Within Korea, as the manufacture of bronze became more controlled, mirrors became more refined, while geometric motifs still prevailed.

In the Early Bronze Age in Korea, personal ornaments in Korean elite burials include necklaces made of green or white tubular stone beads. Virtually identical beads have been discovered in Dongbei graves of the same age and earlier. In the Korean peninsula, such necklaces often have a central curved bead with a suspension hole drilled through the wider end of the bead – a shape called *gogok* in Korean and *magatama* in Japanese. The *gogok* marked high-status burials even in the Bronze Age, and continued to be a symbol of power as states formed in Korea and Japan. *Gogok* are particularly prominent in Silla crowns, which may have hundreds of them amid dangling leaf-shaped and disk ornaments made of gold.

During the Iron Age and Three Kingdoms periods, Silla artifacts continue to reflect sites in the Dongbei, in particular, gold artifacts, such as crowns and belts associated with royalty (Ham 2014b). Horse bells and trappings are often present in Silla burials. Gilt bronze saddlebows with cut-out motifs are only found in royal graves. The leaders emphasized their roles as horse-riders.

Belt plaques were particularly important among the horse-riders of the Steppes, where they sometimes included dangling chains holding tools and weapons (Bunker 1995:23). The royal belts of Silla are similarly constructed of joined plaques with strings of gold pendants, each ending in a symbolic object, such as a fish, a small container, or a *gogok*. While the belts in Korea are made of gold, and are not identical in design to those of the Steppes, they are made of joined plaques in a similar fashion to those of the Xiongnu. The gold and silver belts are found with both males and females in Gyeongju.

The clothing of the north-east included boots and trousers, appropriate for horse-riding. Boots are sometimes indicated by small bronze bosses around the feet of a burial. However, while few actual articles of clothing have survived, paintings from tombs and caves show women's clothing as well as men's. Women are depicted with striped, pleated skirts and short jackets with wide sleeves. In pre-modern Korea, boots and shoes often had upturned toes which may be related to ancient footwear for use with stirrups. Boots and trousers are seen on both men and women in a dancing scene in a Goguryeo tomb (Tomb of the Dancers).

Designs related to the Steppes

Geometric patterns on bronzes are common to both the Dongbei and Korea. The fine-lined geometric patterns on mirrors and weapons are quite unlike designs on mirrors from the Chinese Han dynasty, but have similarities with the less-refined mirrors from Fu Hao's tomb of the Shang dynasty in China (Linduff 2003). Guo (1995:197) characterizes designs on northern bronzes as "chestnut dots, zigzags, and short, slanting lines." The designs occur not only on mirrors and swords, but also on many other kinds of bronze artifacts, beginning in the Bronze Age with the Upper Xiajiadian. Even Neolithic pottery in Korea resembling that of the Dongbei was decorated with similar patterns (Nelson 1990). The Bronze Age

Gyeongju in an East-Asian perspective 123

connection between the peninsula and the Dongbei thus was quite ancient, with long antecedents. Considering the geographic propinquity and similar topography of the two regions, it is not surprising that Gyeongju would have seemed to be an appealing place to settle.

Steppe symbolism

The tall gold crowns for which the Silla kingdom is best known have no counterparts in China south of the Northern Zone, but they are very clearly representations of shamanistic ideas (Henze 1933; McCune 1962; Kim and Pearson 1977). The crowns are constructed with a band around the forehead, to which uprights are attached. The shape of this type of upright unmistakably represents antlers (Lee H. 2012:9). It is notable that in some steppe burials, horses are decked out with antlers as noted by the references just above. Other uprights are more stylized, but they have been interpreted as representing the tree of life, suggesting the shamanism of the forest Steppes (McCune 1962; Balzer 1997).

Materials related to the Steppes

Materials related to the Northern Zone of China include gold, birch bark, reindeer antler, and reindeer leather. Not only were these non-local materials present in Silla graves, the artifacts made with them could be inferred to be special, even sacred.

Gold was less valued than jade in central China, while peoples on the northern borders of China and all across the Steppes used gold lavishly in burials, and presumably for living display as well. For example, burials at Liulihe in the vicinity of Beijing feature gold earrings with fan-shaped ends, a feature also found far to the west (Sun 2006). Gold was abundant in the Silla kingdom, where it was used for jewelry, crowns, and belts. The queen in Hwangnam Daechong in Gyeongju was interred with gold artifacts that together weighed almost 5 kilograms (Kim and Pearson 1977).

The birch tree appears to have had ritual significance in Silla and in the Northern Zone. Some birch bark artifacts in Silla had paintings: one is of a red bird and two depict white horses. The bark may have been imported into Gyeongju, since the birch tree is a northern tree that does not grow in southern Korea. Birch bark containers with lids, and other artifacts including coffins, have been found in various sites in Inner Mongolia, as well as being laid on the floor as planks (Bunker 1997:93).

Still on the theme of the northern forests are reindeer products. Not only do the crowns have gold antlers on them, but reindeer leather for boots is mentioned in the sumptuary laws as being allowed only to the Sacred Bone. Reindeer leather must have been imported from the distant forests. While there were deer in the vicinity of Gyeongju, reindeer are creatures of the northern forests.

Saddlebows found in Silla are similar in shape, although they differ in decoration. The sumptuary rules tell us that women rode horses, but the saddle shape

124 *Gyeongju in an East-Asian perspective*

suggests that women, like men, rode astride. In order to sit comfortably with legs on either side of a horse, trousers are important. As noted above, traditional Korean women's clothing includes baggy trousers under a skirt, possibly a remnant of a horse-riding past. Chong Sun Kim (1977:60) remarks that, "It is interesting to note that the original pattern of the Korean costume resembled the dress worn by the Mongolian groups of North-East Asia, a style which suited their nomadic hunting activities." Boots and trousers are depicted for both men and women on a Koguryo tomb mural, and evidence of boots has been found in the southern part of Korea as well. Whether or not they were originally intended for hunting, trousers and boots were appropriate for horse-riding.

Ideology and the Steppes

Ideology relating the Silla kingdoms to the Steppes includes shamanic beliefs and rituals, reverence for the white horse, and sun worship. However, what is most interesting about the shamanism of Silla is that it seems to have been performed in the service of the state, not in opposition to it.

Shamanism was not merely present, but the ruler (male or female) may have performed the functions of head shaman, interceding with the spirits on behalf of the polity. The title of an early Silla ruler translates as shaman (Iryeon 1972), and the royal headgear implies shamanic rituals, since both shapes of crown uprights (antlers and stylized trees), are references to shamanistic beliefs, as previously noted. Shamanism continues to be active in Korea to this day (Kendall 1985). It is not surprising to see reflections of shamanism in the kingdom of Silla.

Current shamanism in Korea is conducted almost exclusively by women shamans, and it is possible that female shamans were in the majority even in the Three Kingdoms period (Nelson 1993a). Shamanism is specifically mentioned in the *Samguk Sagi* in connection with rituals of song and dance. Chinese documents describe early Koreans as performing rituals with singing, dancing, and strong drink (Parker 1890), activities that are often part of shaman rituals.

A horse (of unknown color) was provided with its own grave, surrounded with stone cobbles, in an elite Iron Age cemetery in Gyeongju. Royal tombs feature saddlebows made of gilded bronze in cut-out patterns similar to one found in Chaoyang, Liaoning Province, China, and in the Fujinoki Tomb in Japan. Horse bells and other embellishments for horses are common finds. Not only were the members of the Sacred Bone rank displaying their wealth and elite status, they also seem to have been honoring the horse. A saddle was placed near the top of the south mound of Hwangnam Daechong, bringing to mind the suggestion in the *Samguk Sagi* that the spirits of the dead Sacred Bone flew to heaven on a heavenly horse (Kim and Pearson 1977).

Social system of Gyeongju

For the people of Gyeongju, family mattered, clan mattered, ethnicity mattered. Gender did not matter in the same way. The entire Silla social system was based

Gyeongju in an East-Asian perspective   125

on bilateral heritage. Ancestry determined not merely who, literally, was entitled to wear the purple, but it enforced the details of a Silla person's entire life. Status was determined by birth and was materially enforced. There is no way of knowing which details about the founding ancestors of each were invented or embellished after the fact, but the intention was to establish illustrious ancestors, the charter on which rank was founded.

Once the social system collapsed, as it did toward the end of Unified Silla, contention among the upper stratum made a free-for-all of the economic and political systems as well as the social system. The elaborate structure of the Silla world had been fragmented, and was irreparable. The conditions for Silla's rise and collapse may be found in the antecedents of the culture.

Manchurian connections

The leading families from Manchuria to Korea and Japan were interconnected, but unrelated to the leading families of central China. Clan or family groups were frequently on the move to new locations, expanding or disappearing, or mixing with other ethnic groups; nevertheless families and clans mattered, and the politics played out according to the needs of families and clans.

When Gyeongju was established, it was on the periphery of East-Asian politics, but beginning in the fifth century the city became an important player in the game of domination, with Silla eventually uniting most of the Korean peninsula. Domination was a continuous game, played by all ethnic groups large enough to participate. As part of this population ferment, as I have argued earlier, ethnic groups from Manchuria settled in Gyeongju, where the newcomers mostly found a place for themselves at or near the top of the hierarchy. Perhaps Silla become a temporary winner among similar polities in the contests for hegemony because of its borderland connections.

Tri-polar ethnicity in Manchuria

Several scholars of north-east China have discussed the inappropriateness of the bipolar dichotomy when applied to the north-east of China. Until recently, many historians who study East Asia have been under the spell of the Chinese historical documents, which are mostly concerned with the relationship between China and the Xiongnu. This presents a bipolar—settled vs. nomads—approach to history (Indrisano and Linduff 2013), which can be enriched and improved by taking into account the third piece of the tripolar history, that of the groups the Chinese called Dongyi. Some of these groups called themselves Xianbei. Even those who are included as "Chinese" dynasties tend to be discounted in the battles for territory in Manchuria, although they also contended with the Xiongnu, and sometimes replaced them in China's northern region, using Xiongnu tactics against China and becoming the "dominant extortionists" of that country.

The Xiongnu (nomadic Turks) and the Xianbei (settled Manchurians) were very different peoples. The names derive from histories written by Chinese

126 *Gyeongju in an East-Asian perspective*

dynasties to designate the "barbarians" north and north-east of an expanding polity that perceived its own history in terms of adherence to rites (Pines 2005).

When the Xianbei became thoroughly assimilated, and moved their capital from the northern region to Luoyang, they were replaced by groups from the Korean peninsula. Gari Ledyard (1983:313) emphasizes "triangular relationships" in north-east China, although his three are China, Manchuria, and Korea. Ledyard is discussing a later time period, but the basic idea is the same. Some of the contestants have been ignored or subsumed in some other group, when in fact they were present and active, and quite separate polities.

Proposing a tripolar East Asia provides a sharper lens through which Korean history can come into focus. In the first century BCE, when the *Samguk Sagi* reports that Silla's earliest king and queen reigned, the Han dynasty of China was struggling with the Xianbei-Tungus peoples of the north, in places where populations speaking Chinese-related dialects had not previously penetrated. Ledyard (1983:318) shows that Xianbei troops helped Goguryeo defeat the Lelang colony. There is more to the regional histories than was recorded in the Chinese annals.

Ethnicity in this period is far from straightforward, but is a tangled web of relationships and even shifting ethnicities, as is suggested by the archaeological record. In particular, the "Chinese" Yan, Wei, Sui, and Tang dynasties were ruled by people of Xianbei descent. During the period of Silla's development, the northern dynasties claimed by China were distant relatives of the people of Gyeongju.

Yangjin Pak (1996:39) notes that the ethnic mixing of this time period was profound. "During the last few centuries BC and first few centuries AD several societies in various parts of the Korean peninsula and north-eastern China went through complex processes of political and social development, and became politically, socially, and culturally quite indistinguishable." Pak does not include "archaeologically indistinguishable," because there are distinctions to be seen in the archaeological record of the Dongbei, especially in terms of burial styles and the artifacts placed in burials. Although there are similarities between sites, the sites suggest different ethnicities, especially in Liaoning and Inner Mongolia, which seem to have been a mixing ground for ethnicities, as well as a place of conflict between them.

Tungusic peoples

The Tungusic peoples occupied a zone of related peoples, all having similar material cultures and beliefs, and speaking similar languages, stretching from the three current provinces of the Chinese Dongbei (Liaoning, Jilin, and Heilongjiang provinces) into the Korean peninsula and north-eastward into the present Russian Far East and even south-eastward into the Japanese islands. Ethnic identity cannot be assumed based on archaeology alone, but documents, archaeology, and linguistics together tend to support this interpretation, making a strong case for a tripolar East Asia as the best model to understand the region. Genetic testing may tell the final tale. Oxenham and Pechinkina (2013:484) suggest Manchurian genes in Korea.

Who the peoples were whose remains are explored in archaeological sites is a delicate subject for the current political situation in the region. Although not expressed in this way, interpretations of the ethnicity of archaeological remains can be inferred as territorial claims (see chapters in Kohl and Fawcett 1995). Museums within China's present borders may interpret the past in idiosyncratic ways (Bennett and Standen 2011).

While this is a delicate situation, avoiding the subject does not make it disappear, and discussing it is important for understanding ancient history. Gwen Bennett (2012) demonstrates the ways in which museums and archaeological interpretations in Xinjiang have been used to make the rule of China over its present ethnic minorities seem ancient, inevitable, and permanent.

Why Gyeongju should never have succeeded

Silla was geographically the least likely group in the Korean peninsula to ally with China, and yet became the force for unifying the peninsula with the help of Tang China. Baekje and Goguryeo were more closely related to the continent in terms of official communications, except for the brief time that Silla was courting Tang to be her ally against the other two Korean kingdoms (Best 2006). Such shifting alliances were the way the political game was played in North-East Asia.

Transportation from Gyeongju to anywhere else was difficult, being either by foot or on horseback, on trails through the hilly Korean peninsula, and then perhaps by boat across rivers and seas. Silla had to create a navy to reach Izumo in Japan and to compete in the Yellow Sea. Distances must have seemed much farther than they do today, but horses with stirrups and saddles gave ethnic groups from the Steppes an advantage—to strike and speed away.

The only choice of written communication among the various ethnicities of North-East Asia was one that utilized the Chinese language. In spite of these limitations in communication, Gyeongju was never isolated, and events there were not independent of the rest of East Asia. People and ideas could and did move through large regions.

Silla becomes a regional power

In the fifth century, when Silla was focused on conquering and absorbing the polities east of the Naktong River, the roads leading out of Gyeongju began to be improved, with post and billet stations along the way. Markets were established, the court was expanded, and official duties became more formalized. Silla was setting the stage for its future glory by adopting Chinese methods of organization and becoming more centralized. Gyeongu's place in North-East Asia was consolidated when the polity of Silla conquered the other two Korean kingdoms in 668 with the help of Tang China and, then, when Tang tried to set up its own commanderies in Goguryeo and Baekje, Silla thwarted Tang's ambitions, driving Tang out of the Korean peninsula.

128 *Gyeongju in an East-Asian perspective*

Archaeology of Manchuria

The archaeology of Manchuria, the original homeland of the Manchu people (some of whom swooped into China to conquer the Ming dynasty of China, thus founding the Qing dynasty [1111–1911]), is beginning to refine the usual Sinocentric version of historical events. Recent archaeological excavations and surveys in Manchuria and Mongolia have refocused the way it is possible to understand the time period from the beginnings of the Han dynasty through the Tang dynasty of China, but so far this work has done little to change the way Korean history is understood.

Beginnings of tripolar Asia

Relationships between the Korean peninsula and China, Manchuria, and the Steppes had begun as early as the Samhan period in the first century BCE. Although Lelang was an important presence on the Korean peninsula, archaeology shows that the impact of China was far less important than the continuity of Silla's nomadic heritage. The proximity of Lelang allowed a few Chinese objects to appear in archaeological sites in and near Gyeongju, but language and culture seem to have played a stronger part than mere objects. As noted by Barbara Seyock (2014), the items from the Lelang colonies in Korean and Japanese graves were more symbolic than practical. Perhaps the Chinese mirrors and tips of umbrellas acquired magical meanings in their new settings. The documents regarding the Samhan imply that the connection between Lelang and the southern parts of Korea was not strong and, in fact, the Chinese documents supply little specific information about Jinhan, Silla's predecessor (Barnes and Byington 2014).

During the Korean Three Kingdoms era (57 BCE to 668 CE) the interactions of Silla were mostly with her closest neighbors. As seen in Chapter 2, Silla was bent on conquest and, after subjugating the area east of the Naktong River, contested the Han River region for an outlet to the Yellow Sea, conquering far up the East Sea coast as well.

In the meantime, related Tungusic groups in Manchuria were challenging both Chinese and Xiongnu groups. It was a tripolar history, not a contest between nomads against farmers, as those tumultuous times were framed by Chinese historians. Tribes of Xiongnu fought among themselves, just as the settled polities of the Korean peninsula did. Contests for power had been part of the nomadic heritage, carried into Korea and retained long after those descendants of nomads had settled into an agricultural life.

Who were the Gyeongju rulers?

The archaeology of Gyeongju suggests that a group from Liaoning established itself in Gyeongju in the Late Mumun period, creating dolmen sites at Hwangseong-dong. To recap Chapter 2, the burials of the ensuing Wooden Coffin period in Joyang-dong and other burial areas of Gyeongju echo graves that have

Gyeongju in an East-Asian perspective   129

been excavated in Liaoning. Mound burials which began in Gyeongju with the arrival of the Kim family were a hallmark of steppe burial. But were the Kims related to the Xiongnu or the Xianbei?

While most of the people of Silla were probably related to the Xianbei, at least some of the Kim clan believed themselves to be descended from Xiongnu ancestors. Wontack Hong notes that,

> According to the *Hanshu*, King Wudi (r. 140–187 BCE) launched an attack on the eastern Xiongnu in 121 BCE, and captured the golden statue that had been sculpted and used in the Rites to Heaven by the Xiongnu king, Xiu-tu. Ri-di (Il-je in Korean), the crown prince, killed his father and surrendered to Han Wudi, who made him *Tu-Ho* in appreciation of his military exploits in suppressing the rebellion. Since the Xiongnu king, Xiu-tu, used to make gold statues for rites to heaven, Wudi bestowed the surname Jin (Kim in Korean, implying gold) upon Ri-di.
>
> (Hong W. 2012:233–234)

Further evidence that the Kim clan of Gyeongju had a tradition of descent from the Xiongnu Kim clan is found in the epitaphs of King Munmu (r. 661–681), and a later epitaph on the tomb of a Silla lady (833–864). King Munmu's epitaph relates that he was descended from "Tu-Hou, the Rites to Heaven," while a long inscription on the Silla lady's tomb says in part, "her remote ancestor was Jin Ri-Di (Kim Il-je in Korean) whose descendants . . . later escaped to Liaodong."

Xiongnu vs. Xianbei in Manchuria

Maodun, leader of the Xiongnu, had challenged the emerging power of the Xianbei in the Eastern Steppes and defeated them in 210 BCE, but the Xiongnu were again expelled from the territory by the Xianbei in 48 CE, who appropriated some of the Xiongnu land as well, becoming "the dominant extortioners [of China]" (Hong 2012:27) until 180 CE. The Tuoba Xianbei began to occupy the lands of what is now Liaoning Province in north-eastern China around 300, establishing the Northern Wei dynasty (386–534). Since it was a Xianbei clan who later ruled in Liaodong as the Tuoba Wei, and the ancestors of the Kim family are linked by gold artifacts and techniques to the sites in Chaoyang, Liaoning Province, some shifting of ethnicity, or perhaps mixing, may have occurred when the Kim family relocated to Liaodong, as expressed in the epitaph of the Silla lady above.

Buddhism

Buddhism was a later mechanism of cementing connections between polities. The Northern Wei (386–534), ruled by the Tuoba Xianbei, brought Buddhism into Manchuria. Their capital at Pingcheng, now called Datong, has some of the most artistic, as well as the most immense Buddhas in China. They are carved into the soft rock, creating artificial grottoes. Buddhism came to Goguryeo and

130 *Gyeongju in an East-Asian perspective*

Baekje through this region, and eventually arrived in Silla from the north, largely through monks from Goguryeo. According to Gwen Bennett (2012), the Xianbei capital at Pingcheng is not acknowledged at all in the museum at Datong. Not only Chinese histories, but also current presentations elide the Xianbei presence in north-eastern China.

Women rulers

The Sui dynasty (581–618) was founded by Xianbei aristocracy who spoke the Xianbei language, wore Xianbei clothing, and kept their three-syllable Xianbei names until late in the dynasty. The Empress Wenming (r. 452–465) changed all that. She was responsible for the "wholesale Sinification of the Tuoba court" (Hong 2012:31). She herself was Han Chinese, married to a Xianbei emperor and happily participating in the Xianbei/Xiongnu tradition of strong women.

The Tang dynasty was also ruled by a woman, Empress Wu (659–705) who presided over an explosion of great art in China, and awarded herself an enormous tomb by having it dug into the top of a high mountain, with a long spirit path. She allied with Silla, another country with a woman ruler at times, in the hopes of annexing the Korean peninsula. In this plot she was thwarted by a timely response from Silla.

New histories of East Asia

Gyeongju's archaeology and the documents that pertain to the kingdom of Silla and the city of Gyeongju clearly need to be related to the larger picture of East Asia, but the details are not yet clear. It *is* clear, however, that Gyeongju's connections with North-East Asia should be factored into the understanding of the entire region.

This has not happened yet. Many recent archaeological writings on the area north of China concentrate on the Steppes, especially on the Xiongnu. Somehow, the forested areas of North-East Asia have almost disappeared from archaeological discourse about this region. While many new excavations in Mongolia have very greatly broadened our understanding of the interactions between China and the (at least partly) nomadic Xiongnu peoples (Allard and Erdenbataar 2005; Wright 2006; Shelach 2008, 2009a; Honeychurch 2015), the relationships between China, the steppe peoples, and the other northern peoples, especially those in the Korean peninsula, are rarely brought into the equation.

While William Honeychurch (2015:253) provides at least a nod to the forests of Manchuria and the Korean peninsula, he does not accord them any particular role. He writes, "These shifts in macro-regional politics may also have had consequences for organization among early Manchurian and Korean complex polities as well." However, Manchuria and Korea were active players in the great game of Chinese politics, not just receivers of consequences. Explaining the interactions of all polities involved will lead to clearer understandings of a complex and shifting situation. Excavations in Mongolia and Inner Mongolia have helped

Gyeongju in an East-Asian perspective 131

Map 10.1 Korea's place in East Asia

greatly to modify the Chinese historical version of events, the only version scholars had until recently. More data from Manchuria and the Russian Far East are now needed to balance the exciting new archaeological evidence from Mongolia and north-eastern China.

Gideon Shelach (2009b) seems to be uncomfortable with the Chinese proclivity for associating archaeological sites with groups named in Chinese documents, but it seems to me that to ignore the interplay of ethnic groups is to miss some of the richness of the mosaic of cultures in the region north of China. The fact that the archaeological sites do not represent undifferentiated "barbarians" or even "nomads" is important for interpreting the archaeological details. Furthermore, Shelach (2006) himself has pointed out the likelihood that distinctive clothing and artifacts are meant as a means of identity, as demonstrated by obvious features such as styles of belts and knives. Requiring visual identification suggests that several other peoples occupy or overlap in the same region, each of them distinguishable by their clothing or artifacts.

Cultural differences make up a good part of China's awareness of "others" on its borders, according to Chinese histories (Pines 2005). If specific ethnic groups

132 *Gyeongju in an East-Asian perspective*

can be identified in archaeological sites, new and more focused information will elucidate the politics and policies of the time. The archaeology of Inner Mongolia is particularly relevant, because these sites indicate a mosaic of various ethnicities (Guo 1995). While some of the sites are clearly related to the Steppes, others, especially in Liaoning Province, could well be sites of the peoples known to the Chinese as Xianbei.

Such a shift in perspective changes the way the Samhan of the Korean peninsula are perceived, as well as the peoples of the Korean Three Kingdoms, and various other states that were formed in the forests and not in the Steppes, such as Buyeo, Gogureyo, Parhae, and Liao. These peoples may have adopted some facets of Chinese culture, but they were not ethnically Chinese, and archaeologically they can be appreciated as different.

Multiple ethnicities in Korea?

Observers of the current Korean population have noted that there are in general two kinds of Korean looks. This was described by Oppert as "two types of faces, the one distinctly Mongolian and the other tending rather to the Malay type" (quoted in Hulbert 1969:27). This observation has been remarked on by Koreans themselves as well as by Westerners. Choong Soon Kim, in defining and defending multiculturalism in Korea, asserts that Korea has always been multicultural. He quotes a remark by a Chinese colleague born in Manchuria, the Chinese-American anthropologist Francis Hsu, who said to him, "You and I look more alike than any other fellow Chinese and I. Your ancestors and my ancestors must have belonged to the same tribe" (Kim Choong Soon 2011:2). DNA testing has not yet produced definitive results, but follows the same trend. Marc Oxenham and Kate Pechenkina (2013:484) note that "a distinct northern central Chinese clustering is seen with offshoots in the population of Korea."

Hong shows that various polities in Manchuria and Mongolia continuously challenged each other for dominance, as well as harassing Chinese states north of the Yellow River. Korean populations, who were descendants of several different groups of Xianbei, jockeyed for power and continued to contest each other's groups after settling in Korea. Once we have cleared our minds of the nomad/civilized dichotomy, there can be a more detailed understanding of the polities in the Korean peninsula. The common heritage of peoples who settled in the peninsula did not prevent different groups from trying to enlarge their own boundaries by conquering their neighbors, in spite of their similar cultures and languages. Silla set out to conquer and make minority groups of the Gaya peoples with a culture so similar archaeologists can scarcely distinguish between them, and ended by conquering the other two kingdoms of Korea. Silla's forays into the Japanese islands left traces of gold crowns and jewelry in Japan. The fact that both cultures included women as powerful rulers may also suggest an ancient relationship (Nelson 1991, 1993a, 2008a, 2014; Piggott 1997, 1999).

The Kim kings and queens of Gyeongju

One possible way to understand the dominance of the Kim clan in Silla is to assume that the Kims arrived with superior horses and weapons. We know that they had stirrups by the third century, almost a necessity for effective fighting from horseback.

There are several reasons to believe that the Kim family, who dominated the rulership after the beginning of the mounded tombs, were latecomers to Saro. Archaeology demonstrates that several traits arrived in Gyeongju at the same time as the Kim family: mounded tombs, worship of white horses, the use of birch bark, and knowledge of gold working. All these were associated with the people of the Steppes, especially Xiongnu, but by this time the Xianbei had acquired these traits as well, making it difficult to distinguish where the influence on Silla originated.

It is very tempting to see the similar but earlier gold crowns and belts that have been excavated near Chaoyang in Liaoning Province, China, as well as the earliest-known stirrups, as making a case for the Kim clan to have come from that location. Perhaps they even gave the name of Jeoyang to the place in Gyeongju after their old homeland, Chaoyang, in Liaoning.

The history of the city of Gyeongju has many facets, and the Silla polity that ruled it for a thousand years is worth much further study. Silla's gold working, its sumptuary laws, its splendid imports from great distances, and its apparent lack of gender discrimination are facets of its history that capture the imagination. There is surely much more to learn about Silla from that which still lies under the ground, waiting for the archaeologist's trowel.

References

Adams, Edward B. (1979) *Kyongju Guide, Cultural Spirit of Silla in Korea*. Seoul: International Tourist.

Allard, Francis and Diimaajav Erdenbataar (2005) Khirigsuurs, Ritual and Mobility in the Bronze Age of Mongolia. *Antiquity* 79:547–563.

Anazawa, Akou and Junichi Manome (1987) Koshiragi Funkyubo Shutsudo no Kantotachi [The Large Ring-handled Swords Found in Old Silla Burial Grounds]. *Chosen Gakuho* 122:168–187.

An, Jiayao (2004) The Art of Glass Along the Silk Road. In J. C. Y. Watt, Jiayao An, Angela F. Howard, Boris I. Marshak, Bai Su and Feng Zhao (eds), *China, Dawn of a Golden Age 200–750 AD*, pp. 57–66. New Haven, CT, New York and London: The Metropolitan Museum of Art and Yale University Press.

Balzer, Marjorie Mandelstam (ed.) (1997) *Shamanic Worlds: Ritual and Lore of Siberia and Central Asia*. New York: North Castle Books.

Barnes, Gina Lee (1997) *China, Korea and Japan, The Rise of Civilization in East Asia*. London: Thames and Hudson.

Barnes, Gina Lee (2001) *State Formation in Korea*. Richmond, Surrey: Curzon.

Barnes, Gina Lee (2007) *State Formation in Japan*. London: Routledge.

Barnes, Gina Lee and Mark Byington (2014) Comparison of Texts between the Accounts of Han in the Sanguo zhi, in the Fragments of the Wei le, and in the Hou-Han shu. Trade and Interaction in Ancient Northeast Asia: Reassessing Archaeological and Documentary Sources. In B. Seyock (ed.), Special Issue of *Crossroads* 9:97–112.

Bartz, Patricia (1972) *South Korea*. Oxford: Clarendon Press.

Bennett, Gwen (2012) National History and Identity Narratives in the People's Republic of China: Cultural Heritage Interpretation in Xinjiang. In C. W. Hartley, G. B. Yazicioglu and A. T. Smith, *The Archaeology of Power and Politics in Eurasia*, pp. 3–22. Cambridge: Cambridge University Press.

Bennett, Gwen and Naomi Standen (2011) Historical and Archaeological Views of the Liao (10th to 12th Centuries) Borderlands in Northeast China. In D. Mullin (ed.), *Places in Between*, pp. 3–21. Oxford: Oxbow Books.

Best, Jonathan W. (2006) The Transmission and Transformation of Early Buddhist Culture in Korea and Japan. In H. Washiizuka, Y. Park and W. Kang (eds), *Transmitting the Forms of the Divinity*, pp. 68–83. New York: Japan Society.

Bunker, Emma C. (1995) The People, the Land, and the Economy. In J. F. So and E. C. Bunker, *Traders and Raiders on China's Northern Frontier*, pp. 17–31. Seattle: University of Washington Press.

References   135

Bunker, Emma C. (1997) *Ancient Bronzes of the Eastern Eurasian Steppes from the Arthur M. Sackler Collection.* New York: Arthur M. Sackler Foundation.

Bunker, Emma C. (2009) First Millennium BCE Beifang Artifacts as Historical Documents. In B. K. Hanks and K. M. Linduff (eds), *Social Complexity in Prehistoric Eurasia*, pp. 272–295. Cambridge: Cambridge University Press.

Bush, Susan (1984) Some Parallels between Chinese and Korean Ornamental Motifs of the Late Fifth and Early Sixth Centuries AD. *Archives of Asian Art* 37:60–78.

Byington, Mark (1997) A History of the Puyo State. PhD dissertation, Harvard University.

Byington, Mark (2009) The Account of Han in the Sanguozhi—An Annotated Translation. *Early Korea* 2:125–152.

Byington, Mark (2016) Some Problems with Early Koguryo–Silla Relations Described in the Samguk Sagi. *Seoul Journal of Korean Studies* 29(1):115–132.

Carlqvist, Anders (2010) The Land-pulling Myth and Some Aspects of Historic Reality. *Japanese Journal of Religious Studies* 37(2):185–222.

Chang, K. C. (1986) *The Archaeology of Ancient China.* New Haven, CT: Yale University Press.

Chapin, Helen (1957) Kyongju. *Royal Asiatic Society* 33:55–72.

Chee, Changboh (1974) Shamanism and the Folk Beliefs of the Koreans. In A. Nahm (ed.), *Traditional Korea, Theory and Practice.* Kalamazoo, MI: Western Michigan University, Center for Korean Studies.

Childs-Johnson, Elizabeth (1988) Dragons, Masks, Axes and Blades from Four Newly Documented Jade-producing Cultures of Ancient China. *Orientations* (April):30–37.

Chin, Hong Sup (1966) Investigation of the Sarira Hole of the Pagoda of Hwangyongsa. *Misul Charyo* 11:17–24.

Cho, Daeyoun and Donghee Lee (2013) Production Specialization of Liaoning- and Korean-type Bronze Daggers during the Korean Bronze Age. *Korean Art and Archaeology* 7:78–89.

Choe, Jongyu (1982) Report of the Fourth Season at Choyangdong, Kyongju. *Archaeology in Korea* 9:35–39.

Ch'oe, Pyong Hon (1981) The Evolution and Chronology of the Wooden Chamber Tomb of the Old Silla Period. *Han'guk kogo hakpo* [Journal of the Korean Archaeological Society] 10–11:137–228 [in Korean].

Ch'oe, Sun-u (1998) Artifacts of Kyongju. In Korean National Committee for UNESCO (ed.), *Kyongju, City of Millennial History*, pp. 143–160. Seoul: Hollym.

Choi, Hochin (1971) *The Economic History of Korea.* Seoul: The Freedom Library.

Como, Michael (2009) *Weaving and Binding, Immigrant Gods and Female Immortals in Ancient Japan.* Honolulu: University of Hawaii Press.

Conkey, Margaret and Janet Spector (1985) Archaeology and the Study of Gender. *Advances in Archaeological Method and Theory* 7:1–38.

Conkey, Margaret and Joan Gero (1991) Tensions, Pluralities, and Engendering Archaeology: An Introduction to Women and Prehistory. In Joan Gero and Margaret Conkey (eds), *Engendering Archaeology: Women and Prehistory*, pp. 1–30. Oxford: Basil Blackwell Ltd.

Covell, Jon Carter and Alan Covell (1984) *Japan's Hidden History.* Seoul: Hollym.

Davy, Jack (2016) Unreliable Narratives: Historical and Archaeological Approaches to Early Silla. *Seoul Journal of Korean Studies* 29(1):7–32.

Deuchler, Martina (1992) *The Confucian Transformation of Korea.* Cambridge, MA: Harvard University Council on East Asian Studies.

136 References

Di Cosmo, Nicola (2002) *Ancient China and its Enemies*. Cambridge: Cambridge University Press.

Egami Namio (1964) The Formation of the Japanese People and the Origin of the State in Japan. *Memoirs of the Toyo Bunko* 23:35–70 [in Japanese].

Francis, Peter (Jr) (2002) *Asia's Maritime Bead Trade, 300 BC to the Present*. Honolulu: University of Hawaii Press.

Gale, Esson M. (1931) *Discourses on Salt and Iron: A Debate on State Control of Commerce and Industry in Ancient China*. Sinica Leidensi. Vol. 2. Leiden, Netherlands: E. J. Brill.

Gero, Joan. M. (1985) Socio-Politics and the Woman-at-Home Ideology. *American Antiquity* 50(2):342–350.

Glover, Ian C. (1990) *Early Trade between India and Southeast Asia*. Hull: Center for South-East Asian Studies.

Glover, Ian C. and J. Henderson (1995) Early Glass in South and East Asia. In R. Scott and J. Guy (eds), *China and Southeast Asia: Art, Commerce, and Interaction*, pp. 141–169. London: Percival David Foundation of Chinese Arts.

Gorman, Michael S. F. (1999) *The Quest for Kibi*. Bangkok: Orchid Press.

Grajdanzev, Andrew J. (1944) *Modern Korea*. New York: The John Day Company.

Grayson, James H. (1976) Some Structural Patterns of the Royal Family of Ancient Korea. *Korea Journal* 16(6):27–32.

Griffis, William Elliot (1882) *Corea, the Hermit Nation*. New York: Charles Scribners' Sons.

Guo, Dashun (1995) Hongshan and Related Cultures. In S. M. Nelson (ed.), *The Archaeology of Northeast China*, pp. 21–64. London: Routledge.

Ham, Soon Seop (2014a) Gold Culture of the Silla Kingdom and Maripkan. In Soyoung Lee and Denise Patry Leidy (eds), *Silla, Korea's Golden Kingdom*, pp. 31–67. New Haven, CT: Yale University Press.

Ham, Soon Seop (2014b) Development of Silla Headband Crowns with Tree-shaped Uprights. *Journal of Korean Art and Archaeology* 8:10–27.

Ha, Tae Hung and Grafton K. Mintz (1972) (trans) *Samguk Yusa: Legends and History of the Three Kingdoms of Ancient Korea*. [Iryeon the Monk (1278)]. Seoul: Yonsei University Press.

Henderson, Gregory (1959) Korea through the Fall of the Lolang Dynasty. *Koreana Quarterly* 131:147–168.

Henze, Carl (1933) Die Schamanen Kronen zur Hanzeit in Korea. *Ostasiatische Zeitschrift* 9(5):156–163.

Hinsch, Bret (2002) *Women in Early Imperial China*. Lanham, MD, Boulder, CO, New York and Oxford: Rowman and Littlefield.

Honeychurch, William (2015) *Inner Asia and the Spatial Politics of Empire*. New York: Springer.

Honeychurch, William and Chunag Amartuvshin (2006) States on Horseback: The Rise of Inner Asian Confederations and Empires. In M. Stark (ed.), *Archaeology of Asia*, pp. 255–278. Lanham, MD: Blackwell.

Hong, Wontack (1994) *Paekche of Korea and the Origin of Yamato Japan*. Seoul: Kudara International.

Hong, Wontack (2012) *East Asian History: A Tripolar Approach*, rev. ed. Seoul: Kudara International.

Hulbert, Homer B. (1969 [1906]) (reprint) *The Passing of Korea*. Seoul: Yonsei University Press.

Humphrey, Caroline (1996) Shamanic Practices and the State in Northern Asia: Views from the Center and Periphery. In N. Thomas and C. Humphrey (eds), *Shamanism, History and the State*, pp. 191–228. Ann Arbor, MI: University of Michigan Press.

References 137

Ikawa-Smith, Fumiko (1986) Late Pleistocene and Early Holocene Technologies. In R. J. Pearson, Gina Lee Barnes and Karl L. Hutterer (eds), *Windows on the Japanese Past: Studies in Archaeology and Prehistory*, pp 199–216. Ann Arbor, MI: University of Michigan, Center for Japanese Studies.

Im, Hyo Jai (2010) Comparative Study of the Okinoshima (Japan) and Chungmakdong (Korea) Ritual Sites. In *World Heritage Promotion Committee of "Okinoshima Island and Related Sites in the Manakata Region"*. Fukuoka: Fukuoka Prefectural Government.

Indrisano, Gregory G. and Katheryn M. Linduff (2013) Expansion of the Chinese Empire into its Northern Frontier (ca. 500 BCE–0 CE). In G. E. Areshian (ed.), *Empires and Diversity*, pp. 164–207. Los Angeles: Cotsen Institute of Archaeology Press.

Iryeon the Monk (1972 [1278]) *Samguk Yusa: Legends and History of the Three Kingdoms of Ancient Korea*, trans. Ha Tae Hung and Grafton K. Mintz. Seoul: Yonsei University Press.

Ito, Akio (1971) Zur Chronologie der fruhsillazeitlichen Graber in Sudkorea. Band 1 and Band 2. Munich: Bayerische Akademie der Wissenschaften, Philosophie-Historische Klasse (in German with English summary).

Jeon, Sang Woon (1974) *Science and Technology in Korea*. Cambridge, MA: MIT Press.

Jeonju National Museum (2009) *Museum Catalogue*. Jeonju: Korea.

Joe, W. J. (1972) *Traditional Korea: A Cultural History*. Seoul: Chung'ang University Press.

Ju, Bodon (2009) Problems Concerning the Basic Historical Documents Related to the Samhan. *Early Korea* 2:95–122.

Ju, Bodon (2010) The Development of the Maripgan Period and the Gold Crowns of Silla. In Hansang Lee (ed.), *Gold Crowns of Silla, Treasures from a Brilliant Age*, pp. 120–133. Seoul: Korea Foundation.

Kang, Bong Won (1984) *Research on Kaya and the Adjacent Area in the Formative Period*. Kyunghee University Thesis Reports No. 12, pp. 7–33.

Kang, Bong Won (2000a) A Reconsideration of Population Pressure and Warfare: A Protohistoric Korean Case. *Current Anthropology* 41(5):873–881.

Kang, Bong Won (2000b) A Test of Increasing Warfare in the Samguk Sagi against the Archaeological Remains in Yongnam, South Korea. *Journal of East Asian Archaeology* 2(3–4):139–198.

Kang, Bong Won (2003) *Burial Site at Hwangsungdong, Gyeongju, Korea, III*. Gyeongju: Gyeongju University Museum.

Kang, Bong Won (2005) An Examination of an Intermediate Sociopolitical Evolutionary Type between Chiefdom and State. *Arctic Anthropology* 42(2):22–35.

Keimyung University Museum (1984) *Excavation of Ancient Tombs*. University Publication No. 2. Daegu: Keimyung University Museum.

Kendall, Laurel (1985) *Shamans, Housewives, and Other Restless Spirits*. Honolulu: University of Hawaii Press.

Kidder, J. Edward (Jr) (1987) The Fujinoki Tomb and its Grave Goods. *Monumenta Nipponica* 42(1):57–87.

Kidder, J. Edward (Jnr) (1989) The Fujinoki Sarcophagus. *Monumneta Nipponica* 44(4):415–460.

Kidder, J. Edward (Jr) (2007) *Himiko and Japan's Elusive Chiefdom of Yamatai*. Honolulu: University of Hawaii Press.

Kim, Byong Mo (1987) Regarding Ho Hwang-Ok. In Hyo Jai Im (ed.), *Papers in Honor of the Retirement of Professor Kim Won-Yong*. Vol 1, pp. 673–681. Seoul: Seoul National University.

138 *References*

Kim, Byong Mo (1997) *Geumgwan-ui Bimil* [Gold Crowns Decoded]. Seoul: Pureun Yoksa.

Kim, Byong Mo and Shim Kwang Ju Lee (1987) *Isong Fortress Excavation Report*. Research Series No. 5. Seoul: Hanyang University Museum.

Kim, Chae Kuei and Eunchang Yi (1975) *A Report on the Excavation of the Tombs at* Hwang*namdong, Kyongju*. Monograph #1. Taegu: Yongnam University Museum [in Korean].

Kim, Che Won and Wong Yong Kim (1966) *Treasures of Korean Art: 2000 Years of Ceramics, Sculpture, and Jeweled Arts*. New York: Harry N. Abrams.

Kim, Choi Guei and Unchang Lee (1975) *Report on Excavation of Ancient Tombs in Hwangnamdong, Kyongju*. Monograph #1. Taegu: Yeungnam University Museum [in Korean].

Kim, Chong Sun (1965) The Emergence of Multi-centered Despotism in the Silla Kingdom: A Study of the Origin of Factional Struggles in Korea. PhD dissertation, University of Washington.

Kim, Chong Sun (1969) Sources of Cohesion and Fragmentation in the Silla Kingdom. *Journal of Korean Studies* 1(1):41–72.

Kim, Chong Sun (1977) The Kolp'um System: Basis for Silla Social Stratification. *Journal of Korean Studies* 1(2):43–69.

Kim, Chong Sun (2004) Silla Economy and Society. *Korean Studies* 28:75–104.

Kim, Choong Soon (2011) *Voices of Foreign Brides*. Lanham, MD: AltaMira Press.

Kim, Gwon Gu (ed.) (2001) *Daegu National Museum*. Daegu: Daegu National Museum.

Kim, Jeong Hak (1978) *The Prehistory of Korea*, trans. R. and K. Pearson. Honolulu: The University of Hawaii Press.

Kim, Won Yong (1973) Silla Pottery Jar with Incised Drawings of Animals. *Kogo Misul* 118:4–9.

Kim, Won Yong (1975) *Archaeology in Korea 1974*. Vol. 2. Seoul: Seoul National University Museum.

Kim, Won Yong (1978) *Archaeology in Korea 1977*. Vol. 5. Seoul: Seoul National University Museum.

Kim, Won Yong (1982a) *Archaeology in Korea 1981*. Vol. 9. Seoul: Seoul National University Musuem.

Kim, Won Yong (1982b) Kyongju, Homeland of Korean Culture. *Korea Journal* 22(9):25–32.

Kim, Won Yong (1983) *Recent Archaeological Discoveries in the Republic of Korea*. Tokyo: UNESCO.

Kim, Won Yong (1986) *Art and Archaeology of Ancient Korea*. Seoul: Taekwang Publishing Co.

Kim, Won Yong and Richard Pearson (1977) Three Royal Tombs: New Discoveries in Korean Archaeology. *Archaeology* 30(5):302–313.

Kim, Won Yong, Hyo Jai Im and Soon Bal Pak (1988) *Mongchon To-song Report*. Seoul: National Museum of Korea.

Kim, Young Won (2009) *Mahan: A Breath of History*. Jeonju: Jeonju National Museum [in Korean].

Kim, Yung Chung (trans. and ed.) (1977) *Women in Korea: A History from Ancient Times to 1945*. Seoul: Ewha Woman's University Press.

Koh, Pyŏng Ik (1958) Korea's Contacts with the "Western Regions" in Pre-modern Times. *Sahoe Gwahak* 2:55–73.

Kohl, Philip L. and Clare Fawcett (eds) (1995) *Nationalism, Politics, and the Practice of Archaeology*. Cambridge, Cambridge University Press.

References 139

Kuzmin, Yaroslav V. (2006a) Paleoeconomy of the Russian Far East. In S. M. Nelson, A. P. Derevanko, Y. V. Kuzmin and R. L. Bland, *Archaeology of the Russian Far East*, BAR International Series No. 1540, pp. 167–174. Oxford: Archaeopress.

Kuzmin, Yaroslav V. (2006b) Recent Studies of Obsidian Exchange Networks in Prehistoric Northeast Asia. In D. E. Dumond and R. L. Bland (eds), *Archaeology in Northeast Asia*, University of Oregon Anthropological Papers No. 65, pp. 61–72. Oregon: University of Oregon, Department of Anthropology and Museum of Natural and Cultural History.

Lankton, James. W. and Laure Dussubieux (2006) Early Glass in Asian Maritime Trade: A Review and Interpretation of Compositional Analysis. *Journal of Glass Studies* 48:121–144.

Lankton, James W. and Insook Lee (2006) Treasures from the Southern Sea: Glass Ornaments from Gimhae-Yangdong and Bokcheondong, Compositional Analysis and Interpretation. *Kogohak* 18 May 2006: 329–355.

Lankton, James W., Insook Lee and James D. Allen (2003) Javanese (Jatim) Beads in Late Fifth to Early Sixth Century Korean (Silla) Tombs. In *AIHV Annales du 16th Congrès*, pp. 327–330.

Lankton, James W., Insook Lee, Gyu-Ho Kim and Hyung-Tae Kang (2006) Bactrian Glass Vessels in KoreanTombs? In *Annals of the 17th Congress of the International Association for the History of Glass*, pp. 578–589.

Lankton, James W., Bernard Gratuze, Gyu-Ho Kim, Laure Dussubieux and Insook Lee (2009) Silk Road Glass in Ancient Korea: The Contribution of Chemical Analysis. In B. Zorn and Alexandra Hilger (eds), *Glass Along the Silk Road from 200 BC to 1000 AD*, pp. 221–237. Mainz: Verlag des Romisch-Germanischen Centralmuseum.

Laursen, Sarah (2014) Leaves That Sway: Gold Xianbei Cap Ornaments from Northeast China. PhD dissertation, University of Pennsylvania.

Ledyard, Gari (1975) Galloping along with the Horseriders: Looking for the Founders of Japan. *Journal of Japanese Studies* 1(2):217–254.

Ledyard, Gari (1983) Yin and Yang in the China–Manchuria–Korea Triangle. In M. Rossabi (ed.), *China Among Equals*, pp. 313–354. Berkeley: University of California Press.

Lee, Hansang (2012) The Gold Culture and the Gold Crowns of Silla. In H. Lee (ed.), *Gold Crowns of Silla, Treasures from a Brilliant Age*, pp. 106–117. Seoul: National Museum of Korea.

Lee, Insook (1987) Report Concerning Prehistoric Gokok. In Hyo Jai Im (ed.), *Papers in Honor of the Retirement of Professor Kim Won-Yong*. Vol. 1, pp. 357–369. Seoul: Seoul National University.

Lee, Insook (1989) A Study of Korean Ancient Glass. *Komunhwa* 34(6):79–95.

Lee, Insook (2012) Of Glass and Gold. In S. Lee and D. P. Leidy (eds), *Silla, Korea's Golden Kingdom*, pp. 115–131. New York: The Metropolitan Museum of Art.

Lee, Jong Wook (1998) Historical Interconnection. In Korean National Committee for UNESCO (ed.), *Kyongju: City of Millennial History*, pp. 15–32. Seoul: Hollym.

Lee, Kidong (2004) The Indigenous Religions of Silla: Their Diversity and Durability. *Korean Studies* 28:49–74.

Lee, Soyoung and Denise Leidy (2013) *Silla, Korea's Golden Kingdom*. New York: The Metropolitan Museum of Art.

Lee, Sung Joo (1998) The Rise of Silla-Kaya Society and its Socio-Political Development. PhD dissertation, Seoul National University [in Korean].140 *References*

Lee, Sung Joo (2016) Recent Discoveries in Silla Settlement Archaeology. *Seoul Journal of Korean Studies* 29(1):33–64.

Leidy, Denise Patry with Huh Hyeong Uk (2013) Interconnections: Buddhism, Silla and the Asian World. In S. Lee and D. P. Leidy, *Silla, Korea's Golden Kingdom*, pp. 143–189. New York: The Metropolitan Museum of Art.

140 *References*

Lena, Kim (2006) Early Korea Buddhist Sculptures and Related Japanese Examples: Iconographic and Stylistic Comparisons. In H. Washiizuka, Y. Park and W. Kang (eds), *Transmitting the Forms of the Divinity*, pp. 68–83. New York: Japan Society.

Lerner, Gerda (1986) *The Creation of Patriarchy*. New York: Oxford University Press.

Lin, Yun (1986) A Re-examination of the Relationship between Bronzes of the Shang Culture and the Northern Zone. In K. C. Chang (ed.), *Studies of Shang Archaeology*, pp. 237–273. New Haven, CT: Yale University Press.

Linduff, Katheryn M. (1994) Early Bronze Age in the Northeast: Xiajiadian and its Place in the Network. Paper delivered at the Association for Asian Studies, Boston.

Linduff, Katheryn M. (1997) Archaeological Overview. In E. Bunker (ed.), *Ancient Bronzes of the Eastern Eurasian Steppes*, pp. 18–112. New York: Arthur M. Sackler Foundation.

Linduff, Katheryn M. (2003) Many Wives, One Queen, in Shang China. In S. M. Nelson (ed.), *Ancient Queens: Archaeological Explorations*, pp. 59–76. Walnut Creek, CA: AltaMira Press.

Liu, Jing Wen (1995) Bronze Culture in Jilin Province. In S. M. Nelson (ed.), *The Archaeology of Northeast China*, pp. 206–224. London: Routledge.

Matsui, Akira (2009) The Use of Livestock Carcasses in Japanese History: An Archaeological Perspective. In N. Matsumoto, H. Bessho and M. Tomii (eds), *Coexistence and Cultural Transmission in East Asia*, pp. 127–139. Walnut Creek, CA: Left Coast Press.

McCune, Evelyn (1962) *The Arts of Korea*. Rutland, VT: Charles E. Tuttle.

McKenzie, Hugh G. and Alexander N. Popov (2015) A Metric Assessment of Evidence for Artificial Cranial Modification at the Boisman 2 Neolithic Cemetery (ca. 5800–5400 14C BP), Primorye, Russian Far East. *Quaternary International* 30:1–12.

McMahon, Keith (2013) *Women Shall Not Rule*. Lanham, MD: Rowman and Littlefield.

Moon Gyoung, Gu (2014) Silla Crowns and Crown Ornaments of the Yeongdong Region. *Journal of Korean Art and Archaeology* 8:28–43.

Mun, Myung Dae (1998) Buddhist Art of Kyongju. In Korean National Commission for UNESCO (ed.), *Kyongju, City of Millennial History*, pp. 111–122. Seoul: Hollym.

Munro, Neil Gordon (1911) *Prehistoric Japan*. Yokohama: [No publisher].

Nelson, S. M. (1990) The Neolithic of Northeastern China and Korea. *Antiquity* 64:234–248.

Nelson, S. M. (1991) The Statuses of Women in Ko-Shilla. *Korea Journal* 31(2):101–107.

Nelson, S. M. (1993) Gender Hierarchy and the Queens of Silla. In B. D. Miller (ed.), *Sex and Gender Hierarchies*, pp. 297–315. Cambridge: Cambridge University Press.

Nelson, S. M. (1995) Roots of Animism in Korea: From the Earliest Inhabitants to the Silla Kingdom. In H. Y. Kwon (ed.), *Korean Cultural Root: Religion and Social Thoughts*, pp. 19–30. Chicago, IL: North Park College and Theological Seminary.

Nelson, S. M. (2003) The Queens of Silla: Power and Connections to the Spirit World. In S. M. Nelson (ed.), *Ancient Queens, Archaeological Explorations*, pp. 77–92. Walnut Creek, CA: AltaMira Press.

Nelson, S. M. (2008a) Horses and Gender in Korea: The Legacy of the Steppe on the Edge of Asia. In K. Linduff and K. Rubinson (eds), *Are All Warriors Male?* Walnut Creek, CA: AltaMira Press.

Nelson, S. M. (2008b) *Shamanism and the Origin of States*. Walnut Creek, CA: Left Coast Press.

Nelson, S. M. (2012) Origin, Significance and Characteristics of the Gold Crowns of Silla. In Hansang Lee (ed.), *Gold Crowns of Silla, Treasures from a Brilliant Age*, pp. 134–144. Seoul: Korea Foundation.

References 141

Nelson, S. M. (2014) Relationships between Silla and Izumo. In B. Seyock and A. Schottenhammer (eds), *Trade and Interaction in Ancient Northeast Asia: Reassessing Archaeological and Documentary Sources*. Special Issue of *Crossroads* 9:83–96.

Oga, Katsuhiko and Sunil Gupta (1995) The Far East, Southeast and South Asia: Indo-Pacific Beads from Yayoi Tombs as Indicators of Early Maritime Exchange. *Journal of South Asian Studies* 16:73–88.

Okauchi, Mitsuzane (1986) Mounded Tombs in East Asia from the 3rd to the 7th centuries AD. In R. Pearson, Gina Lee Barnes and Karl L. Hutterer (eds), *Windows on the Japanese Past: Studies in Archaeology and Prehistory*, pp. 127–148. Ann Arbor, MI: University of Michigan, Center for Japanese Studies.

Osgood, Cornelius (1951) *The Koreans and Their Culture*. New York: The Ronald Press Company.

Oxenham, Marc and Kate Pechenkina (2013) East Asian Bioarchaeology: Major Trends in a Temporally, Genetically, and Eco-culturally Diverse Region. In K. Pechenkina and Marc Oxenham (eds), *Bioarchaeology of East Asia*, pp. 482–498. Gainesville: University Press of Florida.

Pai, Hyung Il (1992) Culture Contact and Culture Change: The Korean Peninsula and its Relations with the Han Dynasty Commandery of Lelang. *World Archaeology* 23(3):306–319.

Pai, Hyung Il (2000) *Constructing "Korean" Origins*. Cambridge, MA: Harvard University Asia Center.

Pak, Yangjin (1996) Archaeological Evidence of Puyeo Society in Northeast China. *Korea Journal* (Winter):39–50.

Pak, Young Sook (1988) The Origins of Silla Metalwork. *Orientations* (September):44–53.

Park, Cheun Soo (2008) Kaya and Silla in Archaeological Perspective. *Early Korea* 1:113–153.

Park, Dong Won (1998) The Environment of Kyongju. In Korean National Commission for UNESCO (ed.), *Kyongju, City of Millennial History*, pp. 47–58, Seoul: Hollym.

Parker, E. H. (1890) On Race Struggles in Korea. *Transactions of the Asiatic Society of Japan* 18(20):157–228.

Patterson, Thomas C. and Christine W. Gailey. (1987) Power Relations and State Formation. In T. Patterson and C. Gailey (eds), *Power Relations and State Formation*, pp. 1-26. Washington, DC: American Anthropological Association.

Pearson, Richard J. (1985) Some Recent Studies in the Chronology and Social Development of Old Silla. In *Essays in Honour of Prof Dr. Tsugio Mikami on His 77th Birthday–Archaeology*, pp. 181-201. Tokyo: Heibonsha.

Pearson, Richard J., Gina Lee Barnes and Karl L. Hutterer (eds) (1986) *Windows on the Japanese Past: Studies in Archaeology and Prehistory*, Ann Arbor, MI: University of Michigan, Center for Japanese Studies.

Pearson, Richard J., Jong Wook Lee, Wonyoung Koh and Anne Underhill (1989) Social Ranking on the Kingdom of Old Silla, Korea: Analysis of Burials. *Journal of Anthropological Archaeology* 8(1):1–50.

Piggott, Joan R. (1997) *The Emergence of Japanese Kingship*. Stanford: Stanford University Press.

Piggott, Joan R. (1999) Chieftain Pairs and Co-Rulers: Female Sovereignty in Early Japan. In H. Tonomura, A. Walthall and W. Haruko (eds) *Women and Class in Japanese History*, pp. 17–52. Ann Arbor, MI: University of Michigan, Center for Japanese Studies.

Pusik, Kim (1145) *Samguk Sagi* [History of the Three Kingdoms].

142 References

Pines, Yuri (2005) Beasts or Humans: Pre-Imperial Origins of the "Sino-Barbarian" Dichotomy. In R. Amitai and M. Biran (eds), *Mongols, Turks, and Others: Eurasian Nomads and the Outside World*, pp. 59–102. Leiden, Netherlands: E. J. Brill.

Rawski, Evelyn (2012) Beyond National History: Seeking the Ethnic in China's History. In *Crossroads: Studies on the History of Exchange Relations in the East Asian World*. Vol. 5, available at http://www.eacrh.net/ojs/index.php/crossroads/article/view/26/Vol5_Rawski_html [accessed 1 November 2016].

Renfrew, Colin (1978) Space, Time, and Polity. In J. Friedman and M. J. Rowlands (eds), *Evolution of Social Systems*, pp. 89–112. Pittsburgh: University of Pittsburgh Press.

Rhee Song Nai, C. M. Aikens, S. Choi and S. N. Rhee (2007) Korean Contributions to Agriculture, Technology and State Formation in Japan. *Asian Perspectives* 46(2): B404–459.

Rhi, Juhyung (2012) The Ancient City of Gyeongju. In S. Lee and D. P. Leidy (eds), *Silla, Korea's Golden Kingdom*, pp. 13–30. New York: The Metropolitan Museum of Art.

Rohrlich, Ruby (1980) State Formation in Sumer and the Subjugation of Women. *Feminist Studies* 6(1):76–102.

Rubinson, Karen S. (2008) Tillya Tepe: Aspects of Gender and Cultural Identity. In K. M. Linduff and K. S. Rubinson (eds), *Are All Warriors Male? Gender Roles on the Ancient Eurasian Steppe*, pp. 51–63. Walnut Creek, CA: AltaMira Press.

Rutt, Richard (1961) The Flower Boys of Silla. *Transactions of the Korea Branch of the Royal Asiatic Society* 38:1–66.

Sacks, Karen (1979) *Sisters and Wives: The Past and Future of Sexual Equality*. Westport, CT: Greenwood Press.

Sample, L. L. (1974) Tongsamdong: A Contribution to Korean Neolithic Culture History. *Arctic Anthropology* 11(2):1–125.

Samson, O. B. (1929) An Outline of Recent Japanese Archaeological Research in Korea, and Its Bearing Upon Japanese History. *Transactions of The Asiatic Society of Japan* 6:5–19.

Sasse, Werner (2001) Trying to Figure Out How Kings Became Kings in Silla. In Li Ogg and Daniel Bouchez, *Melange Offert*, Cahiers d'Etudes Coreennes No. 7, pp. 229–244. Paris: Centre d'Etudes Coreennes.

Sayers, Robert (1987) *The Korean Onggi Potter*. Washington, DC: Smithsonian.

Schulz, Edward J. and Hugh H. W. Kang (2011) Koguryeo Annals of the Samguk Sagi. Honolulu: University of Hawaii Press.

Seyock, Barbara (2004) *Auf den Spüuren der Ostbarbaren*. Bunka. Vol. 8. Tübingen: Lit Verlag.

Seyock, Barbara (2014) Memories from Abroad: Han Chinese and Nomadic Heritage in Korean and Japanese Archaeological Contexts. In B. Seyock and A. Schottenheimer (eds), *Trade and Interaction in Ancient Northeast Asia: Reassessing Archaeological and Documentary Sources.* Special Issue of *Crossroads* 9:5–44.

Shelach, Gideon (2006) Secondary State Formation and the Development of Local Identity, Change and Continuity in the State of Qin. In M. T. Stark (ed.), *Archaeology of Asia*, pp. 202–230. Malden, MA: Blackwell.

Shelach, Gideon (2008) He Who Eats the Horse, She Who Rides It? In K. Linduff and K. Rubinson (eds), *Are All Warriors Male?*, pp. 93–109. Walnut Creek, CA: AltaMira Press.

References   143

Shelach, Gideon (2009a) Violence on the Frontiers? Sources of Power and Socio/Political Change at the Easternmost Parts of the Eurasian Steppes during the Late Second and Early First Millennium BCE. In B. K. Hanks and K. M. Linduff (eds) *Social Complexity in Prehistoric Eurasia*, pp. 241–271. Cambridge: Cambridge University Press.

Shelach, Gideon (2009b) *Prehistoric Societies on the Northern Frontiers of China.* London: Equinox.

Sohn, Pow Key, Chol Choon Kim and Yi Sup Hong (1970) *The History of Korea*. Seoul: Korean National Commission for UNESCO.

Stephenson, F. Richard (2013) Astronomical Records in the Samguk Sagi during the Three Kingdoms Period. *Korean Studies* 37(1):171–224.

Sun, Yan (2006) Colonizing China's Northern Frontier: Yan and Her Neighbors during the Early Western Zhou Period. *International Journal of Historic Archaeology* 10(2):159–177.

Tan, Ying Jui, Xiu Ren Sun, Hong Guang Zhao and Zhi Gang Gan (1995) The Bronze Age of the Song-Nen Plain. In S. M. Nelson (ed.), *The Archaeology of Northeast China*, pp. 225–250. London: Routledge.

Tian, Likun (2014) New Examination of Ancient Stirrups. *Chinese Cultural Relics* 1(1):253–271.

Trocolli, Ruth (2002) Mississippian Chiefs: Men and Women of Power. In M. O'Donovan (ed.), *The Dynamics of Power*, pp. 168–187. Carbondale, IL: Southern Illinois University, Center for Archaeological Investigations.

Watson, William (1971) *Cultural Frontiers in Ancient East Asia.* Edinburgh: Edinburgh University Press.

Watt, J. C. Y. (2004) Art and History in China from the Third to the Eighth Century. In J. C. Y. Watt, An Jiayao, Angela F. Howard, Boris I. Marshak, Su Bai and Zhao Feng (eds), *China, Dawn of a Golden Age 200–750 AD*, pp. 2–45. New Haven, CT, New York and London: The Metropolitan Museum of Art and Yale University Press.

Weatherford, Jack (2010) *The Secret History of the Mongol Queens.* New York: Crown Publishers.

Wendrich, Willemina Z., Roger S. Bagnall, T. J. Rene, James A. Cappers, Steven Harrell, E. Sidebotham and Roberta S. Tomber (2006) Berenie Crossroads: The Integration of Information. In N. Yoffee and B. L. Crowell (eds) *Excavating Asian History*, pp. 15–66. Tucson: University of Arizona Press.

Wright, Joshua (2006) The Adoption of Pastoralism in Northeast Asia, Monumental Transformation in the Eglin Gol Valley, Mongolia. PhD dissertation, Harvard University.

Wylie, Alison (2002) *Thinking from Things.* Berkeley: University of California Press.

Yi, Hyunhae (2009). The Formation and Development of the Samhan. *Early Korea* 2:17–59.

Yi, Ki Baik (1984) *A New History of Korea*, trans. E. Wagner. Cambridge, MA: Harvard University Press.

Yi, Kon Moo, Yong Hoon Lee, Kwang Jin Yun and Dae Gon Sin (1989) Research Report of Excavation of Proto-Three Kingdom Burial Site at Tahori in Uichanggun. *Kogo Hakbo* 1:7–174.

Yi, Young Hoon (2010) Introduction: Silla, the Kingdom of Gold Crowns. In Hansang Lee (ed.), *Gold Crowns of Silla, Treasures from a Brilliant Age*, pp. 6–7. Seoul: Korea Foundation.

Yoon, Dong Suk (1984) *Metallurgical Study of the Early Iron Age Artifacts Found in Korea*. Pohang: Pohang Iron and Steel Co. Ltd.

144 *References*

Yoon, Sangdeok (2012) The Gyerim-ro Dagger and the Riddle of Silla's Foreign Trade. In S. Lee and D. P. Leidy (eds), *Silla, Korea's Golden Kingdom*, pp. 133–142. New York: The Metropolitan Museum of Art.

Youn, Mubyong (1998) Archaeological Sites of Kyongju. In Korean National Commission for UNESCO (ed.), *Kyongju, City of Millennial History*, pp. 101–110. Seoul: Hollym.

Zaichikov, V. T. (1952) *Geography of Korea.* New York: Institute of Pacific Relations.

Zhuschchikovskaya, Irina (2006) Neolithic of the Primorye. In S. M. Nelson, A. P Derevianko, Y. V. Kuzmin and R. L. Bland (eds), *Archaeology of the Russian Far East: Essays in Stone Age Prehistory*, BAR International Series No. 1540, pp. 101–122. Oxford: Archaeopress.

Zozayong (1972) *Spirit of the Korean Tiger.* Korean Art Series. Vol. 2: Seoul. Seoul: Emille Museum.

Index

Page numbers referring to maps and figures are followed by 'map' and 'f' respectively.

agriculture: evidence from dolmen burials 35–6; in Gyeongju's economy 31, 53; natural resources for 7, 9, 16; rituals 24, 25; Seorabeol 10; tools 15, 56, 74; and war 3

An, Jiayao 73

Anazawa, A. 88

animism 15, 93, 99, 100–3

archaeology: agricultural tools 15, 56, 74; assigning sex to burials 51, 83, 88–91; Buddhist sites 2map, 4–6, 52, 106, 108; dolmen burials 35–7, 38f, 39–40, 68, 128; earthen fort villages 19; and ethnicity 131–2; future plans 35, 52; Gyeongju's daily life 10–11; international connections 11, 35, 43, 60, 64, 69–72, 110, 112–14, 117; Kim family origins 30, 128–9; Lelang tombs 21; location 2map, 36map; mounted warfare 32; Namdang 29; Neolithic (Jeulmun) period 24, 35, 39, 66, 122; powerful women 90–1, 93–4, 117; production 33, 43, 52, 53–4, 55, 56, 57–9, 117; wooden chamber burials 36, 38, 40–5, 48, 49, 52, 83, 84; writing materials 27; *see also* mounded tombs; Wolseong-ro

Arikamedu beads 67, 70

armor 16, 32, 40, 44, 50, 56, 91, 113

Aryong (first queen) 28, 87, 100

Auspicious Phoenix Tomb 46, 47, 48–9, 59

Baekdusan 25, 65map, 66

Baekje (Paekche): absorption of Mahan 19; Buddhism 13, 85, 105, 110, 130; continental culture 12; gold headgear 62; Japanese Soga clan 113; location 12map; origins of 11; Saro's conquest of 1, 13, 31, 89, 127; Yamato connections 27, 110

Barnes, Gina 11, 23, 67, 92, 111, 128

Bartz, Patricia 57

beads: Burial 8 (Hwangseong-dong) 43; Chinhan people 23; decorated armor found at Gujeong-dong 40; face bead from Wolseong-ro 45, 69, 70; high status 10, 17, 43, 50, 60, 61, 71, 90, 104, 122; Jatim beads 45, 67, 69; Korean production of 68, 70, 71; Manchurian-Korean similarities 122; pectoral/chestlace (Wolseong-ro, Area C, Ga-13) 43, 59, 78, 79f; religious offerings (Jungmak-dong) 101, 116; Silla's gold-work 57, 58–9; spiritual symbolism 104, 114, 115; Tomb 130 (Sara-ri) 42; trade in 11, 15, 17, 24, 35, 66–71, 114–15; wooden chamber tomb (Namsong-ri) 44

bells: animism and shamanism 99, 103, 105; Bronze Age 55; Buddhism 4, 5, 6f, 106, 108; Emille Bell 56, 108; horse trappings 42, 105, 113, 122, 124; Izumo 112; marking *sodo* 24, 25; Samhan period 37; Wooden chamber tomb artifacts 40, 42

belt buckles 32, 37, 38f, 41, 42, 74, 114

Bennett, Gwen 120, 127, 130

Best, Jonathan 18, 99, 106, 127

146 *Index*

bilateral heritage 86, 87, 91–2, 93, 96–7, 124–5
birds 23, 30, 46, 99, 102
Bokcheondong cemetery 69
bone ranks 33, 37, 51, 76, 78–85, 96, 118, 125
boots 80, 81, 84, 122, 123, 124; *see also* shoes
bronze: Buddha images 106, 109; Chinese metal of choice 61; early burial artifacts 35, 37, 39, 40, 41–2, 44; gilded crowns 17, 32, 47, 59, 60, 62, 90; industry 15, 43, 55–6, 74; large bells 4, 6f, 56, 108; mounded tombs 47, 50; offerings to the sea 101, 116, 117; shamanic artifacts 103, 105; Silla's Chinese connections 11, 14, 41, 55, 74, 121, 122, 124; Silla's Japanese connections 112, 113, 115; sumptuary laws 81, 83; trade 11, 71, 74, 75
buckles 32, 37, 38f, 41, 42, 74, 114
Buddhism: grave goods in Ho-u (Washing Bowl) Tomb (No.140a) 50; import of 13, 16, 85, 99, 105, 106, 129–30; treatment of the dead 38, 51–2; Unified Silla 107; women and gender bias 100, 101f, 107; Wu Zetian 95
Buddhist monuments: Bulguksa 5–6, 7, 83, 107–8; Confucian destruction of 109; Emille Bell 56, 108; gold crowns 62; Gyeongju's landscape 4, 9; historical time periods 28, 32–3; Hwagnyongsa (Imperial Dragon) Temple 2map, 4–5, 52, 106, 107, 108; Mt. Namsan 7–8, 13, 107, 108; pagodas 4, 5, 32, 52, 107, 108; sarira holes and reliquaries 52, 69, 108; Sokkuram grotto 5, 7, 107, 108; tigers 24–5
Bulguksa monastery 5–6, 7, 107–8
Byington, Mark 18, 22, 23, 67, 111, 128

Carlqvist, Anders 110, 115
census data 13, 26, 28, 33, 92, 96
ceramics *see* pottery
Chajang 107
Chaoyang region 40–1, 60, 83, 112, 124, 129, 133
Chapin, Helen 50, 106
Chee, Changboh 100
cheol jeong 56

Cheomseongdae 2map, 5f
China: Buddhism 95, 99, 105; gender bias 89, 92, 94–5, 95, 97; glass beads 68; gold artifacts 76; jade 61; shared ethnicity with Silla 120; Six Dynasties period 10; stone cist burials 39; *see also* Han dynasty; Liaoning Province; Manchuria; Sui dynasty; Tang dynasty
Chinese historical records 18, 22–4
Chinese language 21, 27
Chinhan 20map, 23, 25, 31
Cho, Daeyoun 55
Ch'oe, Pyong Hon 91
Choi, Hochin 33, 54–5
cist burials 35, 39–40, 44
city layout/grid pattern 9, 13
clothing 23, 80–1, 122
cobbles 38, 39, 43, 44, 45, 52, 57–8, 124
Como, Michael 111
compositional analysis 64, 68–70, 73, 77
Confucianism: ascendancy 26; gender bias 89, 92, 95, 97; and native religions 100, 102
copper 33, 55, 56, 75
co-rulership hypothesis 51, 89–90, 97–8
corvée labor 11, 29, 34, 92
cranial deformation 23, 24, 67
cremation 38, 51
crowns: gilt bronze 17, 32, 47–8, 59, 60, 62; *see also* gold crown tombs

Daegu 17, 32, 35, 39, 52
daggers and dagger sheaths: find spot 39, 40, 41, 42, 44, 45; imports of 14, 64, 71, 74–5, 121; Korean production 55, 74, 121
Daifang commandery 20map, 21, 23
Daodunzi cemetery 94, 117
Deuchler, Martina 26, 89, 92, 93
dolmen burials 35–7, 39–40, 68, 128
Dongbei *see* Manchuria
Dongyichuan (DYC) 22
dwellings: Bronze Age 43; Chinhan 23; high status 13–14, 33; Mumun sites 39; sumptuary rules 80, 81, 82–3; tiled roofs 13, 33, 54, 83
DYC *see Dongyichuan*

earrings: Chinese burials 123; gender 88, 94, 117; Gyeongju grave goods 44, 45,

Index 147

49, 50, 88, 90; Inner Mongolian burials 94; origin of Silla elite 114; style 61, 76, 113

Emille Bell 56, 108

ethnicity viii, 16, 119–20, 124, 125–7, 129, 131–2

Eurasian Steppes region: *gogok* 7, 61, 114; gold 17, 47, 60–2, 75–6, 114, 121, 123; Gyeongju's connections to 121–6, 133; horses 12, 63, 76, 82, 121, 122, 123–4, 127; ornament design 37, 41, 47, 75–6, 121, 122–3; raiders 8, 28, 127; religion 17, 61, 62, 99, 103, 105, 112, 114, 121, 123, 124; Silla's ruling elite 60, 112–13, 133; tomb mounds 112, 129; trade routes 15, 64, 65map, 73, 76; women 93–4, 117, 119, 121, 122, 123, 124, 125; Xiongu people 15, 16, 60, 76, 99, 120, 130

face bead (Wolseong-ro) 45, 69, 70

Feng, Empress (442–490) 93

Fifth Head ranks (*Odupum*) 79–80, 81, 82

Flying White Horse tomb 46, 47, 102

Fourth Head ranks (*Sadupum*) 80, 81, 82

Fujinoki Tomb 71, 113, 114

Gaesomoon, Yeon 31

Gaesong 7, 9, 14, 26

Gaya: double-burials 90; glass grave goods 73; iron production 56; legend 67; location 11, 19; Saro's conquest of 1, 13, 31, 32, 132; style of earthenware 43, 53

gender *see* women

geographical features 7–9

Geumseong (golden fortress) 6, 7, 9, 11, 12map, 13, 19, 33, 84

Gimhae-Yangdong cemetery 69

glass vessels 11, 15, 72–3

Glover, Ian 67, 68

gogok: international comparison 60, 61, 114–15, 122; Korean production 71; religious offerings at Jungmak-dong 101, 117; symbolism and status of 10, 17, 43, 50, 60, 61, 71, 90, 104, 114, 122; wooden chamber tomb finds 43, 44, 45, 48

Goguryeo kingdom: Buddhism 13, 85, 105, 106, 129; conquests by 21, 32,

33, 126; crowns 62; culture 12; defeat by Silla 1, 13, 25, 31, 32, 33, 89, 127; Gwanggaeto monument 27; location 12map; origins of 11; raids on Gyeongju 8; silver bowl (Auspicious Phoenix Tomb) 49

golbeum system (bone ranks) 33, 37, 51, 76, 78–85, 96, 118, 125

gold: and the Eurasian Steppes region 17, 47, 60–2, 75–6, 114, 121, 123; Ga 13 (Tomb area C, Wolseong-ro) 43–4, 59, 60, 113; indicating leadership 17, 29, 50, 59, 61, 90, 91, 94, 117; Japanese artifacts 112–14; and the Kim clan 17, 30, 38, 62; production of 7, 16, 30, 57–62; Shamanic symbolism 16, 61, 62, 99, 103, 104, 123; Silla's export of 76–7; sumptuary rules 81; *see also* gold crown tombs

Gold Bell Tomb 47, 48, 53, 59

gold crowns: Buddhist statues and paintings 62; characterizing Silla 2, 59–60, 61, 62; Japanese-Silla connections 112–15; Kim family 17, 30; shamanism 16, 61, 62, 99, 103, 104, 123

gold crown tombs: accidental discovery of 2, 9–10, 47; artifacts related to the Steppes 60–2, 122, 123, 124; Auspicious Phoenix Tomb 46, 47, 48–9, 59; Flying White Horse tomb 46, 47, 102; Gold Bell Tomb 47, 48, 53, 59; Gold Crown Tomb 2, 9–10, 46, 47, 59; Heavenly Horse tomb (Cheonmachong) 44, 47, 49–50, 59, 79f; Kim clan 38; labor requirement 31; and Silla's fame 2–3, 9–10; *see also* north mound of Tomb 98

Goryeo dynasty 4, 7, 9, 14, 26, 92, 93

grave goods: epi-nomadic heritage 11, 12, 49, 58, 74; evidence of production 53, 56, 57f, 58–9; and gender 51, 60, 83, 88, 90–1, 93–4, 117; gold crown tombs 2–3, 10, 46, 47–51, 53, 57, 59–62, 79f, 102; indicating rank 37, 51, 61, 78, 84; international connections 11, 35, 43, 60, 64, 69–72, 110, 112–14, 117; labor implications 31; Lelang commandery 21; for mounted warfare 32; Mumun period dolmen burials 35, 37, 38f, 39,

148 *Index*

68; stone-block tombs of the Buddhist period 38; Wolseong-ro 43–4, 45, 59, 60, 69, 70, 78, 79f, 113; wooden chamber burials 38, 40, 41–2, 43, 44, 45, 48, 49, 52, 83, 84; writing materials 27

Great Silla *see* Unified Silla

Great Tomb *see* Tomb 98

Griffis, William 1, 7, 14

Gujeong-dong archeological site 40, 44

Gupta, Sunil 68, 70–1

Gwanggaeto monument 27

Gyeongju: brief history 9–14, 27–8; capital status 1, 6, 7, 8, 9, 13, 14, 19, 26; environment of 7–9; fame of 2–3; Griffis' description of 1; historical interest in 14–15; maps 2map

Gyerim, alternative name for Silla 15

Gyerim Forest 2map, 11, 30, 45–6, 102

Gyerim-ro dagger sheath 74–5

Hadong 31

Ham, Soon Seop 57, 59, 122

Han dynasty: artifacts from 11, 41–2, 60, 71, 73–4, 105, 112, 122; documents on the Sanhan *see Hou Han Shu Dongyichuan*; historical lens 126, 128; Korean occupation 10, 21; trade monopolies 17, 22; Xiwangmu, the Queen Mother of the West 105, 111

hangul 21

Hata family 111

head-shaping 23, 24, 67

Heavenly Horse tomb (Cheonmachong) 44, 47, 49–50, 59, 79f

Hejo 107

Henderson, Gregory 100, 102–3

Henze, Carl 103, 104, 123

HHS *see Hou Han Shu Dongyichuan*

Himanoyama Tomb 115

Hinsch, Bret 95

historical records: census data 13, 26, 28, 33, 92, 96; Korean histories 25–7; language of 21, 27; ruler selection 19; Sanhan period 22–5; on Silla's immigrant population 25; spiritual beliefs 24–5; validity of 16, 18

"History of the Three Kingdoms" (Pusik) *see Samguk Sagi*

Holy (Sacred) Bone rank (*Song'gol*) 34, 76, 78–9, 84, 88, 89, 91, 105, 123, 124

Honeychurch, William 73, 75, 130

Hong, Wontack 10, 61, 110, 112, 116, 120, 129, 130, 132

horses: buckles shaped as 32, 37, 38f, 41, 114; burial of 45, 105, 124; ceramic vessels 48, 53; Chinese imported trappings 71, 72, 74; Eurasian Steppes region 12, 63, 76, 82, 120–1, 122, 123–4, 127; and gender 82, 83, 84, 89, 93, 94, 122, 123–4; gilded trappings 41, 105, 113, 116, 124; gold crown grave goods 47, 48, 49, 50, 113; introduction into Japan 110–11; iron trappings 35, 37, 74; Japanese grave goods 113, 114; leadership myths 29; and leather production 55; mounted warfare 16–17, 32, 127; ranking and sumptuary rules 51, 80, 81–2, 83, 84, 105, 124; reverence and worship of 99, 102, 105, 112; riding clothes 122, 124; sacrifice of 23, 50, 105; wooden chamber grave goods 41, 42, 44, 45

Hou Han Shu Dongyichuan (HHS) 22, 23, 24, 25, 36, 55, 67, 89

houses *see* dwellings

Ho-u (Washing Bowl) Tomb (No. 140a) 50

Hulbert, Homer 1, 57, 132

Hwacheon-ri archaeological site 52, 54

Hwangnam Daechong *see* Tomb 98

Hwangnam-dong site: wooden chamber tombs 44–5; *see also* Gold Crown Tomb; Tomb 98

Hwango-dong archaeological site 44, 69

Hwang-ok 67–8

Hwangseong-dong archaeological site 35, 36map, 39, 43, 56, 128

Hwangyongsa (Imperial Dragon) Temple 2map, 4–5, 52, 106, 107, 108

Hwarang society 103

Hyeokkeose (King) 29, 43, 87, 100, 105

Ichadon 106

Imperial Dragon Temple *see* Hwangyongsa (Imperial Dragon) Temple

Inariyama–Sakitama Tomb 113

Indian beads 66–7, 68

industry *see* production

Inner Mongolia 17, 25, 76, 94, 117, 120, 121, 123, 126, 130–1, 132
Inwang-dong archaeological site 44, 69
Ipsil-ri archaeological site 36map, 40, 56
iron: artifacts dating wooden chamber burials at Joyang-dong 42; Chinhan 23; epi-nomadic grave goods 49, 71, 74; Han China's monopoly 17, 22; Japanese grave goods 113; Jeulmun site (possible) 39; mounded tomb artifacts 49, 50, 91, 115; mounted warfare 16, 32; Pak clan's castle 29; production 7, 10, 15, 16, 29, 31, 43, 56, 74; rank and sumptuary rules 82; sea goddess offerings 101, 116–17; Sillan export goods 76; wooden chamber tombs 40, 41, 42, 43, 44, 45
Iron Age period *see* Samhan period
Iryeon *see Samguk Yusa*
Iseong Sanseong 32, 41, 114
Ito, Akio 44, 50, 51, 88
Izumo 16, 110, 111, 112, 114, 115–16, 118, 127

Japan: artifacts from Silla 63, 76, 101, 110, 112, 113–14, 132; bead trade 66, 68, 70–1; Buddhist temples 108; Buyeo/Baekje problem 110–11; grave goods in Silla's tombs 44, 54, 124; historical writings of 14, 27, 116; leather production 55; location 131map; *magatama* 122; myths and folklore 110, 112, 115–16; occupation of Korea (1910–1945) 9, 57; powerful women 86, 89, 94, 111, 114, 115, 117–18, 119, 132; raids on Gyeongju 1, 4, 8, 17, 107; sea travel 17, 66, 101, 116–17, 127; shamanism 114, 115; tripolar Asia 125, 126, 128
jar burials 40, 42
Jatim beads 45, 67, 69
Jeongyang Sanseong 52
Jeulmun (Neolithic) era 17, 24, 35, 39, 61, 66, 92, 122
Jindeok, Queen (647–653) 33, 34, 88–9, 90, 91
Jinhan region 18, 19, 24, 25, 31, 93, 113
Jinseong, Queen (887–896) 89, 90
Joseon state 21

Joyang-dong archaeological site 40–2, 56, 60, 112, 128
Ju, Bodon 19, 34, 60–1, 113
Jungmak-dong 101, 116–17

Kang, Bong Won 11, 13, 25, 28, 30, 31, 33, 34, 43, 56
Kibi region (of Japan) 114, 118
Kidder, J. Edward 71, 110, 112, 113–14, 115, 116
kilns 33, 52, 54, 117
Kim, Byong Mo 51, 62, 68, 106
Kim, Chong Sun 26, 51, 53, 68, 78, 79, 80, 81, 87, 89, 92, 93, 95, 96, 100, 124
Kim, Choong Soon 68, 132
Kim Pusik *see Samguk Sagi*
Kim, Won Yong 9, 28, 35, 37, 39, 40, 44, 47, 48, 50, 51, 55, 56, 62, 68, 80, 90, 91, 102, 103, 105, 115, 123, 124
Kim, Yung Chung 88, 89, 104
Kim clan: ethnicity 129, 133; folklore 29, 30, 67–8, 88; fortification of Gyeongju 19; gold 17, 30, 38, 58, 62, 121, 133; Gyerim Forest 11, 30, 45–6; horses 32, 133; mounded tomb period 27–8, 30, 38, 45–7, 91, 96, 113, 129; and rotated leadership 29, 87–8; *see also* gold crown tombs
Korean language 2, 21, 27

labor 31, 34
language 2, 17, 21, 27, 85
Lankton, James W. 69, 70, 71, 73, 75
Laursen, Sarah 58, 59, 61, 76, 121
leather production 23, 53, 55
Ledyard, Gari 110, 121, 126
Lee, Donghee 55
Lee, Insook 50, 61, 66, 67, 68, 69, 70, 104, 115, 120, 121
Lee, Jong Wook 28–9
Lee, Kidong 104, 105
Lee, Soyoung 3, 41
Lee, Sung Joo 29, 30, 119
Leidy, Denise 3, 41, 51, 109
Lelang colony 10, 20map, 21, 22, 32, 71–2, 74, 126, 128
Liao empresses 94
Liaoning Province: bronze style 55, 74; Chaoyang region 40–1, 60, 83, 112, 124, 129, 133; daggers 121; ethnicity 129,

150 *Index*

132; gold 58, 60, 61, 112, 121; mirrors 42, 55, 74
Linduff, Katheryn 60, 61, 122, 125
literacy 16, 27
Lucky Phoenix Tomb 102

McCune, Evelyn 50, 62, 92, 100, 103, 106, 123
McMahon, Keith 93, 94, 95, 111
Mahan 11, 19, 20map, 23, 25, 67
Manchuria: gender equality 119; location of 131map; material culture 14, 51, 63, 71, 73, 76, 114–15, 122; shamanism 51, 103, 104; and Silla-Japan link 110–11, 112; trade 10, 64, 81; tripolar ethnicity 15, 17, 120, 121, 125–6, 128, 129, 130, 132
Manome, J. 88
Maoqinggou burial site 117
Marananda 105
Masan 31
Matsui, Akira 55
"Memorabilia of the Three Kingdoms" (Iryeon) *see Samguk Yusa*
Metropolitan Museum of Art exhibition 3
Michu, King 27, 30, 44, 45, 91
mirrors: depiction of female deities 105, 111; grave goods 37, 40, 41, 42, 44, 71, 72, 112, 113, 115, 128; Jungmak-dong religious offerings 101; Korean style 42, 55, 122; shamanic implements 103; Silla's international connections 11, 14, 41, 42, 60, 63, 73, 105, 112–13, 121–2; typological categorization 74
Mongolia 65map, 124, 128, 130, 131, 132; *see also* Inner Mongolia
Mononobe clan 113, 114
mounded tombs: accidental discovery of 2, 9–10, 47; early examples of 38, 43–4; glass vessels 72, 73; grave goods 2–3, 10, 46, 47–51, 53, 57, 59–62, 68, 79f, 102; Gyerim Forest location 2map, 11, 30, 45–6; Kim clan 27–8, 30, 38, 45–7, 91, 96, 113, 129; labor for 31; period of 11, 17, 28, 30, 38, 97; and rank 37, 78, 80, 84; ruler succession 97; Shamanism 11, 12, 51; and Silla's reputation 2–3; *see also* gold crown tombs; Tomb 98
mountains 2map, 7–8, 9, 13, 29, 107, 108
mountain spirits 51, 100, 101f

Mt. Namsan 2map, 7–8, 9, 13, 29, 107, 108
Mt. Tohamsan 7, 9, 107
Mukhoza 105
Mumun sites 35–7, 39–40, 61, 128
Mun Myung Dae 106, 108
Munro, Neil Gordon 113
Murong Xianbei people 41, 58, 61, 73, 120
Mythology 29, 30, 62, 87, 110, 112, 115–16

Naemul, King (356–402) 17, 28, 30, 51, 60, 91, 95, 96f, 97f, 113; *see also* Tomb 98
Naktong River 7, 8, 31
Namdang 29
Namsong-ri archaeological site 44
Nanshangen burial sites 93–4, 117, 121
Neolithic (Jeulmun) era 17, 24, 35, 39, 61, 66, 92, 122
Nintoku's tomb 113
Northern Wei dynasty 73, 75, 93, 129
North Gyeongsang Province, archaeological finds 35, 38f
north mound of Tomb 98: cobbles 58; date of 91; gold crown 3f, 47–8, 50, 59–60; gold workmanship 76; occupant of 50, 86, 88, 89, 90, 91, 97–8; shamanism 50–1 *see also* Tomb 98
Nosodong graves 69–70

obsidian 66, 77
Oga, Katsuhiko 70–1
Okinoshima shrine 101, 116
Ornamental Shoes Tomb ("Singnichong") 70
Oundong archaeological site 37
Oxenham, Mark 126–7, 132

Paekche *see* Baekje (Paekche)
pagodas 4, 5, 32, 52, 107, 108
Pak clan 29, 43, 87, 92, 113
Pak, Hyeokkeose 29, 43, 87, 100
Pak, Yangjin 111, 126
Pak, Young Sook 76, 94, 121
paper production 53
Parker, E. H. 22–3, 24, 25, 27, 93, 95, 104, 124
Pearson study 81, 83–4, 88, 91
Pechinkina, Kate 126–7, 132
Piggott, Joan 51, 89, 94, 111, 117, 118, 132

Index 151

placer mining 57–8
Poban, Queen 17, 91, 96f, 97f, 98
Pohang 8
population estimates 11, 13, 14, 31, 33
pottery: dating wooden chamber tombs
42, 43, 45; depicting birds 102;
Hwangseong-dong dolmen site 39;
Jungmak-dong site 101, 116, 117;
mounded tombs 48, 49, 50, 51, 53;
Neolithic period 35, 122; production
of 15, 33, 52, 53–4, 117; sea trade
66; *wajil togi* pottery 37, 40, 42;
Wolseong-ro site 39, 43
production: beads made in Korea 68,
70, 71; bronze 15, 43, 55–6, 74; for
court 54–5; gold 7, 16, 30, 57–62, 75;
households 53; iron 7, 10, 15, 16, 29,
31, 43, 56, 74; leather 23, 53, 55; pottery
15, 33, 52, 53–4, 117; silk 23, 28, 33,
53, 55, 64, 77; source of imported beads
66–7, 69, 70; weaving 28, 33, 53, 77
Proto-Three Kingdoms period *see* Samhan
period
Pyonhan 19, 20map, 23, 25, 31

Qin dynasty 7, 15, 23, 25
Queen Mother of the West 105, 111

ranking and sumptuary rules 15, 33, 37,
51, 76, 78–85, 96, 118, 125
religions: animism 93, 99, 100–3;
supernatural ancestry of rulers 29, 87,
88; and women 93, 100, 103–4, 105,
111; written records of the Samhan
period 24–5; *see also* Buddhism;
Buddhist monuments; shamanism
roof tiles 13, 32, 33, 52, 54, 83
Rubinson, Karen 60
rulers of Silla: Aryong 28, 87, 100; Asian
context 71, 86, 89, 93–5, 111, 114–15,
117–18, 119, 122, 123, 124, 130,
132; bilateral heritage 86, 87, 91–2,
93, 96–7, 125; co-rulership case 51,
89–90, 97–8, 114, 118; early shamanic
title (*chachaung*) 88, 103, 124; ethnic
origins 29, 87, 120–1, 125, 128–9, 133;
Hyeokkeose (King) 29, 43, 87, 100,
105; Jindeok (647–653) 33, 34, 88–9,
90, 91; Jinseong (887–896) 89, 90;

Michu, King 27, 30, 44, 45, 91; Naemul
(356–402) 17, 28, 30, 51, 60, 91, 95,
96f, 97f, 113; Poban 17, 91, 96f, 97f,
98; shamanic symbols 17, 61, 104, 114;
supernatural ancestry stories 29, 30, 62,
67–8, 87, 88; three royal clans 19, 29,
87–8; *see also* gold crown tombs; Kim
clan; Seondeok, Queen
Ryusakyu, Tsunoda 113

Sacks, Karen 93
Sacred (Holy) Bone rank (*Song'gol*) 34,
76, 78–9, 84, 88, 89, 91, 105, 123, 124
sacrifice 23, 24, 44, 50, 91, 100, 105
Samguk Sagi ("History of the Three
Kingdoms", Pusik): accounts of raiding
28, 30; animalistic and shamanic beliefs
51, 100, 102–3, 103–4, 124; authorship
25–6, 92; Buddhism 105; Daifang
commandery 23; dating the Joyang-
dong graves 40, 42; gender bias 92,
100; migrations 39, 121; ranking and
sumptuary rules 78, 80, 84; rulers 19,
84, 86, 90, 92, 118
Samguk Yusa ("Memorabilia of the Three
Kingdoms, Iryeon): composition 26;
confederacy of Saro 19, 28, 86–7, 100;
on elite housing 13–14; gender bias 92;
Geumseong's size 33; religious belief
100, 103, 106; rulers 62, 84, 86, 90,
103, 118, 124; Saro's conquests 30;
Yeonorang story 115
Samhan period: artifacts 11, 37, 41, 122,
128; defined 10, 18; Han and Wei
documents 22–4; horse burial 105, 124;
Hwangseong-dong archaeology 43;
international connections 11, 128; map
20map; natural resources 16; rituals and
customs 23–4; Saro's organization 19;
Seorabeol 10–11
Samson, O. B. 40
San Guo Zhi (SGZ) 22, 23, 24
Sara-ri 36map, 42–3, 56
sarira holes and reliquaries 08, 52, 69
Saro, confederacy of 8, 9, 10, 19, 27,
28–9, 40
Sasse, Werner 79, 89, 92
Sayers, Robert 54
seafaring 17, 64, 66, 67, 101, 116–17

152 *Index*

Seondeok, Queen (632–646): alliance with Tang China 13, 34, 85; astronomical observatory of 4, 5f, 104; cleverness of 4, 77, 88; dating the Mounded Tomb period 30; tomb of 2map, 100

Seorabeol 7, 9, 10–11, 15

Seyock, Barbara 19, 22, 32, 49, 68, 74

SGZ *see San Guo Zhi*

shamanism: across the Three Kingdoms 12; and Buddhism 99, 105; gender equality and female practitioners 50–1, 103, 104, 105, 111, 114, 115, 116, 121, 124; gold crowns 15–16, 51, 61, 99, 103, 104, 123; Ho-u Tomb (No.140a) 50; Jungmak-dong 101, 116; and leadership 17, 61, 88, 103, 104, 114, 124; neolithic populations 92; *Samguk Sagi* 102–3, 103–4, 124; Silla-Japan link 111, 112, 114; Silla-Steppes link 17, 61, 62, 99, 103, 105, 112, 114, 121, 123, 124

Shelach, Gideon 94, 117, 130, 131

shoes: elite burials 2, 51, 60, 78, 113, 115; for horse riding 122; Silla-Steppes link 60; state supervised industry 3, 55; straw 53; *see also* boots

shrines: Buddhist 4, 9, 13, 24, 100, 101f, 108; Hyeokkeose (first king) 100, 105; sea goddesses 17, 101, 116–17; Xiwangmu 105

silk: import 17, 21, 33; Korean production 23, 28, 33, 53, 55, 64, 77; sumptuary laws 76, 81, 82, 84; for writing 27

Silk Road 8, 27, 62, 64, 65map

Silla Pon'gi 26

silver vessels 11, 15, 49, 64, 72, 75, 91

Sixth Head rank (*Ryuktupum*) 79–80, 81, 82, 83

social system: bilateral heritage 86, 87, 91–2, 93, 96–7, 124–5; sumptuary rules and ranking 15, 33, 37, 51, 76, 78–85, 89, 96, 118, 125

sodo 24, 25

Soga clan 94, 110, 113, 114, 117, 118

Sok clan 29

Sokkuram grotto 5, 7, 107, 108

statehood 34

Steppes region *see* Eurasian Steppes region

stone beads 66, 67, 68, 122

stone chamber tombs 35, 45, 52

Sui dynasty 85, 120, 126, 130

Suiko of Yamato, Empress (539–571) 94, 117–18

sumptuary rules and ranking 15, 33, 37, 51, 76, 78–85, 89, 96, 118, 125

Sundo 105

swords: Izumo 112, 115–16; mounded tomb artifacts 47, 48, 50, 91; and mounted warfare 32; Steppe design 122; to assign sex to burials 51, 88; wooden chamber artifacts 40, 42, 43, 44, 45

Tang dynasty: Empress Wu 95, 130; ethnicity 120, 126; Silla alliance 1, 13, 14, 33, 34, 85, 88–9, 127, 130; trade 33

Three Hans period *see* Samhan period

Three Kingdoms period: dates for 10, 11, 13, 14, 25; overview 11–13; religion 99, 124

tigers: buckles shaped as 37, 38f, 41, 42; Buddhist shrines 24, 100, 101f; Silla pottery 51; sumptuary laws 82, 84; veneration 24–5

Tillya Tepe (Afghanistan) 60, 62

Tomb 98: artifacts 3f, 47–8, 50, 56, 59, 64, 73, 75, 90–1, 105; and the co-rulership hypothesis 90; double mound of 46, 97; as early mounded tomb 43–4, 46; evidence of local gold production 58–9; excavation 9, 47; imported gold-working techniques 76; location 2map, 44, 46map; rulership 15, 86, 88, 90, 91, 92, 95, 97–8

Tomb 130 (Sara-ri) 42–3

tomb artifacts *see* grave goods

tombs: archaeological value 35; assigning sex to 51, 83, 88–91; cist burials 35, 39–40, 44; connections with China and Japan 110, 112–14; dolmen burials 35–7, 39–40, 68, 128; map of numbered tombs 46map; Silla-Chaoyang region link 41, 60, 83, 112, 124, 129, 133; stone chamber tombs 35, 45, 52; of Unified Silla 51–2; wooden chamber burials 36, 38, 40–5, 48, 49, 52, 83, 84; *see also* grave goods; mounded tombs

trade: beads 11, 15, 17, 24, 35, 66–71, 114–15; between Saro and Japan

31; bronze 11, 71, 74, 75; Eurasian Steppes routes 15, 64, 65map, 73, 76; glass vessels 11, 72–3; Gyeongju's accessibility 8; Han dynasty monopolies 17, 22; metal artifacts 71, 73–6; perishable luxury goods 76; Pleistocene era 66; sea routes 64, 66, 67; shrines for 17, 101, 116–17; Silk Road i, 8, 27, 62, 64, 65map; Silla's export goods 76–7; single burials 37; with Tang China 33

tripolar East Asian model 15, 125–7, 128

True Bone rank 78, 79, 80, 81, 82, 83

Tsukuriyami Tomb 115

Tungusic peoples 17, 61, 126–7, 128

tunnel kilns 52, 54

Tuoba Wei dynasty 22, 73, 83, 93, 121, 129; *see also Wei Zhi Dongyichuan*

Ulsan 8

Unified Silla: decline of 9, 89; industry 33; Kim clan 17; rank and sumptuary laws 33, 78, 80, 125; resistance to Tang China 34, 130; role of Buddhism 107; territoriality 25, 33; tombs of (overview) 17, 51–2; trade 33; victory over Goguryeo and Baekje 1, 13, 14, 25, 31, 32, 33, 34, 88–9, 127; wealth 54

wajil togi pottery 37, 40, 42

water spirits 100–1

weaving 28, 53

Weilüe 22

Wei rulers 22, 73, 75, 83, 93, 120, 121, 126, 129

Wei Zhi Dongyichuan (WZ) 19, 22, 25, 93

Wolseong-ro: agricultural tools 56; archaeological plans for 35; first mounded tombs 11; grave goods 43–4, 45, 59, 69, 70, 71, 78, 79f; location 2map, 29, 36map, 113; Pak clan residence 29; possible Jeulman site 39; raids on 8

women: Buddhist gender bias 100, 101f, 107; in China 89, 92, 94–5, 95, 97; Eurasian Steppes region 93–4, 117, 119,

121, 122, 123, 124, 125; goddesses 17, 51, 87, 93, 95, 100–1, 105, 108, 111, 116; horse riding 82, 83, 84, 89, 93, 94, 122, 123–4; Japan 86, 89, 94, 111, 114, 115, 117–18, 119, 132; rank 51, 79, 81, 82, 89, 96, 118; rulership 29, 34, 51, 86–7, 88–98, 117–18, 119; shamanism 50–1, 103–4, 105, 111, 114, 115, 116, 121, 124; understudy of 119

wonhua association 103

wooden chamber burials 36, 38, 40–5, 48, 49, 52, 83, 84

written records *see* historical records

Wu Zetian (Empress Wu) 13, 95, 130

WZ see Wei Zhi Dongyichuan

Xianbei connections with Silla: horse-riding 17, 120–1; language 120; leadership folklore 29; material culture 41, 58, 61, 73, 76, 120, 133; religion 99, 103, 105, 129, 133; strong women 130; tripolar East Asian context 10, 14, 125–6, 129, 130, 132; written records 21, 22, 23, 25, 27, 120

Xiongnu connections with Silla: horse riding 17; Kim family ancestry 129, 133; leadership folklore 29; material culture 49, 60, 76, 120, 122; religion 99, 103, 105; strong women 130; tripolar East Asian context 10, 14, 15, 125, 128, 130; written records 27

Yamato region 89, 94, 110, 111, 117–18; *see also* Izumo

Yayoi sites 70–1

Yeanni 24

Yeon, Gaesomoon 31

Yeon, Jungto 31

Yeonorang 115

Ye people 20map, 23

Yi dynasty 86, 93

Yongnam 31

Yoon, Dong Suk 44, 56, 74

Youn, Mubyong 35

Yuryaku 113, 115

Taylor & Francis eBooks

Helping you to choose the right eBooks for your Library

Add Routledge titles to your library's digital collection today. Taylor and Francis ebooks contains over 50,000 titles in the Humanities, Social Sciences, Behavioural Sciences, Built Environment and Law.

Choose from a range of subject packages or create your own!

Benefits for you
- Free MARC records
- COUNTER-compliant usage statistics
- Flexible purchase and pricing options
- All titles DRM-free.

REQUEST YOUR FREE INSTITUTIONAL TRIAL TODAY

Free Trials Available
We offer free trials to qualifying academic, corporate and government customers.

Benefits for your user
- Off-site, anytime access via Athens or referring URL
- Print or copy pages or chapters
- Full content search
- Bookmark, highlight and annotate text
- Access to thousands of pages of quality research at the click of a button.

eCollections – Choose from over 30 subject eCollections, including:

Archaeology	Language Learning
Architecture	Law
Asian Studies	Literature
Business & Management	Media & Communication
Classical Studies	Middle East Studies
Construction	Music
Creative & Media Arts	Philosophy
Criminology & Criminal Justice	Planning
Economics	Politics
Education	Psychology & Mental Health
Energy	Religion
Engineering	Security
English Language & Linguistics	Social Work
Environment & Sustainability	Sociology
Geography	Sport
Health Studies	Theatre & Performance
History	Tourism, Hospitality & Events

For more information, pricing enquiries or to order a free trial, please contact your local sales team:
www.tandfebooks.com/page/sales

 | The home of Routledge books

www.tandfebooks.com